The Cybernetic Imagination in Science Fiction

The Cybernetic Imagination in Science Fiction

Patricia S. Warrick

The MIT Press
Cambridge, Massachusetts, and London, England

Second printing, July 1980
Copyright © 1980 by
The Massachusetts Institute of Technology

This book was set in VIP Palatino by DEKR Corporation, printed and bound by The Alpine Press Inc., in the United States of America.

Library of Congress Cataloging in Publication Data

Warrick, Patricia S
    The cybernetic imagination in science fiction.

    Bibliography: p.
    Includes index.
    1. Science fiction—History and criticism. 2. Computers in literature. 3. Automata in literature. I. Title.
PN3448.S45W34   809.3'876   79-28322
ISBN 0-262-23100-X

To JFW
Whose delight in literature complements
his knowledge in science

Contents

Contents

8
Into the Electronic Future   203

Conclusion   231

Notes   238

Nonfiction Bibliography   249

Fiction Bibliography   259

Index   271

Acknowledgments

Parts of this book have been published, with some variations, as articles. They are as follows:

"Ethical Evolving Artificial Intelligence: Asimov's Robots and Computers," in *Isaac Asimov*, ed. Joseph Olander and Martin Greenberg (New York: Taplinger Press, 1977).

"The Labyrinthian Process of the Artificial: Philip K. Dick's Robots and Electronic Constructs," *Extrapolation* 20, No. 2 (summer 1979).

"The Man-Machine Intelligence Relationship in Science Fiction," in *Many Futures, Many Worlds*, ed. Thomas Clareson (Kent, Ohio: Kent State University Press, 1977).

"A Science Fiction Aesthetic," *Pacific Quarterly* 4, No. 3 (July 1979).

I am grateful to the National Endowment for the Humanities for a fellowship in 1973 which enabled me to begin this study. I also want to express my appreciation to several colleagues who both stimulated my thinking and responded with thoughtful criticism to my ideas: Ihab Hassan and Thomas Bontly of the University of Wisconsin–Milwaukee and Martin Harry Greenberg of the University of Wisconsin–Green Bay. Richard DeMillo of the Georgia Institute of Technology gave generously of his time in introducing me to the field of computer science. James Welch of the University of Wisconsin–Madison has my special gratitude for tirelessly and patiently sharing with me his wide knowledge in physics and computer science.

Introduction

The growth of science fiction (SF) has paralleled the development of the natural and human sciences. From its small beginnings in the nineteenth century SF has emerged in the twentieth century as a major literary genre. It has recently begun to receive critical attention in such studies as David Ketterer's *New Worlds for Old* and Robert Scholes's *Structural Fabulation*. These works are wide ranging in their attempts to give an overview of SF. Darko Suvin has defined the genre and differentiated it from the realistic mainstream, the myth, the fairy tale, and the fantasy. He has proposed that the next step in the study of SF is an analysis of subgenres such as the fabulous voyage, the superman story, the artificial intelligence story, time travel, meeting with aliens.[1]

This study has several objectives. The first is to write a history of the subgenre of artificial or machine intelligence (robots and computers). No such history has previously been undertaken, nor has a substantial bibliography of fiction on this theme been published. The second is to analyze this subgenre of SF by discovering and describing recurring images, patterns, and meaning in cybernetic fiction, the term I have used to designate this body of literature. A further analysis of the cybernetic imagination is accomplished by exploring the cross-fertilizations taking place between writers in the subgenre and between the fiction and the developments in theoretical science and technological innovation. The third objective of the study is to make a critical judgment of the literary merit of SF by a rigorous evaluative study of one of its important subgenres, cybernetic SF. Has SF, after a century and a half of development, achieved enough stature to deserve a position beside realistic fiction in the literary tradition?

The literary scholar in SF encounters several problems. A major one is the difficulty of gathering material. The body of literature is large, and much of it is out of print and not easily available. Few comprehensive bibliographies have been compiled, and none according to themes. J. O. Bailey's *Pilgrims through Space and Time* began the task of recording the emergence of the genre, and he makes some use of themes. But he traces the development of SF only until the beginning of World War II; and his study understandably does not mention computers, since the computer did not become prominent until after the war. This study is the first attempt to develop a comprehensive bibliography on a single theme in SF. In my search for titles, I have read commentary and criticism of SF for clues, asked writers and fans for suggestions, called on the wide knowledge of SF book dealers, and searched private libraries.

The literary scholar who undertakes a critical judgment of SF encounters another problem. It is generally agreed that the criteria used to evaluate mainstream fiction are not entirely appropriate for SF, but no consensus has been reached about the proper criteria. Chapter 4 of this study proposes an aesthetic of SF, and the criteria defined in the aesthetic are used to evaluate the literature in the remaining chapters. The aesthetic theory was developed both inductively and deductively. Some works of SF (and here I have focused on works in cybernetic SF) are generally agreed to be outstanding. I have analyzed the elements at work in this body of fiction to determine what constitutes their excellence. In addition, I have used the aesthetic standard, once defined, to judge and comment on fiction that seems to me to be excellent but has not yet been given the critical recognition I feel it merits.

Another difficulty encountered in a critical study of cybernetic fiction, so closely related to theoretical knowledge and technological developments, is that the critic must have some understanding of the field if he is to make informed judgments. To be able to evaluate SF, I have taken courses in computer science and read widely in nonfiction works examining the impact of computers on society. I have also been fortunate in having colleagues in the field of computer science who were generous in sharing their expertise when I needed help in evaluating the scientific background of a fictional work.

A comparison of the fictional worlds of computers and robots with developments in the real world reveals a sharp discrepancy. Much of the SF is dystopian, but no such negative attitude prevails in the field of computer science. How is this discrepancy to be explained? My search for the answer to this question led to some of the most interesting insights about this literature.

The study is based on 225 short stories and novels written between 1930 and 1977. (For a complete list of titles see the bibliography of fiction.) The short stories, with few exceptions, were collected from anthologies rather than from the pulp magazines in which they first appeared. I searched over two hundred anthologies for stories about robots and computers. Because the stories reprinted in the anthologies had already gone through one selective process, they are of somewhat higher caliber than those that might have been selected directly from the pulp magazines. I have tried to be more exhaustive in selecting the novels, and I believe that most of the novels about robots and computers have been included in the study. I have in all instances used the date of original publication, although in some cases the author has indicated that he wrote the story long before publication. I have attempted to trace the history of the development of cybernetic SF, and in assigning credits I have consistently used the date of first publication (not the date of reprinting in an anthology).

The works of fiction were coded according to thirty-three characteristics, such as date of publication, setting in time and space, computer application, and method of plot development. The coded stories were stored in a computer file and analyzed in an attempt to discover correlations between different descriptors. The conclusions expressed in the study are based on this computer analysis of the fiction. The thirty-three descriptors represent the outcome of several attempts to determine which characteristics would be most helpful in the analysis of the fiction. For instance, it was not immediately apparent that the evolution of robots in SF and the evolution of computers followed different paths and therefore needed to be considered separately. Nor was it apparent until after a substantial amount of study that the use of isolated, closed, and open systems would provide a meaningful frame of reference for cataloging the fiction.

For the purposes of the study a computer is defined as an automatic electronic machine for performing calculations and for storing and processing information. A robot is defined as a mobile machine system made of nonbiological materials such as metal, plastic, and electronic devices. The robot may be self-controlled (have its computer within), remotely controlled (have its computer somewhere else), or an intermediate machine, with the robot being partly self-activated and partly remotely controlled. In this study robots have been distinguished from androids, which are defined as humanlike creatures, designed by men, made of biological materials. Robots are also differentiated from cyborgs (a portmanteau of the words *cybernetic* and *organism*), which are defined as entities built by joining mechanisms and biological organisms. Stories about androids and cyborgs have not been included in this study simply because the body of literature that includes robots, androids, and cyborgs is too large.

A pattern that emerges from the study of this large body of fiction creates metaphors of man's relationships with machine intelligence. The images evolve, over the forty-five-year period examined, from the simple to the complex and from optimism to pessimism. Constantly recurring is the Promethean image of man as the creator of a new kind of intelligence through technology. Early optimistic views of man's creative accomplishments are later replaced by destructive metaphors of machines overwhelming and dehumanizing man. Most writers since World War II seemed to have difficulty creating any images except those in which technology destroys man and his environment. The imagination describing these dystopian visions relies largely on extrapolation and works from a closed-system model. In contrast, a much smaller body of fiction is based on an open-system model and makes speculative leaps in creating its bright visions of man's future. In this fiction the transforming imagination pictures a new man-machine symbiosis, symbolized by the man-spaceship metaphor. Man, uniting matter, energy, and information, breaks free from the earth and ventures into the universe.

This study demonstrates that much of the fiction written since World War II is reactionary in its attitude toward computers and artificial intelligence. It is often ill informed about information theory and computer technology and lags behind present developments instead of anticipating the future. Only a small number of the later works demonstrate the sound grounding in science that is characteristic of writers during the golden age of SF in the 1930s and 1940s.

The Cybernetic Imagination
in Science Fiction

Science Fiction as a Form of the Literary Imagination

Storytelling is man's oldest art form, and the urge to tell stories just might be the quality that sets man apart from other forms of life on earth. The storyteller must be able to imagine things not immediately at hand or available to his senses, and he must be able to communicate these mental pictures to someone else. Imagination and language; the teller and the listener; the tale of what happened—a collection of images moving in a patterned process—these are the elements of a story.

Traditionally stories have entertained, recorded history, immortalized men, and preserved wisdoms. At their finest in every culture stories have become myths, visions of the universe proposing an underlying system or pattern operant in the universe. Man has always held that despite the apparent randomness or chaos in the disparate phenomena around us, some mysterious, hidden principle or force beneath the surface binds the universe in a coherent whole. However transient the forms of matter may appear, reshaping themselves in eternal restless movements, the movements have a pattern. The definition of the pattern and the process of its movement is the making of a myth.

Fantasy has long fertilized and embellished the tales lying at the edges of actual events recorded in story form. But science fiction (SF) is a more recent phenomenon. The literary response of the imagination to scientific theory and technological innovation, SF did not appear until early in the nineteenth century. During this period Renaissance intellectual seeds came to fruition. Scientific insight gave a new dimension to man's concept of time and space, and technology a new power to his machines and tools. Mary Shelley's early imaginative response to the potential of science, *Frankenstein* (1818), was the first of many SF tales to create new images of man. All these stories grew from an awareness of the radical future unfolding as man yoked knowledge and mechanical power. The marriage would transform man and his world. Mary Shelley's imagination sparked monstrous horrors; Jules Verne and H. G. Wells built remarkable machines and used them to journey on extraordinary voyages through time and space. Other writers joined Wells and Verne in spinning tales that used the machine as a prime mover to take man where he had never before ventured. Actually the first mover on these remarkable journeys was the human imagination, but it did not rely on magic. The writer used technology to make the imaginary journey plausible. The machine replaced the flying carpet, and future possibility replaced pure fantasy.

Although SF emerged in the nineteenth century, it was a nearly indiscernible literary event, overshadowed by the flowering of the realistic novel. Following its humble beginnings in Samuel Richardson's *Pamela* (1740), the realistic novel achieved respectability in the nineteenth century and replaced poetry as the predominant literary form by the beginning of the twentieth century. It has been proposed that SF is experiencing a later but parallel development. If indeed SF has achieved maturity, it is a very recent event. Critical debate ignites and flames at the possibility of SF's replacing the realistic novel as the predominant literary form by this century's end.

The English literary tradition has generally resisted the American novel's division into mainstream novels and SF. The English tradition recognizes that the novel, whatever its mode, is a response of the literary imagination to science and technology. This stimulation of the imagination actually began much earlier, in the seventeenth century, when modern science was born. Marjorie Nicolson in *Science and Imagination* describes the shift in focus and vision occurring in men like Donne, Milton, and, a century later, Swift. Two technologies that augmented physical vision were developed in this early period: the telescope and the microscope. Man's discovery, through these instruments, of "the vastness and the minuteness of the universe and of man" created a new inner vision. Physical sight altered insight. Reality could no longer be understood as man's unaided senses had perceived it. John Donne's response to the new astronomy was immediate. He had a restless, curious mind, and when it encountered the Copernican theory, his cosmic imagination was stirred. Images begin to appear in his poetry of new stars in the firmament, the wonders of transitory comets, and a "new Philosophy [that] arrests the Sunne and bids the passive earth about it runne." Milton's imagination was also transformed by the new astronomy, stimulated by the sight of the starry heavens through a telescope. It was an experience he never forgot; it is reflected again and again in his mature work; it stimulated him to reading and to thought; and it made *Paradise Lost* the first cosmic poem in which a drama is played against a background of interstellar space." [1] Although less dramatic than the telescope in its immediate impact on the literary imagination, the microscope was equally pervasive in its influence. For example, Jonathan Swift borrowed the device of magnification of anatomical details when he described the larger-than-human inhabitants of Brobdingnag. [2]

In the nineteenth century H. G. Wells was strongly influenced by the evolutionary theories of Charles Darwin. He was introduced to them through his teacher, Thomas Huxley, and Huxley's "cosmic pessimism" is reflected in Wells's first novel, *The Time Machine*. Wells's highly active imagination defined most of the patterns that have served as models for subsequent generations of science fiction writers. He started with the concept or theory that science was enumerating; he translated abstractions into concrete events happening to particular individuals; and he imagined what the impact of the event would be on the man and on his society.

Jules Verne, Wells's fellow pioneering SF writer in France, was more realistic in his starting point and more pragmatic in his imaginative development of ideas. He was more interested in technological innovation, particularly modes of transportation, that might be possible in the near future than in speculations about the nature of the universe. Thus he journeys around the earth, twenty leagues under the sea, and even to the moon. But his adventures never range through cosmic space and time on the vast scope that Wells's do. These innovative giants establish two imaginative modes for SF: extrapolation and speculation. Verne extrapolates; Wells transcends space and time with wildly imaginative speculations.

Although SF employs the forms of mainstream novels and short stories, it does not use the realistic mode. It describes the future as it may be, parallel worlds as they might be, or the past—before recorded time—as it might have been. Time, space, or accepted reality must be altered in some way. This formidable challenge to the human imagination is required to create an image that has never before existed. The only constraint is that scientific plausibility should not be violated.

Should the abundant fiction spawned by the SF imagination be taken seriously? Has it risen from its humble American beginnings in the pulp magazines with their youthful audiences? Does it do more than entertain? Has it accomplished literature's traditional task of mythmaking, mediating between man and his cosmos, creating a pattern to organize chaos and define man's function in the world, suggesting the individual's role in society?

These are the questions I will ask of SF. The scope of the questions and the volume of SF requires limitations if the study is to avoid superficiality and meaningless generalizations. I have elected to impose limits by examining only the literature in the SF genre dealing with machine intelligence. It is an important theme in contemporary SF. Computers and robots are assumed to be part of the artificial environment in which future man acts out his dramas of discovery and survival. Earth has become a computerized world, and computer-operated ships carry man through space to other galaxies and planetary systems. The aliens he encounters may have computers, or mechanical intelligence may even be the form of life on another planet.

What kinds of images does the contemporary SF imagination develop when it plays with the alternatives and future possibilities of computer technology and information theory? Do these images and configurations repeat the patterns of earlier SF writers? These questions will be explored in this study, with an awareness that new processes and patterns may be at work. Because both scientific theory and technological innovation undergo radical developments in the twentieth century, so also may the fiction born from the literary imagination exploring and responding to that science and technology.

The first such development is the revolution in physics. The Newtonian mechanistic world view has been superseded by quantum mechanics on the microscopic level and by relativity physics on the macroscopic level. The implications of these developments are fundamental. Even with the aid of the telescope and the microscope, we cannot observe the worlds that physics is now exploring. We are exploring the universe at its extreme edges, and there is nothing in the observable physical world that provides a model or an understanding of the realms to which scientific exploration leads. Physicist Erwin Schrödinger explains the difficulties we experience as our "mental eye" tries to penetrate worlds it has not seen before: "We find nature behaving so entirely differently from what we observe in visible and palpable bodies of our surroundings, that *no* model shaped after our large-scale experiences can ever be 'true.' This new universe that we try to conquer is not only practically inaccessible, but not even thinkable. Or, to be precise, we can, of course, think it, but however we think it, it is wrong; not perhaps quite as meaningless as a 'triangular circle,' but much more so than a 'winged lion.'"[3] The modern scientist solves the difficulty by giving up trying to "see" in images. Mathematical models replace the earlier mechanical models of the universe. They are, of course, highly abstract. A new and challenging puzzle arises for the contemporary SF imagination: How does it respond—in a creative mode using images—to scientific theory that can only be modeled mathematically?

Second is the development of computers, a technology utilizing electronic circuitry. The process of handling information at incredible speeds within the computer cannot be visualized. All that actually can be observed are metal cabinets, keyboards, visual screens, rows of blinking lights. The electrons that convey information within the computer's circuitry cannot be seen, and the speed of the process, measured in nanoseconds, can hardly be comprehended. This world is much different from the starry firmament whose changes are so slow that they are imperceptible or from the leisurely alteration, through aeons of time, of land forms and living species on earth. The contemporary SF writer about cybernetics is faced with a science much different from that encountered by earlier writers, who imagined what it would be like to be transported through time and space and what adventures might be encountered in this pioneering journey. The cybernetic fiction writer must send ideas or information through time and space, a more formidable undertaking since this knowledge is a construct of the human mind, not of nature.

A challenge for the SF imagination is that writing about artificial intelligence requires dealing with a mechanical form that is in the logical, mathematical mode. Everything in the model is defined, and once these definitions are made, causes and effects and relationships are fixed. Such a mechanistic, closed model is anathema to the creative mind, which tends to work by intuition and not logic. Given the inclination of the SF imagination, can it create fictions about the computer in which the computer is pictured as anything but the villain? If the answer is yes, under what conditions can it do so?

This study concerns not only the possibilities of future man-computer relationships pictured by the SF imagination but also the nature of the literary imagination itself. How does it work? How does it relate to the scientific imagination whose insights are its starting point? Are the creative processes of the scientist and the artist similar?

During the last fifty years both SF and psychology have come of age. Yet psychology has little to say about the human imagi-

nation and the nature of creativity. Since the time of William
James, the subject has generally been avoided in academic psychology.[4] Interest in creativity, however, has recently begun to
appear in another quarter, computer science, as research in artificial intelligence expands. The question is, Can a computer be
programmed to think creatively? Before that question can be
answered, the nature of creativity must be defined.

In one view of this complex subject the human imagination
is believed to work by combining stored pictures or images received from its experiences in the world. Kenneth Boulding has
explored extensively this picture-making function in his *The Image*.[5] The imagination keeps adding images as experience brings
new information or messages from the environment. It creates a
gestalt that might be called its knowledge of the world, but more
precisely it should be referred to as its image of the world. Knowledge implies validity or truth, and the image is highly subjective.
Boulding notes that the image in the mind at birth probably
consists of nothing more than an undifferentiated blur. As the
child develops, his image grows. He perceives himself as separate
in the midst of a world of objects. Consciousness or self-awareness has begun. The behavior of the individual depends on his
knowledge structure, or his image. As long as he continues to
accept new information or messages, his image, and consequently his pattern of behavior, will be altered.[6] The imagination
of the writer may work in just the way Boulding describes. But
it goes one step further. It wishes to communicate its images to
someone, and so it adds the dimension of words to its operation.

The SF imagination is a specialized form of the literary imagination for several reasons. First, the source for its catalytic idea
or image is different from that of mainstream fiction, and that
source is theoretical science and technology. Second, it acts out
its drama in a time other than the present, customarily the future.
And last, it adds a dimension of the unknown. In some form—
new technology, new settings, new creatures—SF creates an image that does not exist in reality as reality is currently perceived.
This creative act has a quality of transcendence. It represents a

struggle to overcome man's present limitations in time, space, and awareness; to transport himself at least mentally to places he has never been, to gain a new world for himself.

As science accumulates information at a startling rate and technological sophistication keeps pace, the SF imagination is challenged. Much early SF, now very naive, must be discarded or preserved only as a historical curiosity. Every advance in science and technology requires the SF writer to reinvent the future. Thus the literary critic must move from defining SF and evaluating its merits to describing its movement and judging the value of its insights and the techniques it evolves in its anticipatory process. This evaluative task demands that the critic note the relationship of the writer's fictional worlds to the real world—the world of empirical reality as it is now understood. To judge cybernetic SF thus requires a familiarity with the function of computers and their rapid evolution in the last thirty years.

Information Theory and Computer Technology

The scientific and technological events that occurred around the middle of the twentieth century are startling. The explosion of the first atomic bombs in August 1945—now recognized as a watershed date in man's history—provoked a powerful literary response: an outpouring of holocaust and postholocaust literature dramatizing the realization that the world would never be the same. We came to understand we had been expelled from the garden of simplicity where we lived before the fall of the bomb.

But several other events occurred during that same period, less dramatic at that time but perhaps more significant in their long-term effects. They are all subsets of the broad category of *cybernetics* which Norbert Wiener, often called its founding father, defines as a new field of science attempting "to find the common elements in the functioning of automatic machines and of the human nervous system, and to develop a theory that will cover the entire field of control and communication in machines and in living organisms."[7] He recognized very early the radical social changes that the computer would cause. Cybernetics comprises all systems, mechanical and biological, in which information plays a role. Information theory, DNA theory, and general systems theory aim at describing the function of cybernetic systems. Cybernetics is an old word; it is derived from the Greek word *kybernētēs*, meaning steersman. Plato used the word in *The Republic* to describe the prudent aspects of the art of government. The Latin word *gubernator* was derived from the Greek, and from it came our word *governor*. A. M. Ampère in his *Essay on the Philosophy of Science* (1838) used the term *cybernetique* for the science of civil government. Not much later, in 1868, J. C. Maxwell presented a paper to the Royal Society analyzing mathematically the governor used on machines.[8] He described the device on a steam engine that controls the steam flow into the engine. The range of cybernetics is illustrated in these early sources. Cybernetics is concerned with governance or control in social systems and in mechanical systems.

Cybernetic systems also occur in nature. Physiologists early in the twentieth century became aware that biological systems have a governing system for maintaining internal control. Cannon's *Wisdom of the Body* (1939) describes the self-regulatory devices used to automatically maintain equilibrium in the physiological systems of the body.

Interest and research in self-regulating systems, both mechanical and biological, increased as the century progressed. In 1948, when Norbert Wiener published *Cybernetics, or Control and Communication in the Animal and the Machine*, he formalized much of the thinking up to that time. In this work and in *The Human Use of Human Beings: Cybernetics and Society* (1950) he identified the common functions of homeostatic, or self-regulating, devices in mechanical, biological, and social systems. He went back to the Greek language for *cybernetics*, the name he gave the new science of communication and control. Later he learned that Ampère had used the word in 1838.[9]

Technology and theory constantly fertilize each other, generating progeny that will continue the creative process. Claude

Shannon's *The Mathematical Theory of Communication* (1948), a mathematical description of the function of a communication system, provided the theoretical base for an information technology so dynamic that it is often described as the second industrial revolution. The theory was rooted in a hundred years of communication technology, beginning with Samuel F. B. Morse's telegraph in 1832. The telephone followed in 1876, radio tubes in 1905, television in 1925, and the digital computer in 1944. The computer has turned out to be one of the most powerful machines ever developed by man. In the thirty-odd years since its first appearance, it has had a major impact; it has altered the lives of individuals and families, changed the structure, methods, and scope of industries and businesses, and affected society as a whole. Coupled with satellites, it links the entire globe in an instant communication system.

The combination of arithmetical and logical operations gives the computer its enormous power. The arithmetical operations—addition, subtraction, multiplication, and division—use the binary system, in which all notations are expressed with either 0 or 1. Logical systems in mathematics and philosophy are two-valued: a proposition is either true or false. In the nineteenth century the British mathematician George Boole worked out the mathematical structure of Aristotelian logic. In 1948 Claude E. Shannon of the Massachusetts Institute of Technology, using Boolean algebra in a study of the logic of switching circuits, noted that two-valued logic can be handled on the same type of electronic circuitry as binary numbers. The binary digits 1 and 0 are represented in the computer by the presence or absence of a current. The logical opposites true and false can be represented in exactly the same way.

The computer can not only perform computations at incredible speeds, it can also compare and make choices. The stored program of instructions allows the computer to do a long series of operations in sequence: to compute, compare, move, position, copy. It is more than an arithmetic machine; it is a big, fast, general-purpose, symbol-manipulating machine.[10] It can be developed to be a flexible, decision-making, problem-solving, perceiving machine: a thinking machine.

Artificial intelligence, a subdivision of computer science, attempts to discover and describe aspects of human intelligence that can be simulated by machines. At present machines can do a number of things that people would say require intelligence.[11] Machines can process information expressed in human languages; play games of strategy (chess, checkers, nim, poker), and in some games (checkers and nim), learn to play better than people; recognize visual or auditory patterns; find proofs for mathematical theorems; solve certain well-formulated problems. Researchers in artificial intelligence grant that their machines currently demonstrate only rudimentary levels of intelligent behavior. But this area of research is relatively new, and enthusiasts like Marvin Minsky at MIT are optimistic that artificial intelligence will someday be able to duplicate much of intelligent human behavior.

The intelligent machine that most nearly simulates human behavior is the robot. The robots of *Star Wars* (1977), R2-D2 and C-3PO, caught the public's fancy and made robots in film popular. But they have always been a part of the SF tradition, where their image is so clear that the term *robot* seems to require no definition. A robot is a machine duplicating man in both appearance and activities. The actual research and development in robotics is recent, and the meaning of the term here is less precise because a variety of robots—simple and complex—exist. At the present time robots do not even approach the level of sophistication portrayed in SF, nor do they resemble the human form. Research in robotics was minimal until the 1960s; thus the field is a very new one. A robot is commonly defined as a teachable, program-controlled, automatic manipulator capable of doing operations without human attendance. The robot consists of three components: (1) the control and memory unit (which may be remotely located or incorporated in the robot as a miniaturized computer), (2) sensing equipment (usually including a TV camera or perhaps only a photoelectric eye), and (3) effector equipment, which usually includes a mechanical arm.[12] The industrial robot in use today is a relatively simple automatic machine; the robots being developed at research laboratories such as those at MIT, Stanford, Johns Hopkins, and Queen Mary College in London are much more sophisticated.

A number of books and articles in the 1960s announced that the age of computers had arrived, and the 1970s seems likely to be the decade ushering in the age of robots. However, neither appeared without technological antecedents. Discovery and development always occur in a continuum, making it almost impossible to define precisely when one age has ended and another begun. Further, technological invention grows from mental images, and mental images seem most often to be expressed first in the literary mode. Thus the division between the literary imagination and the engineering imagination seems artificial. Such tidy, definitive chronologies and categories direct us through unreal times and nonexistent territories. But if we remember that they are only fictional constructs, they can serve as helpful guides when we look from the path we have come in developing machine intelligence to the landscape we have yet to travel.

The first fully electronic computer was developed by J. P. Eckert and J. W. Mauchly at the University of Pennsylvania (1946) and called the Electric Numerical Integrator and Calculator (ENIAC). It had no movable parts; instead it used valves or vacuum tubes. But the origins of this first computer lie as far back as the Chinese abacus (circa 450 B.C.). The idea of a mechanical counting device became more complex with time: John Napier's logarithms (1614), Charles Babbage's difference engine (1833), William Burrough's adding machine (1888), Herman Hollerith's card-punching machine (1890), Vannevar Bush's differential analyzer (1937), Howard Aiken's Mark I digital computer (1944), all predecessors of the ENIAC.

The evolution of the computer accelerated its pace after ENIAC. John von Neumann proposed in 1946 that binary numbering systems be used in designing computers and that computer instructions as well as the data being processed be stored in the machine. UNIVAC, completed in 1951, employed these concepts. Regarded as the first commercial computer, it was used by the Bureau of Census.[13]

In the early 1960s a second generation of computers appeared, using transitors instead of vacuum tubes. The late 1960s produced a third generation using integrated semiconductor circuits. The 1970s introduced miniaturized circuitry and bubble memory and gave a new impetus to computer development. Each new generation of computers has provided faster processing of more information at lower costs.

The use of computers has grown rapidly because they can accomplish some tasks more effectively than humans. They can process computations at a speed beyond human comprehension—1 billion operations per second. They have total recall of data stored in memory, so nothing is ever lost, and their access time to that memory is very fast. They are tireless; they can work round the clock at tasks humans would regard as boring drudgery. Human beings, in contrast, do computations slowly and often inaccurately; have memory lapses; are slow and unreliable in recalling material from their memories; become tired and bored with repetitive tasks.

The limitations of the computer are several. Its storage density is poor when compared to the human brain, so it is a bulky machine; it is inhibited in communication, so the imput of data is a slow process; it is inflexible and can do only what it has been programmed to do, so it cannot handle the unforeseen. In contrast, human brains have developed through natural language a highly effective system of communication; they have easy input and output of data; the storage density of information in the brain is enormous (the three-pound brain has 1000 billion intricate, interrelated cells); humans are creative and flexible and can handle the unforeseen.

This cursory overview makes clear that the computer can be an aid to humans in tasks that require great speed and accuracy, those that are repetitious, and those that involve the processing of large amounts of data. The computer can eliminate the drudgery from mental labor in the same way that the machine removed the drudgery from physical labor during the eighteenth and nineteenth centuries.

The development of robot technology has lagged about ten years behind computer advances. The proliferation in the 1970s of computer technology into all aspects of society will probably be paralleled by a similar proliferation of robots into work and home life in the 1980s. The first step in the development of industrial robots was the remotely controlled mechanical hand that nuclear scientists used for handling deadly radioactive materials through thick walls when they were producing atomic bombs near the end of World War II. The hands were called waldoes, a name derived from a Robert Heinlein story, "Waldo," published in *Astounding* in 1942. In this story (published under the name of Anson McDonald, one of Heinlein's several pseudonyms) mechanical devices used for remote-control manipulation were called waldoes.

The first patent for a commercial robot was granted to George Devol in 1950, and the first prototype, the Unimate, was built by Joseph Engelberger of Unimatation, Danbury, Connecticut, in 1958. A General Motors plant in New Jersey bought the first Unimate in 1961. Expansion of robot production and industrial use has been rapid during the last ten years, although only during the past few years have robots been profitable for their manufacturers. In 1975 the Robot Institute of America was established to facilitate the flow of information between manufacturers and users of robots. According to a study done by James R. Bright of MIT, it takes about ten years from the time a new product is introduced until it is accepted by the market. The introduction of robots into industry seems to be following the same rules, and they are now in the classic exponential growth curve. Growth and development is expanding rapidly not only in the United States but also in Japan, Germany, Sweden, and England. An International Symposium on Industrial Robots has been held annually since 1972. Industrial robots perform jobs such as loading and unloading die-casting machines, spray painting, spot welding, stacking, and assembling, in a highly reliable fashion. They are never late for work, demand no coffee break, and do not complain of boredom when assigned to repetitive tasks. By the 1980s industrial robots will be available with sensors and control systems that allow them to adapt to changing conditions in their environment, thus enabling them to carry out more complex tasks in assembly, machine loading, and areas other than those in which they currently perform.

Robots are also beginning to appear in the home and the classroom where they can both entertain and educate. A robot named 2-XL (to excel), now available from Mego Corporation, can ask questions and accept objective answers such as multiple choice, yes/no, and true/false. The robot's programmable tapes cover a wide range of subjects. Leachim, a robot teacher developed by Michael Freeman and Gary P. Mulkowsky, is being used experimentally in a New York City school. Quasar Industries has built a prototype domestic android which they hope to mass-produce in about two years.

At the same time that electrical engineers were developing systems for coding and processing information in machines, nuclear geneticists were unlocking the puzzle of nature's DNA method of coding information in living systems. In 1953 James D. Watson and Francis Crick constructed their double-helix model and proposed their theory of DNA. They suggested that DNA carries in coded form the genetic information necessary to reproduce the organism. Gregor Mendel, pioneering with his peas in 1832, had defined the gene as the unvarying bearer of hereditary traits. Watson and Crick elucidated the structural basis of the gene's replicative invariances. These are without doubt two of biology's most important discoveries.

During the period when research was proceeding in electrical communication systems and in biological systems, a number of researchers began to realize that their specialized area of study had structures and functions in common with other specialized fields. Ludwig von Bertalanffy, a biologist, introduced the term *general systems theory* after World War II.[14] He suggested that the older reductionist tendency to isolate and study phenomena in narrowly confined contexts was unworkable in dealing with living systems. A holistic approach, which studies the system as an entity rather than as a combination of parts, is more productive.

Biologists, behavioral scientists, and social scientists began to notice that their systems had much in common. Phenomena different in content show isomorphism in their formal structure. General systems theory defines a system as a complex of components acting in interrelation. Systems theory tried to develop principles that apply to systems in general, irrespective of the nature of the systems and their components. In 1972 Ervin Laszlo proposed a return from analytic to synthetic philosophy in his *Introduction to Systems Philosophy*. He sees general systems theory as a theoretical instrument for assuring the mutual relevance of scientific information and philosophic meaning. Systems philosophy integrates "the concept of enduring universals with transient processes within a non-bifurcated, hierarchically differentiated realm of invariant systems as the ultimate actualities of self-structuring nature." [15]

Social and Philosophical Implications of Cybernetics

If SF is to be regarded as serious contemporary fiction, then given the stature of its parent, the mainstream novel, it must move beyond entertainment. It must explore, as art always has, mankind and the individual. It must propose the inner nature and conditions of man; it must define man's social, political, and philosophical problems. But beyond the tasks always required of literature, SF must do more. A literature of anticipatory process, it must suggest a spectrum of future worlds, and by this creative act remind man how transient are the patterns of his contemporary cultural landscape. Those patterns are constructed from a kaleidoscope of scientific ideas, ever shifting and reorganizing into new constructs. Ideas and imagination bubble in a beaker of possibilities in the mental laboratory of the SF writer's head. The yield, if he is perceptive in choosing the germinal ideas and if he is creative enough, will be an array of metaphors offering penetrating insights and throwing helpful illumination down the varied paths into man's future.

SF must, thus, go beyond the realistic novel's accomplishments, because man's view of reality is now so different. In the eighteenth century the ideas of science, the inventions of technology, and the changes in society were limited enough to catch the attention of only the minority; today they engulf us all. The view of a static, enduring world has been washed away by our awareness of accelerating processes and increasing social complexities.

How does the literary imagination exploring cybernetics respond to this challenge of change? Does it move beyond the fascination with gadgets and adventures, typical of early SF, to consider the implications of cybernetic advances; to examine the ways man's environment and his image of his nature and significance will be changed; to speculate on how man may respond to these changes?

These are the questions that will be brought to the body of cybernetic SF being examined in this study. Comprehensive answers depend on an understanding of the social and philosophical implications of advances in information technology as they have been proposed by nonfiction writers.

No one doubts the computer's power as an agent of change. It may well be the most powerful source of change that human technology has ever created. It radically alters man's work life, both the kind of work he does and the amount of time he spends doing it. It alters man's leisure life; it can give to the common man the free time once available only to the aristocrat. It changes man's social and political institutions. It insidiously invades the creative fields, suggesting that machine-made art, produced in mass, can be as aesthetically valuable as the original, unique creation of an individual. Because it so drastically redesigns man's social institutions, from the family to the national government, it challenges many of man's time-tested cultural values. Definitions of right and wrong and of worth that were workable in earlier times hardly seem applicable in a computerized society.

The changes produced by the computer are so diverse that they are almost beyond comprehensive analysis. But some general directions of change can be identified. Social organizations will grow in size, in complexity, and in their power to maintain control. While technological innovations will press toward continued change, bureaucracies will tend to become more rigid as they age. A paradoxical impasse seems likely to develop. Social changes originally catalyzed by computer developments become bureaucratized; bureaucracies grow in size and power with the aid of the computer; finally they become so large and rigid that they cannot respond to the social changes that technology continues to catalyze. While the general direction of change can be determined, there is little agreement about the desirability of that change.

The machine model becomes more pervasive as technological development proceeds. Both man and institutions are understood according to a mechanistic, deterministic model where cause-and-effect relationships are at work. First the machine serves man because he understands how to build it and control it. But the machine begins to dominate. It becomes the *deus ex machina.* Man does not act; he is a passive particle that is acted on. He becomes a robot who can only respond to stimulation and do what he has been programmed to do. In the mechanistic world view the only puzzle is to understand how things work. The mysterious questions of first cause, or prime mover, and the why of the universe, so fascinating to philosophers over the centuries, are no longer asked.[16]

Several consequences inevitably follow from the machine model of both man and organizations. More emphasis will be placed on outputs or products of the system. The end becomes the goal, and the process or means by which the end is accomplished is submitted to one standard: efficiency. Choices are made on the basis of the most efficient way to accomplish an end. The product of most interest will be a material one, since it can be quantified, packaged, distributed. Nonmaterial ends become of little significance.

The effects on institutions and organizations of computerization have been well defined.[17] Automation is instituted in business and industry because it is a cheaper and faster mode of production and therefore more efficient. Data banks and information-processing systems in governmental agencies make it possible to handle more information; bureaucracies expand. Data banks begin sharing their information, and communication networks are established across the nation and then between bureaucracies of various nations. There is general agreement that these results are desirable because they increase efficiency. But what is good for the social organism may be less desirable for the individual organism.

As the size of organizational structures increases, the dimensions of the individual life are reduced. More governmental control means a loss of freedom for the individual. As decisions are increasingly made on the bureaucratic level, the election process loses significance for the individual. He realizes that bureaucratic structures will change little, regardless of which candidate or party is in office. He becomes alienated from himself as a source of power and feels that he is increasingly under the control of outside forces. The development of large data banks means that birth-to-death information about his life is immediately available to bureaucratic officials. His life is no longer a private affair. He feels that he has become only a number in a file of infinite size and that he almost ceases to exist as a unique individual.

More important, perhaps, than any of these is that man's work life becomes altered. Automation results in job displacement. The worker becomes obsolescent and is replaced by either a machine or a more recently educated person who possesses newer knowledge.

Perhaps most devastating of all is man's contemporary image of himself as uncomprehending of the social milieu in which he must exist. Living in a mysterious environment is not a new experience to man. Hunting man and agricultural man inhabited a natural world containing many phenomena beyond understanding. But these were phenomena created by a godhead and presumed to be understood by their creator. If one man could not understand earthquake or eclipse, neither could another. They did not expect to understand the supernatural; however they were certain the supreme being controlled them. But modern man lives in an artificial environment he has created himself. Man-made, it should be comprehensible to man. But it is not; and he must live with the frustration of knowing he cannot understand the understandable.

He presumes that the specialist, expert in his field, does understand. This, however, may no longer be the case. Joseph Weizenbaum in *Computer Power and Human Reason* (1976) notes that gigantic computer systems may well become incomprehensible programs. Often such a program is designed by teams of programmers, whose work may be spread over many years. The program evolves slowly, with subroutines being added and connected by intricate networks. By the time the system comes into use, the original programmer may not be working on it. The new programmer may not be able to predict what will happen when he adds a new program. It may well work, but no one programmer will understand the entire program.[18]

The cost to the individual of expanding, complex systems may be high. Most of the effects seem to provide few advantages to the individual except more leisure time and a higher material standard of living. Could it be that individual freedom and privacy as they have been known in the American tradition can no longer be maintained? Paul Armer, director of the Computation Center at Stanford University, suggests this possibility in a recent article. The enforcement of regulations to control who may have access to data files may well be unaffordable.[19] He proposes that for the common good we may have to renounce some of the rights to privacy that we have regarded as inviolate.

The implications of expanding automation and computer systems for ethical and cultural values become apparent from their social and political effects. Either values traditionally held are being challenged by social change, or new situations arise for which there is no precedent. Questions about values abound, but few answers have been agreed on. First, how much change is desirable? Should we attempt to curtail technological innovation generally, if such a feat is possible? Or, should we attempt to limit only certain kinds of change? Should certain kinds of research be curtailed to halt technological innovation? For instance, would we really want to build a superman robot, one superior to man, if it becomes possible to do so? What would be the effect on man of a superior mechanical intellect? How should a mechanical being mentally similar to a human being be considered? The Polish cyberneticist Stanislaw Lem suggests that ethically such a robot must be regarded as a human.[20]

The value of the work ethic is brought into question as society becomes more automated, allowing more leisure but less meaningful work for most of the population. If work is good, as the Puritan ethic claims, why take it from man and give it to machines?

Much less study of the implications of computerization for the arts has been done. Some interesting projects in computer-produced art have been undertaken. Computers have "created" pictures, written poems, and composed music, and at least one program has been written to produce a novel. Probably more interesting than the art the computer produces are the questions raised by the attempt. What happens to the uniqueness and originality of an art work if it can be created en mass by a machine? What, indeed, is creativity? If it represents some kind of intuitive leap, as is commonly held, then computer intelligence—which functions according to the logic of rational thought—ought not to be able to act creatively. Perhaps, however, intuition, when analyzed, will turn out to be merely a series of infinitely small logical steps. If so, it can be duplicated in a computer. But again, if creativity is a special delight of man, why program machines to do it?

The philosophical implications of cybernetics are several. The development of artificial intelligence in the twentieth century has reopened a lively debate among contemporary philosophers about a question first raised by René Descartes in the seventeenth

century: What is the boundary between the living and the mechanical? Descartes's immediate purpose was to differentiate between man and beast, to propose that man was different because
he possessed a soul, something animals lacked.[21] To accomplish
this he distinguished between mind and body, holding that mind
is something distinct from the body. The body is purely mechanical, a machine. An animal possessed a body but nothing more;
he was the bête (beast) machine. True, man had a body, but he
also had a mind that housed the soul. With his mind man not
only can think but has knowledge that he does. He is self-
conscious. With this analysis Descartes established a dualistic
view of man still not resolved today, although research in molecular biology seems close to providing the answer. Is mind to
be understood as something separate from the material body, or
can mental processes be understood as growing out of cellular
functions?

A few years after Descartes's statements about the nature of
man and animal, the mind-body debate took an evolutionary
turn with Julien La Mettrie. His *L'Homme Machine* swept away
Descartes's dualism and established the analogy of man as a
machine. In response to Descartes's position, La Mettrie agreed
that animals are machines but maintained there is no essential
difference between man and the machine. He suggested that the
human body could be compared to a large watch constructed
with skill and ingenuity. He disagreed with Descartes's claims
for the existence of a soul and argued for a mechanical monism
operating in both man and animal. He held there is no evidence
for a mental self or soul or substance beyond that which may be
considered part of the body itself. Thought, he believed, might
well be one of the properties of matter, like electricity, or the
faculty of motion.[22]

In the nineteenth century Darwin's evolutionary theory established that Descartes's discontinuity between man and animal
was not an acceptable position in light of the conclusive evidence
provided by nature. Man had evolved from less complex forms
of life. But the debate about whether and where a boundary

between the living and the mechanical could be established was not settled. Closely related is the question of the boundary between animate and inanimate matter. The vitalists argued for a dualistic view of the mind and body, while the evolutionists—whose most vocal spokesman was Thomas Huxley—proposed mechanical monism as the most acceptable hypothesis. The debate continues into the twentieth century, and it pervades SF writing about artificial intelligence. In nonfiction literature the mind-body debate is one of the liveliest in philosophical literature exploring the implications of the development of artificial intelligence. [23]

Closely related to the mind-body debate is the long-standing argument about free will and determinism. Gilbert Ryle in *Concept of Mind* (1949) referred to Descartes's view as the paradigm of a ghost-in-the-machine dualism. If man is only a mechanistic system, then it would seem that the deterministic view has been substantiated. But if man is something more—if there is a ghost in the machine—then man may well have the free will that his intuition has always told him he possesses. Arthur Koestler in *The Ghost in the Machine* (1967) advances the debate; he suggests that the dualistic model proposing only an either/or choice has not been resolved because it is the wrong paradigm, and that a more complex model is needed.

In summary, the development of mechanical cybernetic systems raises four tightly related philosophical issues: the Cartesian mind-body dualism, the question of free will, the relationship of human and mechanical systems, and the relationship of animate and inanimate matter.

This brief overview outlines the development of information theory and technology; it also points to the major social changes occurring as a result of these developments and the philosophical issues raised by man's creation of mechanical intelligence. I will now put a series of questions to SF. Does the literature anticipate these developments? Is it aware of the social changes generated by information technology? Are the philosophical issues being debated? If SF about computers and artificial intelligence is to be regarded as serious contemporary literature, one has a right to ask that it keep pace with or be in advance of current technology; that it display a sensitivity to the social impact of computer application; and that it be imaginative in creating alternative futures.

Germinal Literary Images and Early Technologies   2

The Myths

SF portraying robots and computers that are electronically operated was first written early in the 1930s; the actual computer technology was not developed until the late 1930s and early 1940s. But neither cybernetic literature nor technology sprang from a void. Mechanical calculators had been in use for over three centuries. The possibility of creating automata has long intrigued man, as historical records and surviving artifacts verify. Since the early Renaissance, tales of artificially created life forms have occurred in literature and legend. Ancient myths and legends also reveal man's enduring fascination with the creative process and his urge to imagine and make mechanical models of the natural world. In Greek mythology the god Prometheus becomes the prototype for the modern engineer, mechanical or biological, because Prometheus was known as a master craftsman and the creator of life on earth.

The Greek creation myth fascinates the SF imagination almost more than the biblical account of creation. In the Genesis story God with speed and expertise fashioned heaven and earth, animals and man, all in six days, a creative wonder that is static and unchanging. The Greek myth, in contrast, is one of process; heaven, earth, and man come into being through a chain of reactions extending over a long period of time and reflecting a struggle of conflicting forces. Destruction of the old is part of the creation of new forms. The myth is worth looking at in some detail, because SF mirrors so many of its elements.

In the Greek creation chain the universe at first was only
formless chaos, brooded over by unbroken darkness.[1] Mysteriously two children, Night and Erebus, were born of this shape-
lessness. Then came another mysterious act, the most marvelous
of all. The Greek playwright Aristophanes, describes it.

. . . Black winged Night
Into the bosom of Erebus dark and deep
Laid a wind-born egg, and as the seasons rolled
Forth sprang Love, the longed-for, shining, with
     wings of gold.

The sequential chain of creation continued. Love created Light
and its companion, Radiant Day. Then, again marvelously and
inexplicably, Father Heaven and Mother Earth appeared, and
they had children. These children were the first creatures who
had the appearance of life, but their varied forms were not beautiful. They were gigantic, and some were many-headed monsters.
Others, called Cyclops, had one monstrous eye in the middle of
their foreheads. All Heaven and Earth's children tended to be
destructive, except for the Titans, who were destined to father
the next generation of gods. The archetypal pattern of son overthrowing father first appears with the children of these Titans,
children who not only create new gods but also destroy the old.
Three of these Titans are of particular interest to this study:
Kronus, Prometheus, and Epimetheus. From the Greek word
kronus comes the modern word *chronology*, the science that deals
with measuring time by regular intervals. The Greek *menos* means
mind, and it is the root word of Prometheus, meaning forethought, and Epimetheus, meaning afterthought. Metaphorically
time can be understood as becoming part of man's awareness in
this myth. Man's consciousness identifies time, and he realizes
that with his mind he can move backward and forward in time.

In this creation myth Kronus, youngest of the Titan sons,
eventually castrated Father Heaven and became the lord of the
universe with his sister-queen, Rhea. Prometheus and Epime-

theus were on hand as lesser gods. Prometheus was wise, in fact one of the wisest of the Titans, but Epimetheus was a scatterbrain who tended to act impulsively and then regret his actions. Kronus and Rhea had twelve children, the familiar Olympian gods, who lived on Mount Olympus and peopled the well-known Greek myths. One of the twelve, Haphaestus, would become the God of fire and the mastersmith in the new generation of gods, as Prometheus was in the Titan generation. Kronus's sixth child, Zeus, when he was grown, repeated the father-son struggle and went to war with his father in an attempt to gain power. In this war Prometheus sided with Zeus, who eventually unseated his father and became the new ruler of the universe, with the assistance of his Olympian brothers and sisters.

Then came man's creation. One version of the myth says the task of making man and animal was delegated to Prometheus and Epimetheus. Epimetheus impulsively gave all the best gifts—strength, courage, swiftness, cunning—to the animals, which he created first. Too late he realized that he had nothing left to make man a match for the other animals. He turned the task of creation over to Prometheus, who fashioned man from clay in a graceful, upright form like the gods. Then Prometheus went to heaven and stole into the palace of the Sun where he lit a torch and brought it back to earth. Fire was his gift to man. It was a marvelous gift, providing man with a limitless source of energy. With it he could master many crafts.

Zeus, a jealous god, on hearing what had happened, swore revenge on mankind and on mankind's benefactor, Prometheus, for stealing a secret of the gods and giving it to man. He created Pandora, the first woman, and sent her to his brother gods with a box of gifts that she was forbidden to open. She little suspected that each god had put something harmful into the box. Prudent Prometheus was suspicious of a gift from Zeus, but Epimetheus, ever lacking in forethought, accepted Pandora and her box. She in turn, possessed of a lively curiosity, opened the box. Out flew all the mischief. In terror Pandora slammed the lid shut—too late. But one thing remained—Hope. It was the only good among all the evils in the box, all that man has to comfort him when surrounded with misfortune.

For Prometheus Zeus also had a punishment. He ordered him taken to the Caucasus and chained to a mountain top where vultures perpetually gnawed at his liver. Zeus had another objective besides punishing man's creator; he knew that a son fated to dethrone him would sometime be born. Only Prometheus knew who was destined to be the mother of this son. Zeus hoped to force Prometheus to tell, but Prometheus stubbornly remained silent. His body might be bound, but his spirit was free, and he refused to submit to the tyranny of Zeus. An interesting duality of mind and body is suggested here, a metaphor that appears in SF. It was this Promethean quality of spiritual resistance to authority that fascinated Percy Bysshe Shelley in the nineteenth century and led him to write *Prometheus Unbound*. And, in turn, it was Shelley's interest that led Mary Shelley to write the first science fiction novel, *Frankenstein: or the Modern Prometheus*, transforming the old myth into a new shape.

The Promethean myth of creation provides several themes that reappear in the contemporary mythology of SF. First, the creative process in the universe is ongoing, handed on from generation to generation of gods. Next, man, created by the master craftsman and artificer Prometheus, is given fire—a source of energy and a secret of the gods. This energy, along with Promethean knowledge and craftsmanship, gives man the potential for creation through his technology. But the gods have mated man with Pandora of the curious mind; indeed he may have more curiosity than wisdom in using his technology. Thus man's beginnings are not all framed in grace. They are also attended by Epimetheus, who failed in creation because he forgot to plan and husband his resources. Man may use his fire both creatively and destructively, like the god who gave him the gift. The son of Prometheus, he also is the master of technic: he may suffer torment as his father did.[2]

For French literary critic Gaston Bachelard, the Prometheus myth is still vital. His *The Psychoanalysis of Fire* (1938) speaks of a subconscious of the scientific mind which can be reached only through poetic images revealed by the imagination. A philosopher of science as well as a literary critic, he explores the invention of images and the daydreaming of the poet and the scientist and finds them similar. His study, in which fire symbolizes the imagination, proposes that man has a will to intellectuality, a need to understand. He gives the name *Prometheus complex* to the need that drives men to know as much as their fathers, to surpass their fathers, suggesting that the Prometheus complex is the Oedipus complex of the intellect. According to Bachelard, in Western cultural tradition the fire world was the world between heaven and earth. The spirit descends from heaven in tongues of fire; man, through fire, attempts to ascend to the world from which he fell. The fire of the imagination, creating and transforming images, is one means of ascension.

Another Greek myth on which SF writers draw is that of Daedalus, the artificer who builds the labyrinth and then, imprisoned in it, escapes with his son, Icarus, through flight. Icarus ventures too near the sun and is destroyed when his wings melt and he falls into the sea. Legend says that Daedalus, the prototype of the inventor and mechanical genius, also built a robot named Talos that kept invaders from the shores of Crete.

Early Automata

Early man was a maker not only of myths but also of mechanical devices like automata. The complex clockworks built in the late Middle Ages are often assumed to be the first intricate machines designed by man. Recent research shows this to be an incorrect assumption. Derek de Solla Price, a historian of technology, points out that fascination with mechanization is a phenomenon appearing much earlier than the late Middle Ages and early Renaissance. The urge to design mechanisms simulating the natural world seems to be a deep-rooted urge. The mechanical fragment found in the water near the island of Antikythera, Greece, dates to the first century B.C. It is a relic of a complex, geared astronomical machine. Surviving records indicate that the early Babylonian and Chinese cultures also built amazingly complex mechanisms. It is generally assumed that the mechanistic philosophy appeared in the eighteenth and nineteenth centuries as a result of the influence of Newton's mechanical model of the universe and the development of mechanical devices during that period. Actually, Price proposes in "Automata and the Origins of Mechanism and Mechanistic Philosophy" that the process seems to have occurred in reverse.

It seems as if mechanistic philosophy . . . led to mechanism rather than the other way about. We suggest that some strong innate urge toward mechanistic explanation led to the making of automata, and that from automata has evolved much of our technology, particularly the part embracing fine mechanism and scientific instrumentation. When the old interpretation has been thus reversed, the history of automata assumes an importance even greater than before.[3]

Early man's urge to simulate the natural world by designing mechanisms expressed itself in two types of artifices: simulacra, or devices that represent the natural world, and automata, or devices that move by themselves. The designs of the simulacra were derived from two sources in nature, celestial bodies and biological forms. Man created pictorial representations of the starry firmament and of biological forms such as birds, animals, and man himself. Then he built models, and the models were automated. Greek myths and legends tell of these movable artifices; Hephaestus built handmaids of gold and mobile tripods that served in the divine dining hall, performing their functions automatically. Daedalus mechanically imitated the flights of birds and built statues that moved.[4]

Cosmological simulacra apparently appeared somewhat later than biological models. Drawings, carvings, and sculpture came first. But as early as the first century A.D. water clocks and sundials were in existence, and their primary purpose was apparently not telling time. According to Price, "their design and intention seems to have been the aesthetic or religious satisfaction derived from making a device to simulate the heavens."[5] Celestial clockwork continued to develop in Europe. In 1364 a great clock was built in Padua, Italy; it modeled the heavens, showing each of the planets moving through its orbit around the earth and providing other astronomical data through multiple gear wheels. The clock had only one small dial for telling time, suggesting that this was not its primary purpose. The purpose of this clock and other elaborate models that followed in the next three centuries does not seem to have been primarily a utilitarian one. Rather the clock models appear to have been remarkable machines simulating the Creator's design by modeling his astronomical universe.[6]

Legend has it that an automaton in human form was built by the Bavarian Scholastic philosopher Albertus Magnus (1204–1282). He reportedly worked on the robot for thirty years; when it was completed, it could answer questions and solve problems.[7] Only the tale of this medieval robot survives, but there is more reliable evidence that armor makers by the fifteenth century were building articulated suits for knights, a form suggestive of metal men. Technological innovation seems from earliest times to have been fathered by warfare.

As early as the Greek period of civilization, astronomy and physics had produced their automata, movable models of the heavens. Mathematics came of age in the seventeenth century. One would predict the next step to be automation of the mathematical process. This is exactly what happened. Actually the first step in building mechanisms to model logical thought had occurred in the thirteenth century. Ramon Lull (1234–1315), a Spanish mystic, wanted to transform philosophy by removing theology as its supporting base and replacing it with reason. He devised a logic machine that he called *Ars Magna,* a device consisting of a series of concentric circles with words designating ideas arranged on them in a certain order. Lull hoped his machine would be an aid in bringing reason to bear on all subjects. The *Ars Magna* has been described as the first step in the direction of a complete and automatic language for reasoning.[8] Not until several centuries later, in 1645, did Blaise Pascal (1623–1662) create a robot mathematician, a calculating machine that could add and subtract. Twenty years later Gottfried Leibnitz read Lull and studied Pascal's calculating machine and dreamed of building a machine that could not only do arithmetical operations but reason as well. His dreams never materialized, but in the nineteenth century Charles Babbage designed just such a machine, although the technology to build it did not become available until the twentieth century.

While these mechanistic artificers were building simulacra and automata modeled on heavenly bodies, mechanisms that calculated time and numbers, another line of artificers continued its simulation of biological forms. The ancient Greeks had claimed heads that made oracular pronouncements, such as the speaking head of Orpheus at Lesbos. The Bible records (Ezech. 21:21) that Nebuchadnezzar consulted mummified heads that spoke. The Egyptians had statues that reportedly replied to questions with a nod of the head.[9] Many occult philosophers, cabbalists, and alchemists in the Middle Ages hoped to build an automaton, not of stone or metal, but of flesh and blood. The literature sometimes refers to such a creature as a homunculus, on other occasions as a golem. The alchemist Paracelsus (1493–1541) provides a recipe for growing a homunculus from semen and human blood incubated for eighty days in a medium of horse dung.[10] The golem legend is associated with the Jewish folklore of the city of Prague. Jewish literature contains various references to a golem, but the most famous is the one attributed to Rabbi Judah Loew, who was chief rabbi of Prague in the sixteenth century. Tradition has it that the golem first did housework but then became unmanageable. It was feared that he would annihilate Prague, and so he was disanimated.[11]

The figure of Dr. Faustus embodies the preoccupation of all these artificers, legendary or historical. They wished to escape the traditional limitations of man's knowledge and to acquire the mysterious knowledge of the gods—the secret of man's creation.

Christopher Marlowe's sixteenth-century *Dr. Faustus* dramatizes the risk of transcending those limits; the price of the secret knowledge belonging to the gods is eternal damnation. Marlowe retold but did not invent the tale of Faustus. A real Georg Faust (1480?–1540?) lived in Germany, a man of learning who also dabbled in alchemy and magic.[12] In the fourth century St. Augustine described in his *Confessions* his youthful fascination with the teachings of Faustus, a Manichean possessing secret knowledge and wisdom.[13] Apparently the first reference to the Faust figure is recorded in the Book of Acts (8:4–25). The magician Simon Magus claimed to have secret knowledge from God, making it possible for him to perform miracles.[14]

Thus the Faustian legend of the man who learns the secrets of the gods has seeded itself and sent up literary shoots through the centuries, suggesting that man's urge to have knowledge of the creation of life is an eternal desire. Faust appears in SF as the contemporary magician, the man of science whose discoveries lead him to the secrets of the universe. Some of the stories suggest that the tragic consequences of Faust's quest for knowledge may also be the consequences of the quest of modern science for knowledge.

The making of intricate and marvelous mechanisms metamorphosed and flowered in the eighteenth century. A menagerie of mechanical animals—tigers, horses, dogs, cocks, songbirds—entertained and amazed the aristocracy with their ingenuity in simulating life and motion. One of the most famous was the illustrious duck of the toy maker Jacques de Vaucanson (1709–1782), which moved, ate, drank, and in most convincing fashion simulated the activities of a real duck.[15] Evidence seems to suggest that Descartes, responding to these lifelike mechanisms, proposed that animals might indeed be mere machines like these automata, but man was different because he also had a mind. So began the mind-body dualism that flared into the arguments between the vitalists and the mechanists in the nineteenth century. The controversy generates fiery philosophical debate today, rekindled by the development of computers and the claims of researchers in artificial intelligence.

Automata in human form, ranging from small to life-size figures, poured from the workshops of inventors and clock makers: dancing dolls, marching soldiers, bugle, flute, and piano players. That most of these devices were toys for entertainment indicates that the experimentation was more imaginative play than purposeful research.

Invention and imagination thus interact, each mirroring new possibilities to the other. The artificer makes forms, first in verbal images and then in mechanical constructs; image and construct pursue each other, like children playfully chasing each other. Book and industrial exhibition provided viewing sites for each new form. An exhibit of automata in Dresden in 1813 seems to have inspired the German writer E. T. A. Hoffman to write his tales of mechanical inventions. Jacques Offenbach's *Tales from Hoffman* (1881), an opera about a life-size dancing doll, was based on Hoffman's fiction. Thus the theater again became a display case for automata, as it had for classical theater with its deus ex machina.

In America the same cross-fertilization between the imagination of the literary and the mechanical artificer designing automata was taking place. Thomas Edison, the Wizard of Menlo Park, built a talking doll in 1894. L. Frank Baum, in his famous Wizard of Oz series (1900–1921), created the Tin Woodsman and the Tik-Tok Machine Man.[16]

The cycling of ideas between art and technology continues in the twentieth century. Isaac Asimov wrote his first robot story, "Robbie," after seeing a robot on display at the New York World's Fair in 1939, and he says he was undoubtedly influenced by the automaton at the exhibition.[17] Joseph Engelberger, builder of the first industrial robot, Unimate (1958), attributes his long-standing fascination with robots to his reading Asimov's *I, Robot* when he was a teenager.[18]

In the twentieth century, movies have become another form of theater displaying automata. Mara, the demonic female in Fritz

Lang's *Metropolis* (1926), is the most famous of the early robots in film. The first robot appeared in an 1897 French film, *The Clown and the Automaton.*[19]

Frankenstein and His Nineteenth-Century Followers

Several substantial works of nineteenth-century fiction can be seen as the literary antecedents of modern SF portraying machine intelligence. Two written early in the century and two written at the end of the century are worth study because they contain themes, metaphors, techniques, and questions that are signficant in the contemporary SF about computers and robots. Their authors, fascinated with the possibility of artificial intelligence, also sense the audacity of man and the risks he takes in building automatons.

The first work is Mary Shelley's *Frankenstein: or, the Modern Prometheus* (1818). It is generally regarded as the first work of SF because its protagonist, Dr. Frankenstein, has been educated as a scientist, and he builds a creature not through any unexplained magic but through his knowledge of chemistry, anatomy, physiology, and electricity.

A number of recent critical studies of Mary Shelley's *Frankenstein* are finally giving it the recognition it deserves.[20] Its themes are substantial, and it is more than a Gothic horror story. It is a remarkable work to have been written by a teenage girl in the nineteenth century. But Mary Godwin was not an ordinary girl. Her parents were gifted intellectuals. Her father, William Godwin, was a radical political philosopher interested in revolution and social change. His *Political Justice* (1793) was widely read and found a particularly responsive audience in Percey Bysshe Shelley. Mary's mother, Mary Wollstonecraft, was a novelist and the author of *Vindication of the Rights of Women* (1792), the first great feminist document. At sixteen Mary formed a liaison with Shelley, whom she eventually married. He served as a model for Dr. Frankenstein and for Frankenstein's friend Clerval. Mary gave

Shelley's deep interest in science, particularly chemistry, to Dr. Frankenstein. She gave his poetic nature to Clerval. At the time she was writing the novel, Shelley was at work on his *Prometheus Unbound,* and she used the Prometheus story as a source for her ideas. The novel first appeared under a pseudonym, and the common belief was that Shelley wrote it.

Mary Shelley later identified herself as the author of *Frankenstein.* In an introduction to the 1831 edition she describes the events leading to the creation of the story. Summering in Switzerland, Shelley, Byron, his physician Dr. Polidori, and Mary decided one day that each should write a ghost story. "Invention," Mary explains, "does not consist in creating out of a void, but out of chaos; the materials must, in the first place be afforded: it can give form to dark, shapeless substances, but cannot bring into being the substance itself." The materials from which Mary created are readily apparent: Shelley's interest in science; his discussions with Byron about Erasmus, Darwin, and Galvani and the chemical and electrical properties of matter; William Godwin's social concern and his view that evil in man is not innate but caused by social conditions; Shelley's work on his Prometheus poem.[21]

The creative act itself came intuitively, almost as a revelation. Mary describes how one night she lay in bed, not sleeping, nor really thinking:

My imagination, unbidden, possessed and guided me, gifting the successive images that arose in my mind with a vividness far beyond the usual bounds of reverie. I saw—with shut eyes, but acute mental vision—I saw the pale student of unhallowed arts kneeling beside the thing he had put together. I saw the hideous phantasm of a man stretched out, and then, on the working of some powerful engine, show signs of life, and stir with an uneasy, half vital motion. Frightful must it be, for supremely frightful would be the effect of any human endeavor to mock the stupendous mechanism of the Creator of the world. His success would terrify the artist; he would rush away from his odious handiwork, horror-stricken.[22]

Thus Mary suddenly saw the entire story of *Frankenstein*. Afterward she wrote the story step by step, working over a period of two years before she completed it. But the vision for the story came whole, complete, and in an instant.

Moving beyond the literal level of the plot and viewing the story as richly symbolic—approaching the level of mythmaking—reveals several significant metaphors. Dr. Frankenstein is modern scientific man, and the creature he makes is man's technology. Four themes in this novel are repeated again and again in modern SF.

1. *The Promethean theme*   Dr. Frankenstein is patterned after the mythical technologist, Prometheus. Like Prometheus, he goes beyond what has been done before and, entering forbidden territory, steals knowledge from the gods. He develops techniques for creating life, a secret and mysterious act previously known only to the gods. But he develops these techniques only after long study. Future SF will present many versions of the Promethean scientist, full of curiosity, pushing the limits, doing what previously only the gods had done. However, his artifices are accomplished not through magic but through knowledge. The scientist affirms what Francis Bacon pointed out: knowledge is power. In SF man uses this power to manipulate and control the natural environment. He manipulates through obedience to the laws of nature, but like Prometheus, he is a creative trickster, a master of technics. Man's machine inventions work as a kind of trap for nature. In *Mary Shelley's Frankenstein* Christopher Small notes: "A machine is nothing more than one or more of the 'forces of nature' tricked, so to speak, into driving itself." [23]

2. *The ambiguity of technology*   The creature at first is gentle and kind; later he becomes a destructive monster. Dr. Frankenstein presumes he is doing no wrong as he makes the creature. In fact, Frankenstein is a modern Epimetheus more than a modern Prometheus; he does not foresee the consequences of his crea-

tive act, and he abandons his creation impulsively, failing to take full responsibility for it. Having loosed the monster on the world, Frankenstein after much reflection comes to regard his act of creation as an unforgivable evil. Ihab Haasan offers an insight into the process by which creation becomes destruction.

Prometheanism, I think, veers toward the demonic when it denies the female principle of creation . . . . (Significantly, Mary Shelley's Frankenstein never consummates his relation to Elizabeth, nor is his relation to any man or woman but perfunctory.) There is a dark, moon-like side to Promethean nature . . . , a side shaped by maternal forces. That side Prometheus can never afford to ignore.[24]

Frankenstein, man of science, denies this intuitive, unconscious element and recognizes only the rational intellect. Although he undertakes this work with the best of intentions, his creation becomes evil.

3. *The effect of man's rejection of the products of his technology*   The creature, in his first days on earth, is gentle and helpful and yearns to be loved. He becomes a malignant, uncontrollable monster only after Dr. Frankenstein rejects and deserts him.

4. *The shifting roles of master and servant, creator and created*   Dr. Frankenstein is clearly the master and creator at the beginning of the story. But as he becomes obsessed with destroying the technology he has created, he becomes enslaved by it. Losing his independent will, he can only pursue the monster wherever it may lead him. Modern SF about man and machine intelligence repeatedly portrays this reversal of the master–servant relationship between man and the robot he creates. The process echoes the Greek creation myth. What the gods create turns against them and becomes the new god.

Frankenstein states in symbolic form most of the issues that are of paramount importance to twentieth-century man in his struggle to live in harmony with and control his technology. These issues appear again and again in modern SF about robots and computers.

The seeds of SF germinated in the intellectual ground of the romantic poets. Mary Shelley was schooled by both Shelley and Byron, and they in turn were influenced by Wordsworth and Coleridge, who hailed the power of the imagination to create divinely inspired poetic metaphors. An interesting reversal in method and content in the two forms of fiction—mainstream and SF—has taken place in the past two centuries. Mainstream fiction in its realism and cause-effect narrative logic uses the methodology of science, although it remains in the literary tradition and continues to explore the subjects common to that tradition. SF, in contrast, continues the methodology of the poetic tradition, eschewing realism and plumbing the imagination for metaphors, but its content is new: the ideas and inventions of science and technology. Speculation about the future of the novel suggests that mainstream fiction and SF are likely to reunite by the end of the century.

As the romantic poet Shelley is connected with an early literary image of artificial intelligence through his relationship with Mary Shelley, so another romantic poet is indirectly related to an early technology. Lord Byron had one daughter, Augusta Ada, who became Lady Lovelace when she married. A gifted child, she showed mathematical precocity as well as literary talent. She became well acquainted with Charles Babbage (1791–1871), whose analytical machine was the first mechanical computer. The paper she wrote about this machine is one of the most detailed discussions of Babbage's work surviving from the nineteenth century.[25]

Edgar Allen Poe's short story "Maelzel's Chess-Player" is an interesting early work about an automaton primarily because of the narrator's methodology. Today computers can be programmed to play chess quite successfully, but Poe's chess player turns out to be a hoax. Careful observation and logical thought reveal the trick. Poe is said to be the father of detective fiction, and his deductive method of solving a mystery is at work in this story. The chess player has been advertised as pure machine, but a highly intelligent machine that can beat all challengers in chess. The narrator describes the methodology he will use in answering the question whether the automaton is genuine or whether a human hidden within the machine determines the moves. "Certain *data* being given, certain results necessarily and inevitably follow. These results have dependence upon nothing, and are influenced by nothing but the *data* originally given. And the question to be solved proceeds, or should proceed, to its final determination, in a succession of unerring steps liable to no change and subject to no modification." [26] Using this methodology, the narrator can solve the problem of the authenticity of the automaton and convincingly prove that it is a fake. The method of plot development in this story is quite different from that used in *Frankenstein*. *Frankenstein* uses the traditional conflict that commonly supports dramatic narrative. Man is pitted against monster. Much of the science fiction examined in this study uses this mode of plot development, and the usual formula is for man to struggle against the computer. Poe's story, in contrast, uses not conflict but the puzzle- or problem-solving mode. This is the second pattern of plot development found in cybernetic science fiction. Patterns and meanings cluster and are associated with each mode of plot development: conflict and puzzle solving.

The second story about a chess player, "Moxon's Master," written by Ambrose Bierce in 1894, is essentially a philosophical questioning of the relationship between mechanistic and living systems. The issues unfold as the narrator discusses with Moxon the implications of the question, Can a machine think? Moxon is an inventor who constantly tinkers in his machine shop. He begins his dialogue with a dictionary definition of a machine: Any instrument or organization by which power is applied, and made effective, or a desired effect produced. This definition, Moxon contends, also describes a man—or a plant, or a flight of wild geese, or a crystal formation. Moxon concludes "that all matter is sentient, that every atom is a living, feeling, conscious being. There is no such thing as dead, inert matter; it is all alive . . . ."²⁷ Moxon then asks, What is life? He thinks it is a process, somehow tightly related to consciousness and intelligence. The discussion ends without answer. When the narrator later returns to continue their talk, he discovers Moxon playing chess with an automaton he has built. The mechanical man, angry at being checkmated, attacks Moxon and kills him.

The questions the story raises are still fundamental. What is the relationship between man and mechanism, between the animate and the inanimate? Is it dichotomous, or do the two exist in a continuum? What is the role of consciousness in the thinking process? Could consciousness ever be created in a machine?

The last nineteenth-century precursor fiction to be examined is Samuel Butler's *Erewhon* (1872). Chapters 21–23, entitled "The Book of the Machine," demonstrate a pattern that is repeated in twentieth-century dystopian fiction: What the literary imagination creates as a tool for satire has a habit of later turning into actuality. This phenomenon can be seen in *Erewhon*. Butler's aim was probably only to satirize the idea of evolution and ridicule reason when it is used to an extreme. To accomplish this he employed exaggeration and irony. But his description of the evolution of the machine was remarkably prophetic.

Butler's method is to push the development of the machine to extremes, extrapolating from two views prevalent in the nineteenth century. One was the faith in technological progress, and the other was the Darwinian view of evolution. He combines the two and traces the evolution of the machine and the dangers of letting mechanical evolution proceed unchecked. In his satire the land of Erewhon has banished all complex machines because one of its philosophers has argued that machines will eventually develop a consciousness of their own and come to control man, just as man eventually came to dominate and exploit the more primitive forms of life from which he evolved. Just as early forms of life have developed into increasingly complex organisms and expanded their consciousness, so machines will develop complexity and consciousness.

The narrator in *Erewhon* says he fears not the existing machines but rather what machines will become if allowed to develop unchecked. He says although we praise man's "power of calculation," we already have machines that can "do all manner of sums more quickly and correctly than we can." The machine "is brisk and active, when the man is weary; it is clear-headed and collected, when the man is stupid and dull; it needs no slumber, when man must sleep or drop." "Man's very soul is due to the machines; it is a machine-made thing; he thinks as he thinks, and feels as he feels, through the work that his machines have wrought upon him, and their existence is quite as much a *sine qua non* for his, as for theirs . . . . "[28]

The narrator continues his comparison of machines and men, pointing out that machines are taking on many of the characteristics of the biological organism, even to reproduction, for now machines are able to produce new machines. Man becomes increasingly helpless as he builds more machines and comes to depend on them. Machines may well develop a consciousness of their own and come to control man. Just as consciousness developed in biological forms as they moved from the primitive to the complex, so the same process may be repeated in machines. Machines become extensions of man's body. As the development of the machine "progresses," man regresses, and his body is reduced to a piece of flabby muscle, his mind to a mechanism serving the superior mechanism developed by the machines. The Erewhonians, after listening to the arguments of the philosophers, decide to destroy all the inventions that have been discovered in the preceding 271 years.

"The Book of the Machines" is an ambivalent work. The comparison of man to a machine first seems to be merely a literary metaphor but later becomes a scientific hypothesis. Butler was interested in examining Darwin's theory of biological evolution, not in writing a history of machines. But his attitude toward mechanistic biology vacillated. He seemed to accept Darwin's theory of evolution but preferred to think that evolution occurred through the spontaneous volitional activities of a life force or creative unconscious rather than through the impersonal operation of mechanistic laws.[29] Whatever his ambivalent intent when he wrote it, the delight of the work today, as Herbert Sussman notes in *Victorians and the Machine*, is Butler's "ability to play with the modern machine as philosophical metaphor for the central paradox of Western philosophy, the conflict between the deterministic implications of science and the inward apprehension of volitional freedom."[30] There is also an uncanny reversal of satire into later fact. Much of the argument presented as satire can be read one hundred years later as a literal, although obviously unintentional, description of the developments in computer technology in the last twenty years. Computers are now used to build more complex computers (Butler's machine reproduction), and in the automated factory man is a mere tender of the machines. Although consciousness in machines does not yet exist, the definitions and possibilities of machine consciousness are now seriously discussed by both philosopher and computer scientist.

Butler's uneasy questioning of the machine was a minor irritant in a century enthusiastic about technological development. But other voices later joined Butler's. In the period following World War II an avalanche of literary protest against science and technology poured forth, and one of its major targets was the computer.

Twentieth-Century Antecedents

The nineteenth century was essentially a time of optimistic faith in progress. Science, aided by industrialization, was expected to fulfill the potential for creating a good society that Bacon had outlined in his *New Atlantis* (1627). In America these utopian aspirations were summarized in Edward Bellamy's widely read *Looking Backward* (1888). Wells, in England, wrote *A Modern Utopia* in 1905. But a suspicion of the total beneficence of scientific knowledge implemented through technology began to express itself in dystopian doubt, a skepticism appearing earlier in England than in America. This uneasy questioning of science and mechanization was found in the writings of Mary Shelley and Samuel Butler.

The twentieth century brought an accelerating avalanche of dystopian literature that by the 1960s had almost buried optimism in SF. The earliest and still one of the most powerful twentieth-century dystopias is E. M. Forster's "The Machine Stops" (1909). Forster's future society is the promise of a hypothetical answer to a two-part question: What if the rational, mechanistic utopian model of the good society could be implemented through engineering expertise? What if that society turns out to be a nightmare instead of a utopia? A plethora of fiction since Forster has created a variety of dystopian answers to this question, but his vision remains one of the most brilliant.

The story is told with great precision and effectiveness. In only thirty-odd pages Forster creates an image of a mechanized society and its collapse, one of the finest examples of literary economy in science fiction. Without laboring to pile up details, he creates in a few sure strokes a setting vivid enough to make his automated world convincing. The story is divided into three parts. Part I draws a picture of group social life in an artificial environment, where every element is regulated automatically by machine. Part II pictures one atavistic individual who attempts to break out of his synthetic, mechanistic world and rediscover the world of nature and the stars. Part III records the death of a society when its mechanical systems gradually disintegrate and fail.

"Imagine, if you can, a small room hexagonal in shape, like the cell of a bee."[31] With this opening sentence Forster begins his image of life in a mechanized society. It is a hive existence where the unseen all-powerful Central Committee, operating through the machine, provides the control that instinct does in an insect society. Part I is told from the point of view of Vashti, an intellectual who exemplifies the hive mentality. She is happy with her mechanized environment. It is an underground utopia where all needs and desires are fulfilled at the touch of a button. Each individual remains isolated in his cell, physically inactive, engaging only in intellectual activities. An elaborate global communications network using voice and picture permits remote communication with anyone in the world. No direct experience or communication is necessary or even desirable. Every event is tightly scheduled, controlled, predictable, efficiently accomplished. Clock and machine rhythms replace natural rhythms. Vashti has become a part of the mechanistic heartbeat.

She made the room dark and slept; she awoke and made the room light; she ate and exchanged ideas with her friends, and listened to music and attended lectures; she made the room dark and slept. Above her, beneath her, and around her, the Machine hummed eternally; she did not notice the noise, for she had been born with it in her ears. The earth, carrying her, hummed as it sped through silence, turning her now to the invisible sun, now to the invisible stars. She awoke and made the room light.[32]

She suffers in her underground cell from an excess of rationalism. Dostoevsky's *Notes from the Underground* in the nineteenth century drew a contrasting picture of an underground man; he lived below the surface with passions and irrationality and defied his own best interests for the perverse pleasure of expressing his free will. Dostoevsky's underground man has disappeared in Vashti's future world. She has no will of her own and relishes the security of a world where a machine does her calculations for her, where 2 + 2 can be depended on to add up to 4 every time.

Part II is told from the point of view of Kuno, Vashti's aberrant son. Atavistic and individualistic in his views, he yearns to break out of his underground isolation, to make direct contact with his mother, to venture to the world of nature and the stars. He tries to explain to Vashti.

Cannot you see, cannot all your lecturers see, that it is we who are dying, and that down here the only thing that really lives is the Machine? We created the Machine, to do our will, but we cannot make it do our will now. It has robbed us of the sense of space and of the sense of touch, it has blurred every human relation and narrowed down love to a carnal act, it has paralyzed our bodies and our wills, and now it compels us to worship it.

The Machine develops—but not on our lines. The Machine proceeds—but not to our goal. We only exist as the blood corpuscles that course through its arteries, and if it could work without us, it would let us die.[33]

Acting on his yearning, he does go above ground but finds he cannot survive. His physical capacities have atrophied, and he is no longer able to breathe the natural air.

In Part III the Machine's failure is so insidious that for a long time no one is conscious of the significance of the increasing number of technical difficulties. The piped musical system becomes erratic, the lights occasionally fail, then the air becomes foul, and breathing is difficult. Finally the entire world communication system breaks down, and society disintegrates as entropy claims the machine. None of the underground population lives; but Kuno dies remembering that in his brief trip to the earth's surface he encountered a few humans who had escaped earlier from the underground machine world. They were learning again to survive in nature.

Forster's antiutopia is clearly a reaction against the optimistic view of scientific and technological progress most powerfully expressed in H. G. Wells's *Modern Utopia*, written four years earlier. Mark R. Hillegas in *H. G. Wells and the Anti-utopians* (1967) provides extensive documentation for Forster's use of images from Wells's fiction while attacking Wells's optimism. Forster's future city is much like the one Wells outlined, but Wells had hailed machines and the products of engineering,[34] while Forster attacks them.

Another widely influential dystopian novel, Yevgeny Zamiatin's *We*, was written in Russian in 1921. Zamiatin was trained as an engineer and spent eighteen months in England (1916-1917), supervising the construction of Russian icebreakers. He seems to have become acquainted with Wells's work during this time. In 1922 he published a book entitled *Herbert Wells*, in which he expressed his admiration for Wells's "social-scientific fantasy" and his opinion that this was a significant new literary genre.[35]

The future city that Zamiatin created in *We* is reminiscent of Forster's in "The Machine Stops" because both used Wells as their source of images. But Zamiatin, like Forster, rejects Wells's optimistic vision of the future world that science and the machine could build.

Zamiatin's story is in the form of a journal written by an engineer building a spaceship, *The Integral*, whose purpose is to carry the plans for his perfect society to the whole universe. The novel uses the device of a naive narrator, for the engineer regards his tightly regimented, synthetic, mechanized city as the best of all possible worlds. In this future world the machine has become God, and homage is paid to it. People have numbers, not names, *We* (the mindless group) is good, and *I* (the individual and his imagination) is evil. Finally mankind has achieved the perfect state, where there is stability, peace, order, perfection, reason, and presumably happiness. Utopia has arrived. But into this paradise comes a disruptive event. The narrator, D-503, meets and falls in love with I-303 (the imagination and creativity). Having discovered and become intoxicated with the emotions and the imagination, he also discovers unhappiness. He recognizes that human nature is violated when the individual is programmed to function on a clockwork schedule, when life is reduced to production-line efficiency.[36] D-503 is no longer willing to perform merely as a standardized part in a giant machine. Nor can he function only as a reasoning creature, basing his life on mathematical logic, for man is also a creature of feeling and intuition and creativity.

A revolution finally occurs as a little group of dissidents— headquartered in the green natural world beyond the crystal wall that encapsulates the perfect city—attempt to assert their right to the poetry, intuition, individuality, and creative imagination that have been banned in the "perfect" state built according to reason. Imagination is unique; it creates new forms, changes result. The revolution is speedily put down by the authorities, who perform lobotomies on all Numbers to excise imagination.

While the novel goes to Wells for its images, it goes to Dos-

toevsky's *Notes from the Underground* for its philosophical concerns.[37] Zamiatin recognized that Dostoevsky's suspicions of
nineteenth-century utopian optimism were well grounded. Dostoevsky held that man is not solely a rational creature who, acting
out of enlightened self-interest, is capable of creating and living
happily in the perfect society. Beneath the man's reason lies
seething irrationality; man's greatest desire is to exercise his freedom, even at the cost of unhappiness.

Zamiatin's novel is the first, and I believe the best, in that
trinity of outstanding twentieth-century dystopias: *We, Brave New
World,* and *1984. We* was clearly a major influence in Orwell's
novel, as he acknowledges,[38] and Huxley apparently had heard
of it when he wrote *Brave New World,* although he claims not to
have been influenced by it. Because Zamiatin was educated as
an engineer, he was particularly sensitive to the implications of
mathematical logic, and in fact the mathematical imagery is one
of the most interesting aspects of the novel. The machine that
dominates the society is not called a computer, but it functions
as a computer would. The novel thus dramatizes powerfully the
fears of machines and automation that haunt people today. It
defines the humanistic values of individuality, freedom, and creativity, themes that recur repeatedly in modern antimachine science fiction. Zamiatin concludes that man's individuality, freedom, and creativity make revolution and change inevitable. The
possibility of establishing a permanent and static utopia must be
discarded if man's unique qualities are to survive.

Another classical dystopian work, Karl Capek's *R.U.R.* (1921),
was written at the same time as Zamiatin's work. It is a drama,
rather than a novel, and is not a fully developed dystopia as are
the works of Forster and Zamiatin. It is more reminiscent of Mary
Shelley's *Frankenstein.* It is set in Prague, and not surprisingly it
draws on the Jewish legend of the golem associated with the city.
R.U.R. stands for Rossum's Universal Robots, and Capek in this
work contributed the word *robot* to the English language. Robot
is the Czechoslovakian word for servant.

R.U.R. is a play about the manufacture of robots specialized to do one thing—work. The robots were designed to be intelligent, but they have no souls, emotions, wills, or need for affection. They are servants who perform all the necessary labor in society. But as time passes, changes occur in man and robot that upset the social equilibrium. Human reproduction begins to cease and the population declines. The robots begin to develop sensitivity and become irritated at being allowed to function only as servants. They revolt against dwindling mankind, who fight the robot rebellion by ceasing the manufacture of more robots. In the altercations the secret formula for making robots is lost. In the epilogue to the play only one man remains alive, laboring as the robots' servant to rediscover the secret formula so that the robots will not become extinct as man will soon be. In the final scene of the play two robots, male and female, begin to experience emotions of love, laughter, and sexual attraction. A new Adam and Eve, they offer promise that life will continue, albeit in a new form.

The play is essentially a satire attacking capitalism and the alienation of the masses and not an exploration of the development of artificial intelligence. (In fact, the robots are built of organic materials; thus, according to modern science fiction terminology, they should be called androids rather than robots.) The robots are most meaningfully seen as a dehumanized proletariat whose enslavement by the bourgeois is aided by science and technology. Old Rossum (the Czechoslovakian word *rozum* means reason or intellect) in his youth was an outstanding physiologist engaged in research to create living protoplasm through chemical synthesis. Thus he hoped to prove a belief in God unnecessary. He never imagined mass production of robots. Young Rossum, his son, is an engineer and a shrewd industrialist whose goal is to provide cheap labor, so he simplifies the robots, eliminating their souls and their emotions. He aspires to create an efficient laborer whose only desire is to work. Comin, the next manager of the plant, dreams of transforming the world so that man will be free and supreme. But man, by his definition, is someone who does not labor at the task of production, so the living machines in the factory are not part of his dream, even though they look so much like humans that it is difficult to tell man from robot. Men eventually begin using robots in war, and it is after the robots are taught to fight that they turn on their masters.

Advancing industrialism, as Capek pictures it, will accelerate under man's guidance until—mechanized warfare having developed—the means is at hand for man's destruction. Capek commented that in writing the play, "he wished to write a comedy, partly of science, partly of truth."[39] Because it is a comedy, the play ends on a bright note. The two robots, having learned responsiveness and love, suggest that the regeneration of the robot masses may be possible. The managerial class of man has disappeared, and the way is cleared for a new kind of man. R.U.R. is best read as a study of the effects of increasing mechanization in a capitalistic system. When man is treated like a machine, Capek suggests, he is transformed into a machine. Another transformation in the novel is worth noting: theoretical knowledge is shaped into technology. Old Rossum, the scientist, is totally oblivious to the effect that his research may have on society when it is implemented by his engineering son, who is motivated by increased efficiency and profit.

The first three decades in American literature produced no science fiction comparable to the three European works "The Machine Stops," We, and R.U.R. But a few works published in the 1920s are worth noting because they present the first images of robots and artificial intelligence to appear in American fiction. They are generally crude adventure-type fiction, full of exciting suspense but devoid of the penetrating social insight found in the European works. The first, A. Merritt's The Metal Monster (1920), introduces into science fiction the theme of intelligence housed in inorganic material. The story is set in the mountains of Asia where four American adventurers encounter huge threatening metal monsters that have both consciousness and intelligence. Electrical energy pulsates through metal and crystals to create this intelligence. The form of the story is pure fantasy, but the building materials and energy Merritt uses are those of the modern computer.

Edmond Hamilton's "Metal Giants," published in *Weird Tales* in 1926, is influenced by Merritt's metal monsters. Hamilton portrays a scientist who builds a brain of metal and activates it with T-waves. The brain learns to think and solve scientific problems; finally it builds metal giants, three hundred feet high, and remotely controlled by the brain. The giants attack and destroy a town and are setting out to conquer the world when the scientist is finally able to stop them by destroying the central brain. Jack Williamson also read and was influenced by Merritt. His "Metal Man," published in *Amazing* in 1928, is another version of intelligence in inorganic form. In this story a scientist is turned into a metal man when he encounters a strange form of artificial intelligence. The intelligence is housed in crystalline structures, and it sends out radioactive emanations that turn all objects into metal.

S. Fowler Wright's "Automata," published in *Weird Tales* in 1930, is a short three-part story presenting an evolutionary view of life on earth where machine intelligence plays a key role. Part I, set in the present, pictures a world where machines begin to fulfill their promise of freeing man from the necessity of work. Part II shows a future world where this promise is totally fulfilled, and all household tasks are performed by automata (Wright does not use the term *robot*). Part III, in the far distant future, pictures the last man on earth; he works for the automata, now the predominant species. In a universe where "law and order rule," in a universe that "is itself a machine, worked by mathematical, unchanging law," machines function more harmoniously than erratic, emotional man, so they have survived and man has died out. Wright's reflective little story is one of the earliest to present a theme that will be developed in a variety of patterns in cybernetic fiction: the machine as the next stage in the evolutionary process.

To deliver a robot from the womb of the imagination into the mundane world, not a fictional reality, requires a sophisticated homeostatic machine capable of processing information. Only if an SF writer creates both the image of an intelligent machine and an engineering design that might make such a robot feasible does he deserve credit for advancing cybernetic tales from fantasy to SF. Just such an man, one destined to become a major influence in shaping SF in America, would break into print with his first story in *Amazing* in 1930.

Science Fiction Images of Computers and Robots

Isaac Asimov Develops the Genre

From their beginnings in the 1940s computers have evolved through several generations of development; production has expanded, and today computers are pervasive in society. What has been happening in SF during the last thirty years while the development of computer technology has advanced with such astonishing speed? It both reflects and anticipates the technology, but in a reversed way. In the real world the development of computers has occurred much earlier than the development of robots. Research and development on robots have proceeded at a much slower pace, and commercial applications, although expanding, are still limited to specialized industrial robots performing repetitive tasks. The robot form is nonhuman, most often a mechanical arm. In SF the development of computers and robots has been exactly the opposite. Robots (here a robot is assumed to be a metal, electronically operated mechanical device—in contrast to earlier organic robots) are the focal electronic mechanism in cybernetic SF.

The names of two men dominate early SF about computers and robots: John W. Campbell and Isaac Asimov. These two men were once closely related. Campbell's story "When the Atoms Fail," published in *Amazing* in January 1930, was the first to portray a machine that is clearly a computer. He soon followed with another computer story, "The Last Evolution" (1932), which portrays a machine that can reason independently. Campbell continued to write stories about the development of sophisticated machines and their impact on man for several years.

Campbell began writing SF in 1929, the early days of American SF, when he was a nineteen-year-old student at MIT. One of his professors was Norbert Wiener. Sam Moskowitz in *Seekers of Tomorrow* notes:

Few of the students at MIT during that period seemed to be interested in SF, but Campbell did secure the friendship of Norbert Wiener, professor of mathematics who is today hailed as the godfather of "thinking machines." Wiener helped the young author with the scientific background of some of those early stories and may have been the inspiration for the "thinking machine" ideas.[1]

Isaac Asimov is deservedly regarded as the father of robot stories in SF. He has produced more robot and computer stories than any other writer, and the quality of his fiction is consistently high. Three stories using electronically operated robots appeared before Asimov's first robot story, "Robbie," was published in 1940. They are Harl Vincent's "Rex" (1934), Lester del Rey's "Helen O'Loy" (1938), and Eando Binder's "I, Robot" (1939).[2] Asimov continued to write robot stories. Most of his subsequent robot stories were published in *Astounding*. Campbell, who had been the editor of that magazine since 1937, became Asimov's mentor. Asimov in *The Early Asimov* (1972) indicates that Campbell was a significant influence in the development of his ideas and his fiction. Thus the father of cybernetics, Norbert Wiener, and the father of cybernetic SF, Isaac Asimov, are linked through Campbell. The influence may have gone both ways: Norbert Wiener wrote some SF, and one wonders whether he became interested when he knew Campbell as a student at MIT. I have not been able to find documentation for this possibility, and Asimov indicates that when he and Campbell were discussing robots, he cannot recall ever hearing Campbell mention Wiener.[3]

Frederik Pohl, recalling the early SF images of electronic robots, paid tribute to Campbell, who demanded that his writers for *Astounding* demonstrate rigorous and comprehensive thinking about the implications of robot technology. Pohl recalls that

Campbell rejected Asimov's first robot story, "Robbie," because it did not meet Campbell's standards. Pohl, who was then editor of *Super Science*, published "Robbie" in that magazine under the title "Strange Playfellow." Pohl cites two other writers of robot stories who were coached by Campbell: Lester del Rey and Jack Williamson. Although Campbell published Williamson's "With Folded Hands," he was not entirely pleased with it and pointed out to Williamson the implications that he had not considered. Williamson then wrote a sequel, "And Searching Mind," and the two robot stories later became the novel *The Humanoids*. [4]

Because the imaginative literature about computers and robots is so extensive, it is helpful to be familiar with its images, themes, and issues. For this overview there is no better source than the cybernetic fiction of Asimov. He has written thirty-five works of fiction about computers and robots, a far greater number than any other writer. The fiction extends over a long period of time: the first was published in 1940, the most recent in 1976. Asimov has been both comprehensive, thoughtful, and imaginative in creating his substantial body of fiction.

Asimov is optimistic about the relationship of man and intelligent machines. Asimov has labeled the fear of mechanical intelligence the "Frankenstein complex." He does not have this fear, nor does he approve of those who do. He believes that machines take over dehumanizing labor and thus allow humans to become more human. In his words, "the electronic computer is far superior at those mental tasks that are dull, repetitive, stultifying and degrading, leaving to human beings themselves the far greater work of creative thought in every field from art and literature to science and ethics." [5] His optimistic attitude is notable because it is the exception to much of the SF written since World War II.

The literature about automation from the early antecedents to the present reveals an interesting pattern of oscillation. From the Greeks through the Middle Ages and into the Renaissance, man's imagination created optimistic visions of the fruits of technological innovation. Then the opposite view began to appear in works like *Frankenstein* and "The Machine Stops." (These works were children of the European imagination.) Early American SF, splitting away from mainstream fiction in the twentieth century, was optimistic. But since about 1950, it has become negative. This negative attitude extends beyond SF to the general population. Technology can now create almost anything man can imagine; and man is horrified and fearful when the products of his imagination become actual.

This resistance to technological innovation is not new; one is merely more conscious of it because more technological innovation has occurred in the twentieth century, and particularly since World War II, than ever before in history. Asimov became aware of this resistance early in his career. In 1939 he was helping a sociology professor collect references for a book about technological innovation. He said, "It occurred to me that if there had been people who objected to every single technological advance in man's history, from the introduction of metal and of writing, to the development of the airplane, why shouldn't there be people who would oppose space exploration?"[6] So he wrote the story "Trends" (1939), in which people are not interested in efforts to reach Mars but prefer that mankind should concern itself with its affairs on Earth.

In his robot stories most of the population resents robot research and resists the use or robots, so most of the development and testing goes on in outer space. In "Profession" (1957) he summarizes this phenomenon of resistance to change by creating a future world where the phenomenon has become part of the system. In this imaginary world most people have their brains wired to tapes and are programmed like machines to function in a routine, nondeviating fashion. Rare, creative individuals are set apart in a special house where they follow the creative thrust of their imagination. Asimov's view is clear: Most members of society are rigid, like machines, and resist change; the rare individual with a creative mind is the exception. The nineteenth-century Luddites, smashing weaving looms in England, were as programmed to a fixed pattern as the machines they attacked.

Asimov's cybernetic fiction can be divided into three phases. During the first, from 1940 to 1950, he wrote a dozen stories primarily about robots, with only two computer stories. Nine of these stories were collected and published as *I, Robot* in 1950. During his second period, from 1951 to 1961, he wrote another dozen or so stories and the novels *The Caves of Steel* and *The Naked Sun*. Many of the stories and the two novels were collected and published under the title *The Rest of the Robots*. In 1958 he turned from writing SF to writing about science, and not until the mid 1970s did he write more fiction about computers and robots. *The Bicentennial Man* (1976) contains a half dozen stories marking his third period and demonstrates the evolution of his ideas about the key role computers will play in man's future.

The Asimovian view gives a kind of unity to all his fiction about computers and robots, from the first story in 1940 to the last in 1976. This view holds that man will continue to develop more sophisticated technology; he will become more skillful at solving societal and environmental problems; he will expand outward and colonize space. Many of the stories share the same characters and settings. U.S. Robots and Mechanical Men, Inc. builds the first robot in 1998 and the progress of the corporation is guided for many years by Dr. Susan Calvin, "the brilliant roboticist who had, virtually single-handedly built up the positronic robot from a massive toy to man's most delicate and versatile instrument. . . ."[7] The most recent stories are set two hundred years later, Susan has died, and the new roboticist is Mervin Mansky.[8]

The stories are often concerned with the same themes: the political potential of the computer, the uses of computers and robots in space exploration and development, problem solving with computers, the differences between man and machine, the evolution of artificial intelligence, the ethical use of technology. This last theme is explored through Asimov's Three Laws of Robotics, first fully stated in "Runaround," Asimov's fifth robot tale. They appear in many other stories and are crucial to three stories in *The Bicentennial Man*.

Asimov handles machine intelligence both realistically and metaphorically. In stories about computers, technology functions very much like existing technology. Large stationary machines store, process, and retrieve data; do mathematical calculations at incredible speeds; play mathematical games; make logical decisions. Asimov is knowledgeable in the concepts of computer science, and his portrayals are always intelligent and accurate. He has been wise enough to omit specific descriptions of computer technology, and consequently the material does not become dated—something that can easily happen if the writer portrays details of the technology because it is changing so rapidly in the real world. Asimov's robots are much more metaphorical than his computers. In the real world no robots comparable in form to those he pictures have been built, nor is there much possibility that they will be in the near future. Only specialized industrial robots performing limited functions are being developed. The all-purpose robots that Asimov pictures might be possible, but the specialized ones are economically more feasible. It is more meaningful to regard his robots as a metaphor for all the automated electronic technology—in a variety of forms—that will replace most of man's physical and routine mental work in the future.

Asimov rarely uses dramatic conflict to develop his plots; instead he relies almost entirely on puzzle or problem solving to create suspense and to move his plot forward. Through all his fiction runs the theme of faith in the ability of human reason to solve problems. His fiction is cerebral, grounded in sound science and logic. The action is more often mental than physical. In a typical story a problem or puzzle is defined; as much data as possible is collected and evaluated; a hypothesis is formed, providing a basis for a set of predictions about the solution to the problem; finally the predictions are tested. If they are incorrect, the process is reexamined until the difficulty is discovered. This procedure, of course, is the scientific method. The universe for Asimov is more mysterious than threatening. His use of the puzzle paradigm, rather than the conflict paradigm, seems related to his optimistic view of computer and robots. His short story "The Evitable Conflict" reflects his attitude toward conflict. The future world is one in which society has learned to avoid war. In his fiction Asimov also avoids the conflict mode.

Asimov's earliest cybernetic fiction, "Robbie," is set on earth at the end of the twentieth century, where robots are manufactured as playmates for children. This starting point is reminiscent of Capek's robot factory in *R.U.R.*, but Asimov's robots contrast sharply with the Czech robots, who revolt, destroy mankind, and take over the world. Asimov's robots in "Robbie" are programmed with the First Law of Robotics: A robot may not injure a human being or, through inaction, let a human being come to harm. Robbie, the hero of the story, is a dependable playmate for an eight-year-old girl named Gloria, even though her mother dislikes him because she distrusts robots. The robot eventually saves Gloria's life.

The next group of robot stories are set in space. Feelings against robots have grown so strong on earth that they are banned. In these stories two engineers, Powell and Donovan, solve a set of problems and puzzles using robots. The robots serve a variety of functions in space. They help maintain a space station, they perform ore-mining operations on an asteroid, they operate a spaceship sent to explore Jupiter. Because these stories are set in space, not on earth, little conflict between man and robot occurs. In the hostile environment of space, machine intelligence is vital to man, and so he welcomes it.

The situation is different on earth, where the later stories are set. In "Evidence" (1946), one of Asimov's most profound cybernetic stories, the general population resents robots. Stephen Byerly, who is running for mayor, is charged by his opponents with being a robot and therefore unsuitable for public office. Two questions arise: Is Byerly really a robot? If so, can a machine govern effectively?

The first question gives Asimov a good opportunity to explore the logic of proof, and here he demonstrates his education and intellectual inclination. He is ever the scientist, using the scientific method of hypothesis and proof. To the second question Asimov answers *yes*. His robots and computer are programmed with the Three Laws of Robotics, which ensure that they will always aid and serve man. "Evidence" contains a substantial discussion of those laws. Byerly points out that they incorporate the ethical principles of the world's great religions. Because a robot mechanism cannot violate these laws, it is a more reliable device for governing than a politician, who may be motivated by ambition and greed. At the end of the story Byerly is elected mayor and performs effectively for five years. Then he becomes a regional coordinator. In 2044 the regions of Earth form a federation and Byerly becomes world coordinator. By that time the machines are running the world. Byerly's term as world coordinator is described in "The Evitable Conflict" (1950), the final tale of *I, Robot*.

"The Evitable Conflict" is one of science fiction's most superbly imaginative stories in envisioning the creative use of machine intelligence. In this story, set in the twenty-first century, the world has been divided into four geographic regions, with the economy of each maintained in balance by a huge computer. As a result war has been eliminated. But small errors in production schedules begin to occur. The question is whether the resulting imbalance is caused by machine error or by human error—deliberate or otherwise. An antimachine group has arisen, and its leaders may be trying to sabotage the computer by feeding it inaccurate data. Byerly's problem is to explain and then correct the imbalance in production.

As it turns out, the computer—programmed to operate heuristically—soon corrects the problem itself. It detects the inaccurate data, and then dictates the removal of the economic supervisors opposed to machine control. They are motivated not by a concern for the good of the whole but by a drive to dominate and control, a drive that will lead to war. The computer's capacity for detecting and removing the potential creators of conflict before they can cause trouble thus prevents war. Conflict is evitable; only the machine is inevitable. Asimov in this story suggests that machine control is superior to economic and sociological forces, the whims of climate, and the fortunes of war. Mankind, he intimates, has never been free; machine control is just a different—and superior—form of control.

The short fiction in *The Rest of the Robots* is generally not as strong as the *I, Robot* stories. The comments by Asimov linking the stories in this second robot anthology work less effectively than the Susan Calvin frame in *I, Robot*.

In his interstitial comments Asimov notes that when he used the word *robotics* in his stories, he did not realize he was coining a word. Later he discovered that the word did not appear in *Webster's Unabridged Dictionary*. It still does not appear. However, the term is commonly used in the field of computer science, and it now appears in the *Barnhard Dictionary of New English Since 1963*, with credit to Asimov. His robots have positronic brains. Positrons are minute particles of matter discovered about the time Asimov was creating his robots. He borrowed the term and gave it to his robot brains.

The two robot detective novels, *The Caves of Steel* and *The Naked Sun*, illustrate Asimov's faith that man and machine can form a harmonious relationship. Machines can perform dependably as accurate logic machines, handling large masses of data and doing mathematical calculations at fantastic speeds. They are incorruptible because they are without emotions and consequently have no ambitions, loves, or other distractions to subvert the functioning of logic. Man, in contrast, is capable of creative problem solving and can exercise judgment in choosing between alternatives. His intuition can be of value if his insights are supported and developed through the mathematical logic that the computer provides.

The Caves of Steel, the novel Asimov regards as his best, is detective fiction, a mode that lends itself neatly to his scientific mind since the methodology of science is to define a problem, collect evidence, and then reason through to a solution. Elijah Baley, the human detective in the novel, solves murder mysteries with the aid of robot detective Daneel Olivaw, who can provide all kinds of data and process it rapidly when necessary. He can apply logic to a situation, but a man can add judgment to logic, and this capacity to be reasonable makes man superior.

Asimov says SF is the most demanding form of writing that he has undertaken because the SF writer must create a convincing setting alternative to existing environments. Making that setting convincing is a formidable challenge to the imagination. The technological setting of *The Caves of Steel*—an enclosed future city in an automated world of high population density—displays Asimov's inventive brilliance at its best.

Asimov's cybernetic fiction uses the electronic brain in a variety of ways, none malignant. The computer is an aid in the research and development of space travel; it performs all mathematical calculations for society, predicts election results, aids in the educational process. It solves a variety of problems, and the greatest problem it undertakes is that of decreasing entropy in the universe. In what is often considered the classic computer story, "The Last Question" (1956), it reverses the entropic process and recreates the cosmos. In this tale man keeps asking the computer, How can entropy be reversed? He asks it six different times, first on earth, then on various galaxies, as he continually expands through the universe. The computer keeps answering, Insufficient data to give meaningful answer. Finally, trillions of years later, as entropy becomes absolute and the last star goes out, he asks it the seventh time. The computer finally has sufficient data to give the answer: Let there be light! The story is a beautiful myth of cyclic creation. Man—himself once created—creates the machine. The machine, a greater creator, finally acquires all the information in the universe. Then, omniscient like God, the machine is able to re-create the universe.

What is a man? What is a machine? These questions intrigue Asimov. Man sees himself as distinct from animals because of his higher intelligence and his ability to store information and to pass it from individual to individual and from generation to generation. Each new generation begins with the accumulated knowledge of all the previous generations. But what happens to man's image of himself when machines begin to acquire some of these characteristics? If machine intelligence can perform the functions of human intelligence, is man then nothing more than a machine?

In his early fiction Asimov assumes that man and machine intelligence share many characteristics—hence the continued use of the human-appearing robot as a symbol of artificial intelligence. At first glance man and robot look alike, but deeper probing reveals the difference. Machines do some things that a man can, but man possesses unique characteristics that make him more than a machine. This is why a machine is always subservient to a human, as assured in the Second Law of Robotics.

The differences between humans and machines provide subject matter for a number of stories. One difference is that human intelligence is coupled with emotion; machine intelligence is not. In "Liar" (1941) Susan Calvin falls in love, and when she finds that the man loves someone else, her love turns to anger. Herbie, her faithful robot, is baffled; he does not know how he can best serve her because he cannot comprehend emotions and so does not know how to deal with them. In "Satisfaction Guaranteed" (1951) the neglected wife of an overworked engineer falls in love with her handsome household robot. While he can perform faithfully the duties he is programmed to handle, he cannot respond emotionally. Feelings are not an element of pure intelligence.

Another difference is that machines cannot handle ambiguity. In mathematical logic one symbol can denote only one thing. A figure of speech, where the individual meanings of a group of words are different from their sum, creates havoc for the computer. In this respect human language is unlike computer language. Any human easily grasps the meaning of a figure of speech from its context. Not so a computer. Asimov loves to play with this difference, just as he delights in puns, which are also beyond the capacity of the computer. The delight in incongruity or contradiction is the essence of humor, and Asimov's puckish humor often shimmers just above his hard, scientific thinking. But his robots are incapable of laughter because they take everything literally and thus have no sense of humor. Asimov often uses this fact as the basis for a story. In "Little Lost Robot" (1947) a frustrated engineer tells an overly helpful robot to "go lose yourself," and the robot does just that.

Creative problem solving is another area in which machine intelligence differs from human intelligence. Asimov explores this difference in "Risk" (1955), in which a robot is used as a test pilot in an experimental spaceship. When difficulties develop on the ship, the robot is replaced by a man because the robot can solve only problems it has been programmed to solve, while a man is able to solve unanticipated problems.

One of the differences between human and artificial intelligence is that machines do not possess consciousness or self-awareness. They may perform operations that humans define as intelligent, but they are not aware of what they are doing. They do not observe themselves in the process of thinking as humans do.

In the fiction of his first two periods Asimov raises but does not pursue the question of consciousness in his robots. As early as his second story, "Reason" (1941), he creates a robot who exhibits signs of intellectual activity associated with sentient creatures. The robot is curious about its own existence and how it was created. The two engineers, Powell and Donovan, argue theories of creation with the robot when it becomes interested in religion, activities that have to be interpreted as displays of consciousness. When Asimov was later asked about consciousness in his robots, he replied that he does think of his robots as being conscious.[9] But the fiction of his first two periods fails to probe the ethical and moral implications of consciousness in artificial intelligence. If a robot does have consciousness, in what significant way is he different from a human being? If he is not significantly different, is it ethical to treat him like a nonhuman? Is it moral to use him as a slave when humans value their freedom so highly? What about death? Should the robot be portrayed in SF as dying or merely wearing out? Can a human "kill" a robot? In "Liar" Susan Calvin deliberately programs a robot so that he collapses and goes insane. Should she be condemned for driving him insane? These are complex questions that have never been considered because man has never moved so close to the technological reality of constructing artificial intelligence. Asimov raises them in the fiction of his first two periods, but not until the fiction of his recent period does he give the thoughtful reflection that consciousness, death, and freedom—either in human or high-level artificial intelligence—deserve.

The Three Laws of Robotics have attracted more attention than any other aspect of Asimov's cybernetic SF. In SF religious tales are rare. So are stories debating the niceties of various moral codes. SF has traditionally based itself on the natural and social sciences, which aim to be analytic not normative. Certainly no writer grounds his fiction more solidly in science than Asimov, yet he has formulated an ethical code now famous in and out of SF. Two recent texts on artificial intelligence make references to the Three Laws, and one of the authors says he sees no reason why the laws cannot be programmed.[10] Adrian Berry's *The Next Ten Thousand Years* (1974) also cites the Three Laws. Even Asimov himself expresses amazement at the wide influence of those Three Laws. "It is rather odd to think that in centuries to come, I may be remember (if I am remembered at all) only for having laid the conceptual groundwork for a science which in my own time was nonexistent."[11] The laws are as follows:

1. A robot may not injure a human being nor, through inaction, allow a human being to come to harm.

2. A robot must obey the orders given it by human beings except where such orders would conflict with the First Law.

3. A robot must protect its own existence as long as such protection does not conflict with the First or Second Law.

The Three Laws are an important element in at least a dozen stories. Asimov explains that "there was just enough ambiguity in the Three Laws to provide the conflicts and uncertainties required for new stories, and to my great relief, it seemed always to be possible to think up a new angle out of the sixty-one words of The Three Laws."[12] In "Robbie" (1940) the First Law apparently served no purpose other than to assure man that a robot was harmless. But six years later, in "Evidence" (1946), Asimov was fully aware of the ethical implications of the laws. Susan Calvin explains their significance.

If you stop to think of it, the three rules of robotics are the essential guiding principles of a good many of the world's ethical systems. Of course, every human being is supposed to have the instinct of self-preservation. That's Rule Three to a robot. Also every "good" human being, with a social conscience and a sense of responsibility, is supposed to defer to proper authority; to listen to his doctor, his boss, his government, his psychiatrist, his fellow man; to obey laws, to follow rules, to conform to custom—even when they interfere with his comfort or his safety. That's Rule Two to a robot. Also, every "good" human being is supposed to love others as himself, protect his fellow man, risk his life to save another. That's Rule One to a robot. To put it simply—if Byerly follows all the Rules of Robotics, he may be a robot, and may simply be a very good man.[13]

She concludes:

I like robots. I like them considerably better than I do human beings. If a robot can be created capable of being a civil executive, I think he'd make the best one possible. By the Laws of Robotics, he's incapable of harming humans, incapable of tyranny, of corruption, or stupidity, or prejudice (p. 181).

Several of Asimov's most recent cybernetic stories, collected in *The Bicentennial Man* (1976), explore the Three Laws on a more profound level than did the works in his first two periods. Thirty-five years after his early stories, his knowledge and perceptions have evolved considerably. So has the level of machine intelligence he describes and the implications of the Three Laws for that intelligence. The most significant aspect of the Three Laws, however, is not the ways that Asimov uses them fictionally but the influence they have had in the real world. He has suggested that man needs to consider ways to implement the ethical use of technology and has provided models for doing this. Mere fictional model? Certainly fiction, but much more than that. As

Asimov's stories are always grounded in accurate scientific fact, so here his ethical possibilities rest on actual capabilities of computer programming.

Asimov uses a behavioral definition of ethics and suggests that computer programs be written to operationalize that behavior. If the behavior regarded as ethical can be described, a program for it can be written. Writing such a program is well within the capability of present computer programming. Asimov follows the approach of the behavioral psychologists. Not motives or consciousness but the behavior of the individual is examined. Skinner proposes in his operant conditioning that desirable behavior be defined and that the individual be programmed to respond, through positive reinforcement, with that behavior. Similarly, Asimov's computer would be programmed to respond in a prescribed way, the only difference being that it is much easier to program a computer than a human.

The difficult part of the task is to decide what is desirable. Who will define the ideal? It seems likely that John Stuart Mill's concept "the greatest good for the greatest number" would have to be the essential criterion for designing the ideal.

Thus, while not a simple task, defining ideal behavior and writing a computer program to obtain it would be possible. The program would control the performance of the technology, not the performance of man himself. However, man increasingly expresses himself through technology. Programming the technology to operate according to ethical principles would be a great step toward an ethical society. The world's great religious systems have attempted to program man's mind with an ethical system, but they have been only partially effective because man's emotions, ambitions, and aggressions often override the programming. Overriding would not be a problem, however, in the computer program.

Such an ethical technology would be desirable, of course, but it would come at some cost. The model of behavior would inevitably reflect the values of the modelers. Many persons might disagree with those values. Given the diversity of human nature, any model of ethical behavior will be defective from some points of view. The implementation of the model would mean some restriction of individual liberty; a degree of conformity would be the result. It would require a trade-off—the loss of some individual freedom for the sake of some social order and freedom from violence and war.

Any discussion of computer programming of ethics is still highly speculative. But there is no reason why speculations could not someday become realities. Asimov's significant accomplishment is that the drama he has created with the Three Laws has set us thinking. Perhaps in the real world ethical concepts could be operationalized in computer technology. No other science fiction writer has given the world that vision.

Asimov's imagination constantly spirals forward into new possibilities. Robbie, his first robot, was a giant toy programmed to entertain and protect a child. Later his robots labored in space. In his most recent writing robots acquire characteristics previously ascribed only to humans—characteristics like creativity and the capacity to make judgments. Finally the complexity of the robots leads Asimov in *The Bicentennial Man* to suggest that ethical considerations concerning man may need to be extended to include machine intelligence.

Several of the short stories in *The Bicentennial Man* pair with earlier fiction; comparison shows how Asimov's thinking has evolved over the last thirty-five years. "Evidence" (1946) considered whether a robot might not be as efficient a mayor as a human. In "Tercentary Incident" (1976) a robot serves as president of the United States. In both instances the general public is unaware of the substitution of machine for man but enjoys the benefits that result from more efficient government.

Another pair of stories pictures a world governance structure operated by computer. In the early story, "The Evitable Conflict," the world economy has been stabilized, underemployment and overproduction have been eliminated, and famine and war have disappeared. The recent "Life and Times of Multivac" also pictures a world system operated by computer, but the details of the process are more specific. Multivac is "a global presence knit together by wire, optical fiber, and microwave. It had a brain divided into a hundred subsidiaries but acting as one. It had its outlets everywhere and no human being . . . was far from one." [14] Robots perform all necessary work, and mankind has an abundance of leisure time. But human nature, ever perverse, is unhappy in its peace, leisure, and economic abundance. The majority feel that their freedom has been confiscated and that they are being forced to live in slavery under the rule of Multivac. The protagonist of the story, listening to the pleas of the majority, devises and carries out a plan that irreversibly shuts down the computer system. Then he and his fellow men face one another in solemn shock at what they have done: traded peace and security for freedom.

In "The Life and Times of Multivac," as in all his other stories, Asimov has a comprehensive grasp of the issues raised by the development of artificial intelligence. Machine systems can remove the drudgery of work; they can be used in planning and decision making; they can store and process vast amounts of information, thus augmenting man's mental power. But these benefits have a cost. Man must replace his image of himself as a rugged individualist free to do as he wills with an image of himself as a systems man living in symbiosis with his machines. In *The Caves of Steel* Asimov calls this supportive relationship a C/Fe culture: carbon (C) is the basis of human life and iron (Fe) of robot life. A C/Fe culture results from a combination of the best of the two forms. [15]

In the stories of the third period artificial intelligence has evolved substantially beyond its level in the earlier works. The goal of the computer scientists in "Feminine Intuition" (1969) is to develop a creative robot. The principle of uncertainty, explains Research Director Bogert, "is important in particles the mass of positrons." [16] If this unpredictability of minute particles can be utilized in the robot design, it might be possible to have a creative robot. "If there's anything a human brain has that a robotic brain has never had, it's the trace of unpredictability that comes from the effects of uncertainty at the subatomic level . . . this effect has never been demonstrated experimentally within the nervous system, but without that the human brain is not superior to the robotic brain in principle" (p. 9). If the uncertainty effect can be introduced into the robot brain, it will share the creativity of the human brain. The research is successful, and U.S. Robots produces the first successful design of creativity in artificial intelligence.

"Stranger in Paradise" (1974) describes another aspect of the evolutionary process augmenting the capability of artificial intelligence. A robot, designed for use on Mercury, is operated via radio control by an Earth-based computer as complex as a human brain. The robot results from the collaborative research of a specialist in the human brain and a specialist in computer science. When the robot lands on Mercury, he capers in joy at reaching the paradise for which he was designed. Here is a new form of intelligence rejoicing in the environment of outer space so inimical to man's survival. Asimov suggests that the machine form may be ideal for housing intelligence as it journeys among the stars.

"That Thou Art Mindful of Him" (1974) pictures the development of the positronic brain with the capacity for judgment. Judgment is developed in the robot because it is required to cope with conflicting orders from two humans. The Second Law says he must obey—but which order? The answer is that he must obey the human most fit by mind, character, and knowledge to give that order.[17] However, once the capacity for judgment is designed into the robots, they begin to use it in unanticipated ways. The robot George Nine decides he will "disregard shape and form in judging human beings, and . . . rise superior to the distinction between metal and flesh" (p. 83). He concludes, after exercising his judgment, that his fellow robots are like humans, except more fit. Therefore they ought to dominate humans. The possibility that machine intelligence may be both superior to human intelligence and likely to dominate human intelligence appears for the first time in this story.[18] Asimov's robots have now evolved a long way from that first clumsy Robbie in 1940.

The last design for the evolution of artificial intelligence appears in "The Bicentennial Man" (1976). Here pure intelligence, irrespective of carbon or metal form, appears. This story, awarded both the Hugo and Nebula awards in 1977, is Asimov's finest fictional work. It is the longest story (fifteen thousand words) that he has produced in seventeen years. Despite its length, it is still very terse—dense with ideas—and might well benefit from expansion to novel length. Told in twenty-three episodes, it covers two hundred years in the life of the robot Andrew Martin. Asimov's approach to the puzzle of intelligence, human or machine, gives the story its power. Inverting the obvious approach—man examining artificial intelligence—he has Andrew explore the nature and implications of human intelligence. As the story opens, Andrew is an obedient household servant for the Martin family, much the role of Asimov's early Robbie. But Andrew is a mutant robot form with an unusual talent: he is creative. He produces exquisite wood carvings. Just as he has transcended the patterns of previous robots, so he aspires to transcend the limits of the role they occupied in society. He desires to be free, not a slave to man, but this seems a clear violation of the Second Law.

Andrew's struggle to evolve beyond his programmed obedience is dramatized with great economy. The Martin family represents the small group of humans who realize the potential of artificial intelligence and take actions to foster and expand it. The U.S. Robots Corporation symbolizes the economic system supported by the mass of men who wish only to exploit robot technology for profit. They feel no ethical responsibility to this emerging form of intelligence.

After a long struggle the courts declare Andrew free. Then, bit by bit over the ensuing years, Andrew moves toward fulfilling his aspiration to become like his masters. His potential, his determination, and the support of a few dedicated individuals yield slow progress.

Having gained freedom, Andrew uses it to acquire knowl-

edge. He makes his hesitant first trip to the library to begin his
task of self-education. Threatened by humans on this trip, he
realizes he must have a law protecting his right to survive.
George Martin, his protector, appears before the court and argues
for the rights of nonhumankind to survive.

If a man has the right to give a robot any order that does not
involve harm to a human being, he should have the decency
never to give a robot any order that involves harm to a robot,
unless human safety absolutely requires it. With great power
goes great responsibility, and if the robots have Three Laws to
protect men, is it too much to ask that men have a law or two to
protect robots? [19]

Andrew wins his court battle after the fervent pleading of
George Martin, and the law finally assures his right to survive.
Then he begins to write a history of robots, a means of learning
about his past. And he begins to yearn for an organic body like
humans have.

Andrew is not alone in his learning activities. The research of
man into artificial intelligence and sophisticated mechanical devices continues. The science of prothestology develops rapidly
and becomes increasingly skillful at replacing human parts—kid-
ney, heart, hands—with mechanical parts. Andrew draws on this
new technological expertise to have his positronic brain trans-
planted into an android body.

With Andrew's increasing intelligence comes increasing
awareness of the price he pays for approaching humanity. Complexity yields ambiguity. The moral simplicity of his early life
when he was an obedient servant is gone. To achieve what he
has, he had to ask others to lie for him. He resorted to pressure
and blackmail. But given his aspirations to become a man, he is
willing to pay the price. Because his robot intelligence is never
muddied by emotions, he can reason clearly and with utmost
logic. He finally sees that he cannot be declared a man as he had
hoped, despite his freedom, intelligence, and organic body, because his brain is different. The World Court has declared a

criterion for determining what is human. "Human beings have an organic cellular brain and robots have a platinum-iridium positronic brain . . . ." (p. 168). Andrew is at an impasse. His brain is man-made; the human brain is not. His brain is constructed; man's brain is developed.

Finally Andrew pushes the implications of this statement to its ultimate meaning. The greatest difference between robot and man is the matter of immortality. He reasons, "Who really cares what a brain looks like or is built of or how it was formed? What matters is that brain cells die; *must* die. Even if every other organ in the body is maintained or replaced, the brain cells, which cannot be replaced without changing and therefore killing the personality, must eventually die" (pp. 170–171). He realizes that the price of being human is to sacrifice his immortality. In the final moving episode of the story he submits to surgery that rearranges the connection between organic nerves and positronic brain in such a way that he will slowly die. When he performs this ultimate act of sacrifice, the court at last declares him a man.

"The Bicentennial Man" is a powerful, profound story for several reasons. Foremost is what Asimov leaves unsaid. The story follows the movement of mechanical intelligence toward human intelligence and death. But Andrew's progress toward manhood and death unfolds against man's development of technology and movement toward artificial intelligence and immortality. Knowledge or information eventually dies in the organic brain, but it can survive indefinitely in a mechanical brain. Thus the inorganic form may well be the most likely form for the survival of intelligence in the universe. As machine intelligence evolves to human form, human intelligence is evolving toward machine form. A second implication of "The Bicentennial Man," again unstated, is that a line between the animate and the inanimate, the organic and the inorganic, cannot be drawn (p. 152). If the fundamental materials of the universe are matter, energy, and information patterns (or intelligence), then man is not unique. He exists on a continuum with all intelligence; he is no more than the most highly evolved form on earth. This view implies that ethical behavior should extend to all systems because any organizational pattern—human or nonhuman, organic or inorganic—represents intelligence. A sacred view of the universe, the result not of religious mysticism but of pure logic, emerges from this reading of "The Bicentennial Man."

The Role of Consciousness

What is the relationship of consciousness to intelligence? When the SF imagination creates machine intelligence, this question must be faced. Is the robot or computer to exhibit signs of consciousness? If it has consciousness, does it have free will? In the real world of cybernetics the question has generally been avoided. It is regarded as a philosophical question not germane to the field of computer science. There the questions are more likely to be, How does the brain work? Can a model of it be built?

Asimov's stories deal with the question of robot consciousness in an ambiguous manner. If he assumes that his robots are conscious, he ignores the question of the significance of consciousness in nonhuman intelligence. His stance reflects the prevailing attitude of science toward consciousness, not only computer science but biology and psychology as well. The computer scientist need not concern himself with consciousness because he is interested only in artificial intelligence, and he readily admits that machine intelligence is still primitive compared with human intelligence.

Consciousness was once the domain of psychology. The original meaning of the word *psychology* is the study of the mind, and the concept of mind implies the existence of a consciousness, an experiencing self. *Consciousness* can be defined as a person's total subjective awareness of the world and self. William James (1842–1910) regarded consciousness as an appropriate study for a psychologist.[20] But J. B. Watson brought an end to that study in 1913 when he declared, "The time has come when psychology must discard all reference to consciousness . . . its sole task is the prediction and control of behavior; and introspection can play no part of its method."[21] As a result of Watson's pronouncement, the behaviorist-mechanistic school of psychology, the predominant one until recently, ceased to deal with consciousness, mind, free will, imagination, emotions. In the name of scientific methodology the behaviorist school has tried to measure behavior by describing activity. B. F. Skinner is today the leading disciple of Watson.

Behaviorism became the dominant paradigm in psychology for the next sixty years. Thomas Kuhn defines a paradigm as a shared set of implicit assumptions in a scientific community about what is possible, the boundaries of acceptable inquiry, the limiting cases.[22] A successful paradigm allows a scientific community to maintain and share criteria for the selection of problems. This paradigm is valuable, but it also means that questions outside the acceptable areas of research will not be explored and evidence that apparently contradicts the paradigm will tend to be ignored. Eventually, however, the paradigm may be challenged and possibly overthrown.

The beginnings of such a revolution in the area of consciousness seem to be occurring now. A growing group of researchers, among them Robert Ornstein at the Langley Porter Neuropsychiatric Institute, are insisting that consciousness is worthy of scientific study. With the gate finally unlocked, a variety of hypotheses about the nature and function of consciousness are pouring out; one is Julian Jaynes's *The Origins of Consciousness in the Breakdown of the Bicameral Mind* (1976). These hypotheses represent the twentieth-century version of the mind-body debate created by Descartes in the seventeenth century. A number of positions are currently being enunciated, and often a particular view is associated with an academic discipline.

The mechanistic-physical view holds that intelligent activities can be completely explained in terms of the physical properties of the neuronal mechanism in the body. Consciousness is a passive phenomenon; it does not do anything. A single body of natural laws operating on material particles accounts for the properties of living organisms as well as nonliving aggregates of matter. Man is no more than a complex machine. The human brain and the computer are similar; the human brain is a complex network, a large number of multiple interconnected neurons. The output of each neuron is determined by the input received from the other neurons with which it is connected. The computer is similar, except that instead of neurons, it uses a large number of interconnected electric switches.[23]

Given this mechanistic paradigm of a completely physical biology, free will simply does not exist. It is an illusion. As Woolridge concludes:

Obviously, it cannot, if conscious personality is not more than a derived, passive property of certain states of organization and electrochemical activity of the neurons. On this basis our thoughts and actions must be as rigidly controlled by the operation of inexorable physical law among the material particles of the universe as is the movement of wind and wave.[24]

Differing from this view, Ornstein holds that there are two modes of consciousness in man, one analytical and one holistic or intuitive. These are related to man's bimodal brain. The right hemisphere of the brain subtends different functions and processes information differently from the left. The right hemisphere utilizes an intuitive mode that grasps the relationship between the parts directly rather than as a sequence of deductions. This holistic process underlies art, music, the sense of the body in space. The left hemisphere, in contrast, operates in the linear, sequential mode underlying language and analytical thought.[25] The left cerebral cortex seems to function in a manner similar to that described by Woolridge as the total basis for conscious thought. Woolridge's interpretation does not allow room for the existence of intuitive thought—that sudden jump into the consciousness of a complete new awareness—or insight.

The views of the humanists on consciousness generally differ from those of the scientist. The objective scientist assumes that he merely describes and does not make value judgments. The humanist, however, does not hesitate to identify his view as subjective. He proposes that other subjective views also exist and that some are better than others. Concomitantly man' has free will, allowing him the possibility of making the best choices among the available alternatives. In contrast, the materialist-behaviorist view denies the existence of consciousness as a significant entity and therefore denies the existence of free will and the ability to choose among alternatives. This view is anathema to the humanists. Pratima Bowes presents an excellent study of the problem in *Consciousness and Freedom* (1971). He first considers the mechanistic (or materialist-behaviorist, as he calls it) view. Then he examines the phenomenological-existentialist view, using Husserl, Sartre, and Merleau-Ponty as his representatives. Finally he turns to eastern philosophy and presents two Indian views. Bowes concludes that phenomenological-existentialism and Eastern philosophy share many ideas and that both disagree with the mechanistic view in that they claim an independent and absolute status for consciousness and freedom.[26]

The views of a few men appear to mediate between the position of the humanists and the objective scientists. Physicists such as Louis de Broglie and Erwin Schrödinger seem to support Ornstein's view that consciousness and thought are more complex and mysterious than they are held to be in the mechanistic model comparing them to a computer.[27] Schrödinger suggests that consciousness cannot be discussed apart from the unconscious.

Any succession of events in which we take part with sensations, perceptions and possibly with actions gradually drops out of the domain of consciousness when the same string of events repeats itself in the same way very often. But it is immediately shot up into the conscious region, if at such a repetition either the occasion or the environmental conditions met with on its pursuit differ from what they were on all the previous incidences. Even so, at first anyhow, only those modifications or "differentials" intrude into the conscious sphere that distinguish the new incidence from previous ones and thereby usually call for "new considerations."[28]

Schrödinger concludes that consciousness is a phenomenon in the zone of evolution. "This world lights up to itself only where or only inasmuch as it develops, procreates new forms. Places of stagnancy slip from consciousness; they may only appear in their interplay with places of evolution."[29] Consciousness, then, makes the individual aware of alternatives, and from these he can make choices. So ethics is born of consciousness.

Arthur Koestler adds another dimension to the complex question of consciousness when he suggests that it is not "an all-or-nothing affair but a *matter of degrees*. There is a continuous scale of graduations which extend from the unconsciousness that results from being hit on the head, through the restricted forms of consciousness in dreamless sleep, dreaming, day-dreaming, drowsiness, epileptic automatisms, and so on, up to bright, wide-awake states of arousal."[30]

Anthropologist Gregory Bateson suggest that consciousness has an important role in the ongoing process of human adaptation. He sees consciousness as an important component in the coupling of three homeostatic systems: the individual human organism, the human society, and the larger ecosystem.[31]

This discussion of some of the current views on consciousness is not comprehensive or exhaustive, but it brings into focus the lively debate that has developed as a result of the cyberneticist's research and development in information processing and artificial intelligence. A variety of fields—computer science, biology, physics, psychology, anthropology, philosophy—are concerned with the debate and they are beginning to talk with each other because they realize that they are all looking at the same topics, from different angles. This study will add the point of view of the SF imagination and explore the question, What range of views does this imaginative literature offer on the subject of consciousness?

Many of the stories that I will examine suggest that some relationship between consciousness and high-level intelligence does exist. Neither consciousness nor its part in the function of intelligence is defined in the early fiction; consciousness in robots and computers is assumed and modeled. In almost half the stories the robot or computer is given consciousness. The nature and function of consciousness in artificial intelligence receive more attention as the subgenre of cybernetic SF matures. In later novels, Herbert's *Destination: Void*, for example, consciousness is one of the major themes. Finally in the aesthetic theory that I am using to evaluate the fiction, the success of the imaginative metaphor in expanding the reader's consciousness will be an important criterion. To use Schrödinger's words, the reader's "world lights up to itself" when the writer's imagination succeeds in its attempt to convincingly "develop" and "procreate new forms." The lens of SF helps the reader's imagination see future time and space as the microscope and telescope aid physical vision.

An Aesthetic of Complementary Perception

To evaluate cybernetic SF requires aesthetic criteria, but none comparable to those used in mainstream literary criticism has been developed. Yet, SF is serious literature, critics now generally agree. Robert Scholes in *Structural Fabulation* (1975) recognizes SF as a significant literary form and suggests that its growth is related to the death of realism. The faith in realism held by writers earlier in the century no longer exists because they now recognize that reality cannot be recorded. "All writing, all composition, is construct. We do not imitate the world, we construct versions of it. There is no mimesis, only poiesis." Scholes sees SF as an emerging literary form and defines it as "the fictional exploration of human situations made perceptible by the implications of recent science."[1] Pointing out the need for an aesthetic theory, Scholes cites Darko Suvin's "On the Poetics of the Science Fiction Genre" (1972) as the best essay he has read on the subject.

Suvin in turn expresses his indebtedness to Bertolt Brecht, who wrote "plays for a scientific age" and who used the technique of estrangement. According to Brecht, "a representation which estranges is one which allows us to recognize its subject, but at the same time makes it seem unfamiliar."[2] Suvin defines SF as an art form that estranges conceptually. He calls this *cognitive estrangement*. The necessary and sufficient conditions for SF are "the present and interaction of estrangement and cognition"; the main formal device of SF is "an imaginative framework alternative to the author's empirical environment."[3]

Because SF is a unique genre of fiction, it cannot be judged by the usual literary criteria. In 1975 SF writer and critic Joanna Russ set forth her criteria for judging SF in "Towards an Aesthetic of Science Fiction." Her first requirement is a standard of plausibility derived "rigorously and systematically from science."[4] She suggests the similarity of SF to medieval art. The SF protagonist is collective, as was the hero in pre-Renaissance literature; SF is didactic, although it teaches scientific truth not religious truth; like medieval painting, SF addresses itself to the mind not the eye; SF is often awed and worshipful, as is medieval art.[5]

Russ is perceptive in the equation she makes. "Science is to science fiction (by analogy) what medieval Christianity was to deliberately didactic medieval fiction." Her rejection of the methodology of contemporary literary criticism as a tool for dealing with SF is also sound. The mainstream critic can ignore science; the SF critic cannot. Russ raises a key question: "Without knowledge of or appreciation of the 'theology' of SF—that is, science— what kind of criticism will be practiced on particular SF works?"[6]

Building on the work of Suvin and Russ, I have expanded the criteria, grounded them in science, and given special consideration to the attribute of good SF that Suvin labels cognitive estrangement and Russ terms a sense of awe. I want to propose that SF achieves this sense of awe or wonder when it creates a metaphor of complementary intellectual perception—a model in which the reader's consciousness is engaged in a dynamic of transcendent awareness that ends in a moment of illumination.

Plot, character, setting, symbols, narrative technique—the elements of the traditional novel—are present in SF, but they are secondary to other elements that are the central concerns of SF. The work succeeds because the writer has effectively incorporated these elements, or the work fails because the writer has disregarded them or handled them poorly. Although SF uses characters involved in an action in a particular place, these elements are not ends in themselves but vehicles to accomplish other purposes. Characterization, narrative technique, style, structure are often disappointing when an SF novel is judged by the criteria used in traditional criticism. Then what elements lead

to a novel's recognition as a good SF novel? A number of elements are present in successful SF. They work a dynamic and
accelerating process, culminating in the reader's experiencing a
sense of wonder.

First, the work is *grounded in scientific knowledge.* While the
fictional world may not be possible according to present-day
knowledge, it appears plausible because of the possibility of some
future scientific discovery or development. The imaginary world
may violate one or two aspects of reality as science now defines
reality, but it cannot ignore scientific knowledge, or it becomes
fantasy, not SF. The imaginary world must create a plausible
setting in which events happen not magically but for reasons and
causes.

Second, the fiction incorporates *a sense of novelty.* It does not
repeat exactly what has been written before. It may treat but not
duplicate the idea that another work has used. The subsequent
work on the same idea develops another permutation. SF's requirement of novelty reflects in a more informal way the importance of originality of published research in science.

Third, the fiction imagines *some dislocation in space or time* from
present reality. Darko Suvin calls this present reality the "zero
world" of "empirically verifiable properties around the author."
The fiction creates a moment that surpasses the usual perception
of time and space; in this characteristic it differs markedly from
realistic fiction. The disjunction of space moves the reader to
momentarily conceive of space as different from the spatial world
that his visual perceptions bring him. He must, therefore, "see"
with his mind's eye, his imagination. Traveling through a setting,
either in the void between planets or in a foreign setting on
another planet, is often the technique used by the writer to
achieve the dislocation in space. The creation of a believable
imaginary setting becomes one of the essential tasks of the writer;
it is more essential to the success of the fiction than the creation
of convincing character. The disjunction of time may accompany
the disjunction of space, or it may serve as a substitute in accom-
plishing the necessary destruction of the reader's commonplace

view of reality. In its treatment of time and space SF borrows from the world of dreams, where movement through time and space defies the reality of the waking world. Indeed SF is almost conscious dreaming—a contradictory term, but contradiction is necessary to the imaginative process of SF.

Fourth, the fiction moves the reader toward an *awareness of unity* in the world and toward a higher level of abstraction. In defining this movement toward abstraction, Werner Heisenberg has been the most perceptive of all the scientists writing on the philosophical implications of new scientific knowledge. What he says is addressed to the relationship between art and science generally and not to SF specificially, but it offers insight into the abstraction present in SF, an element often misunderstood as poor writing by the critic who comes to SF expecting to find the sharp delineation of character found in mimetic fiction. In "The Tendency to Abstraction in Modern Art and Science" Heisenberg describes the striving toward unity present in intellectual thought today.

The tendency to feel the earth or the universe to be the habitat to which our own destiny is related will certainly become strong in the future. It answers to the tendency in science to regard the whole of nature as a unity and to formulate laws that hold good throughout all its spheres. . . . The realization of the program has pushed the sciences on to ever higher levels of abstraction, and to that extent it might well be imagined that the relation of our life to the whole spiritual and social structure of the earth will also be capable of artistic presentation only if we are ready to enter into regions more remote from life.[7]

Heisenberg sees an analogy between the phases of development in modern art and modern science.

If we assess the tendencies of modern art from the standpoint of this analogy . . . the tendency toward universality would have to be reckoned the most strongly positive feature. Art can no longer bind itself to the tradition of any particular culture, but seeks to present a sense of life which perceives man in relation to the whole earth, and sees earth in the cosmos as if from other stars.[8]

This movement toward universality and abstraction (also a characteristic of monotheistic religion, as Joanna Russ notes) is clearly present in SF; as a consequence, characterization does not assume the same dimension as in mainstream fiction. Not the unique individual in society but man, unique in the universe, is the concern of SF.

Fifth, the fiction *addresses itself to the mind.* This aspect of SF has received general recognition. It is variously referred to as the literature of ideas or as cognitive fiction and reference to the idea as hero is common. The literature is didactic; it aims to teach its reader about scientific knowledge and suggest imaginatively the implications of that new knowledge for the human condition. The extent to which the literature sparks an intellectual and imaginative response in the reader is a measure of its excellence. When it succeeds, it leads its reader to experience a purely mental structure that nonetheless illuminates the real world. The idea is of primary importance (another reason why the tools of contemporary criticism, concerned as they are with form, are not appropriate for SF). In a discussion of form and content in SF, analogy with its parent, science, may be illuminating. Heisenberg notes that in science the form is always secondary to the content. "Mathematics is the form in which we express our understanding of nature; but it is not the content of that understanding. Modern science and, I think, also the modern development of art are misunderstood at a crucial point if we overestimate the significance in them of the formal element."[9]

The sixth criterion in the aesthetic involves a complex process, but it lies at the heart of my theory. When the writer achieves the right mix of the first five elements, *the reader experiences a new awareness,* a moment that surpasses his previous perceptions of time and space. Coleridge, defining the literary imagination, suggested that the writer succeeds when he leads the reader to a "willing suspension of disbelief." I propose that successful SF activates a more complex process in the reader's mind. He does not leave his world of reality to enter an imaginary world (perhaps this happens in fantasy). Along with the willing suspension of disbelief, the reader of SF also practices a willing maintenance of disbelief. This complementary mode is essential to the function of the fiction. Grounded in the present reality of this world, the reader must know that the imaginary world is not true. But grounded in the reality of the world he enters with his imagination, the reader must know that world is true—for the duration of his reading of the work. Thus the creation of a credible alternative setting becomes one of the major tasks of the writer.[10] When he succeeds, a process or event or action occurs in the reader's mind. (Here I am well aware that I am borrowing from quantum theory and the epistemological analysis given by Niels Bohr.) A field of expanded consciousness momentarily exists, built from a complex of interactions. The critic, attempting to describe the process, faces the same difficulty as the physicist trying to observe matter. If he describes a particle's position in space, he violates its essential nature because it is not fixed but in motion. However, when he describes its motion, he also asserts an untruth because the particle has mass. Language is no longer adequate to describe our perceptions of reality.

A diagram of the metaphor of complementary perception I am delineating may be helpful (figure, p. 86). The reader's consciousness moves between his present awareness of reality and the alternative reality the writer creates. For the creative act to succeed, both writer and reader must participate. The writer creates; the reader re-creates. An element of destruction as well as of creation is at work. The imagination (both reader's and writer's) must be willing to destroy momentarily its present perception of reality, if the mind is to retain momentarily an alternative possibility as a reality. But it must also simultaneously destroy the truth of the alternative metaphor. A double negation occurs; present reality and alternative reality are both true and not true.

The SF creative process encompasses an element of indeterminacy. It assumes that the future has not been fixed by the

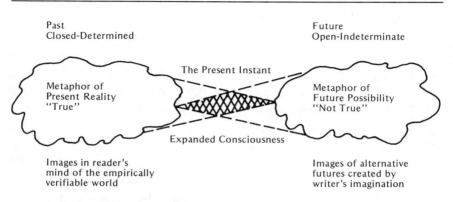

Past   Future
Closed-Determined   Open-Indeterminate

Metaphor of   The Present Instant   Metaphor of
Present Reality   Future Possibility
"True"   "Not True"

                    Expanded Consciousness

Images in reader's   Images of alternative
mind of the empirically   futures created by
verifiable world   writer's imagination

SF Metaphor of Complementary Perception

past; the future is open. It assumes that the observer will alter reality. The future of man will be different because he has become conscious of alternatives from what that future could have been had his consciousness not evolved to this level of awareness. Here one is reminded of the biblical myth of the fall. Man's fall is a fall into consciousness and freedom—within natural laws— to determine his future. An interaction, such as the one that I have just outlined in the aesthetic, occurs between the human imagination and the inevitability of the laws of matter.

Any hypothesis defining the function of the SF imagination is beyond proof. But the insights of a number of contemporary thinkers suggest just this view of the creative process at work in the world of ideas. Alfred North Whitehead proposes that creativity is to the mind as energy is to matter. Energy transforms matter; imagination transforms ideas. Arthur Koestler defines a creative process that he calls *bisociation*. It involves the combining of "two hitherto unrelated cognitive matrices in such a way that a new level is added to the hierarchy, which contains the previously separate structures as its members."[11] Ihab Hassan's "Beyond Arcadians and Technophiles: New Convergences in Culture?" is full of keen insights about Western culture's present intellectual ferment, a ferment that seems to reflect the outdating of our present models of reality because of man's transcendent nature. He suggests:

Man, the self-transforming animal, transforms reality, which responds mysteriously to his mental forms; his mind is the place where unities and contradictions meet. This is surely no sudden development. It may have begun three or four million years ago when the human brain exploded into biological evolution. The evidence is already there in the ancient caves of Altamira and Lascaux. But the best evidence may still lie buried in our dreams. For it was "dream that opened man's eyes to new possibilities in his waking life," Lewis Mumford speculates about our prehistoric progenitors; and perhaps it is still dream that deeply informs our arts and rituals, our sciences and technics. First comes the Dream—is it both Mythos and Logos? [12]

In the last step of the unfolding of the aesthetic, good SF *creates a moment of illumination*. When the writer's metaphor of the future works, it creates in the reader's mind a new possibility as to the nature of the cosmos. He experiences a shining forth of a connection where none had previously existed for him. The connection may be between present reality and future possibility, previous knowledge and new knowledge, previous consciousness and new consciousness. This moment of illumination, the sense of wonder, is not unlike the one that the scientist experiences when he achieves a new insight in his understanding of nature. [13] The intellectual insight provokes an emotional response and a momentary synthesis of mind and emotion occurs. One is reminded of the radiance of Stephen Dedalus's epiphany—a momentary shining forth of truth, as Joyce describes it in *A Portrait of the Artist as a Young Man*. The SF epiphany adds a time dimension to Joyce's moment of illumination: not this is the way things are, but this is the way things might be in the future. The SF imagination is appropriately called the Promethean imagination. It is the rebel consciousness destroying our present understanding of reality, stealing the fire of awareness from the gods, and uniting Mythos and Logos in a momentary explosion of new understanding. For the duration of the reading, the mind is pushed beyond its present limits of understanding into the shadow regions of the cosmos where matter, energy, life, consciousness, and intelligence germinate mysteriously.

The Problem: Too Much Material

Since the beginnings of cybernetic SF in 1930, the amount has increased throughout the decade. With the exceptions of Campbell's tales about computers, the early stories are all about robots. Harl Vincent's "Rex," Eando Binder's "I, Robot," Lester del Rey's "Helen O'Loy," and Asimov's "Robbie" were all written at the end of the 1930s, and a plethora of robot stories followed. Like organisms that feed on each other, the imagination of each SF writer feeds on that of the others. Almost every substantial writer in the 1940s wrote at least one, and usually more than one, robot story. By the 1950s anthologies of robot stories began to appear, reprinting stories that had first been published in the pulp magazines. There was Isaac Asimov's *I, Robot* (1950), Henry Kuttner's *Robots Have No Tails* (1952), Martin Greenberg's *The Robot and the Man* (1953), Groff Conklin's *Science Fiction Thinking Machines* (1954), and Lester del Rey's *Robots and Changelings* (1957). Conklin's anthology includes eighteen stories about robots and androids, and only four stories about computers, a selection that reflects the preponderance of robot stories during the first two decades of cybernetic SF.

Computer stories began to appear more frequently a decade later, in the fifties. Reflecting this change, anthologies published in the sixties and seventies contained a higher percentage of computer stories. There was Sam Moskowitz's *Coming of the Robots* (1963), Robert Silverberg's *Men and Machines* (1968), Damon Knight's *The Metal Smile* (1974). Finally, in 1977 two anthologies appeared containing only stories about computers: Abbe Mowshowitz's *Inside Information: Computers in Fiction* and Dennie Van Tassel's *Computers. Computers. Computers.*

A new phenomenon appeared in American SF following World War II—the novel. Prior to that time SF had been essentially a short story form, with publishing possibilities limited to the pulp magazines. Novels portraying the computer began to appear early in the 1950s. Two excellent novels, Kurt Vonnegut's *Player Piano,* and Bernard Wolfe's *Limbo,* both published in 1952, drew a pessimistic picture of future automated worlds. More dark cybernetic visions followed. Kendell Foster Crossen's *Year of Consent* (1954) envisioned a future world where total political control was accomplished through the use of a giant electronic brain called SOCIAC. (In 1951 the UNIVAC was used by the U.S. government in tabulating the census.) Two years earlier than Crossen's novel, Poul Anderson's famous short story "Sam Hall" (1952) had created an equally pessimistic picture of a computer-aided police state.

The computer novels continued, and the themes most often explored were political and military applications of computers. Mordecai Roshwald's *Level 7* (1959) showed computerized warfare accelerating relentlessly to culminate in a nuclear holocaust. Eugene Burdick and Harvey Wheeler's *Fail-Safe* (1962) also explored a worldwide military catastrophe. Jay Hadley's *The Joy Wagon* (1958) examined the impact of computers on political campaigns and the election process.

The 1960s produced two major novels examining the role of the computer in space travel: Frank Herbert's *Destination: Void* (1965) and Arthur C. Clarke's *2001: A Space Odyssey* (1968). As the decade of the 1960s ended and the 1970s began, substantial novels appeared exploring the social and political implications of a computerized world: John Boyd's *The Last Starship from Earth* (1968), Mack Reynold's *Computer World* (1970), Ira Levin's *This Perfect Day* (1970), John Sladek's *The Muller-Fokker Effect* (1971), Alfred Bester's *Computer Connection* (1974), John Brunner's *The Shockwave Rider* (1975), Frederik Pohl's *Gateway* (1977), James Hogan's *The Genesis Machine* (1978) are only a few of the titles.

In addition to the use of the computer in military, political, and space operations, a wide range of other computer applications is reflected in the fiction: applications in scientific research, law, education, medicine, industry, business, decision making, game playing, the creation of art. The fiction ranges as widely in time and space as it does in applications. The stories may be set as near as a few years in the future or as far as millions of years. The settings in space range from earth, through the planetary system, and on to distant galaxies.

How is one to classify, analyze, and evaluate so much material covering such a wide range of possibilities? This question faces the SF critic whenever he wishes to deal with more than a single work or two. Science fiction is essentially a literature using the short story form to explore new ideas and possibilities having their roots in science. The genre experiences the same information explosion that overwhelms all fields of the sciences.

Not only the amount but also the nature of SF poses difficulties for the critic. The literature departs from mainstream fiction in its form. The capacious novel has primarily been the form of mainstream fiction from the time the first works appeared in the eighteenth century. Richardson could leisurely devote a thousand pages to exploring the changing relationship of Clarissa and Lovelace, and the result was a memorable novel with rich character development. SF cannot be memorable in the same way, first because its major form has been the short story. Even though the changed status of SF today makes the publication of novels economically feasible, the results have not been memorable novels in the mold of mainstream novels. Ideas and setting are more significant in SF than characterization, and they are usually not as easily recalled.

The chronicler of SF tends to be forced into making long lists of authors, titles, dates, and plot summaries. Examples are J. O. Bailey's *Pilgrims through Space and Time* (1947), Brian Aldiss's *Billion Year Spree* (1973), and James Gunn's *Alternative Worlds* (1975). These works are excellent and necessary histories of SF, but they are tedious reading and are most useful as reference works.

How can one overcome this problem of abundance? Limiting one's study to a single theme or idea in SF may be one answer. But the permutations of the artificial intelligence theme, the subject of this study, are too many and varied to permit an effective limitation of the material. One again begins to make lists, either chronological or thematical, as I did at the beginning of this section. Even the selection of representative samples from each category yields too much material for the mind to process effectively.

I have elected to use an approach that puts the material in a manageable form and allows one to arrive at some interesting insights about the way the literary imagination functions when it considers the theme of cybernetics. This approach is to analyze the fiction on the basis of the *systems model* underlying the imaginary world created in the fiction. The systems approach is certainly not the only workable approach; a different approach might yield quite different and profitable insights. But the systems models allow me to productively explore a phenomenon that I immediately noted when I began studying the fiction. I was struck by the fact that the literature divided itself so strongly into two categories. A small amount of the fiction was positive in its attitude toward the computer, but most was very negative and the climax of the story was often a computer-smashing scene. This fictional model appeared again and again—in a literature concerned with the future of science and technology. At the same time in the real world, science and technology advanced the development and application of computers at a breathtaking rate, without even one report of a smashed computer.

The first and obvious explanation is that popular opinion since World War II has turned increasingly against science and technology. SF merely reflects the disillusionment with the promise of "better living through science" that most people are now experiencing. This explanation is certainly not to be discounted, because it undoubtedly contains some truth, but it seems an oversimplification. When one compares the anticomputer fiction with that reflecting a positive attitude, one discovers a more complex set of variables at work, variables that raise many questions. Does the form of the short story or novel affect the attitude toward computer technology? What about the setting in time? in space? the method of plot development? the use of extrapolation or speculation to create the imaginary world? Clearly there is not a simple cause-and-effect pattern at work here; it is much more complex.

The fiction is about the relationship of man and machine. The analogy with man-machine systems designed by engineers jumps to mind. Will the models of physical systems be productive in examining the imaginary systems created by the literary mind? The use of the analogy has an additional support. The development of communications, culminating in the computer, led to a theory of the function of communication and control in a system, either a machine or a biological system. Cybernetics is the effort to understand the behavior of complex systems. Imaginative literature exploring this subject might be fruitfully approached using systems theory.

A Systems Approach Using Isolated, Closed, and Open Systems

The twentieth century is an age of specialization in science. The result is that knowledge has been pursued in depth but not in breadth. This in-depth study is not to be demeaned. By reducing seemingly complex sets of events to their elementary interactions, and then carefully studying each part, scientists have accumulated a vast store of valuable information. In this atomistic approach, originated by Newton in the seventeenth century, the physical universe is seen as a giant mechanism obeying deterministic laws of motion. This universe is reducible to simple relationships between forces or bodies.

Along with the rigorous in-depth study of highly specialized areas, the twentieth century is seeing the beginning of a trend toward synthesis of phenomena once regarded as disparate. This trend recognizes that the characteristics of a complex whole are more than a mere sum of the parts. The emerging paradigm is called the systems view. A system can be defined as an organized collection of related elements, characterized by a boundary and functional unity.

The idea of systems is not new. A variety of systems have long been identified and studied—physical, chemical, geological, biological, social, political, military, educational systems. What is new is the recognition that reductionism (reducing a system to its parts and studying each part in isolation) is not productive in studying biological and social systems, although it has seemed to work well in inanimate systems like those of astronomy or physical chemistry. Such systems concern themselves with linear causal trains, two-variable problems, or with unorganized complexity. Here the second principle of thermodynamics applies.[14] In contrast, living systems are concerned with problems of organized complexity, interactions of a large but finite number of variables.[15] Living systems also seem to be involved in an evolutionary process that moves them toward increasing complexity, in contrast to inanimate systems, which move toward increasing entropy or randomness.

In the last two decades researchers in biological and social systems have increasingly recognized that structural likenesses or isomorphs appear in different systems. These similarities relate to the structure and function of systems. A general theory of systems has been developed, and the biologist Ludwig von Bertalanffy is regarded as its founder. His *General System Theory* (1968) presents the foundations, development, and applications of the theory. Ervin Laszlo's *Introduction to Systems Philosophy* (1972) is a comprehensive treatment of the philosophical concepts underlying a systems approach.

The general systems model posits an open, hierarchical system. This open system maintains a nonequilibrium steady state through the input and output of information. Ervin Laszlo explains the value of the systems approach: "General systems theory identifies a host of basic properties and functions, all of which are independent of the physical constitution and particular origin of the system. It is thanks to such isomorphs between dynamically analogous systems that knowledge obtained in regard to one system can be transferred to facilitate the investigation of another."[16]

The open-system model of the general system theory contrasts with the closed-system model of classical physics. A brief glance at the history of the development of that earlier mechanistic model reveals the difference between open and closed systems. The implications for the literary imagination of working from an open- or a closed-world view are crucial to this study of cybernetic SF. Thus it is important to hold clearly in mind the differences between an open- and a closed-system view. No scientist has been more sensitive than Jacob Bronowski to the significance of the human imagination and to the similarity of its function in science and art. It is to him that I turn for this overview of the scientific revolution of the seventeenth century and the impact of Isaac Newton's machine model of the universe.

A model is a concept, expressed either visually or mathematically, that seems to explain nature or some aspect of it and to give a unity to what otherwise seems an incomprehensible and chaotic complexity. The model explains the reality lying beneath the appearances perceived by the senses. But the model is not the reality. It is not, therefore, true or false. It is functional or nonfunctional.

Bronowski points out that the structure of thought in the Middle Ages is so different from concepts today that it is difficult to grasp.[17] The notions of matter were quite different from those held by science today. Matter appeared in four forms—earth, water, air, and fire—and each was driven by a will, a kind of obstinate animal will. The idea of order was also much different. There was a hierarchical design, stretching from earthy things to airy, heavenly things. When the right order was finally achieved by all the parts, they would come to perfect rest.

Newton replaced this medieval view with a view of the universe as a machine, a kind of gigantic clockwork. It was a mechanism that explained effects in terms of causes. His whole concept was of a natural law built on cause and on force. It explained the movements of planets in terms of the mechanics of billiard balls. He defined his system in three general laws of motion that could be expressed mathematically. Bronowski, summarizing the impact of Newton's model, concludes that the world became a machine. The earlier world of matter with a will and hierarchical order was replaced by the "modeled world of Newton which is built upon a substratum of undefined particles and simple laws, yet which clocks in triumphantly at each revolution upon the orbits of the real world. The notion of cause is an essential cement within both these, within the machine and within the model." [18]

Newton established the science of physics in the seventeenth century. In the eighteenth century, a century with a rage for order, the Swedish naturalist Linnaeus undertook the development of a system of classification of plants according to species and families, and the science of botany was born. The classification of animals followed, and the science of biology appeared. It is a tenet of science that the processes that it studies are machines. "A machine in science is a concept with definite properties which can be isolated, can be reproduced in space and in time, and whose behavior can be predicted." [19] A mechanism of cause and effect is ever at work in science. Darwin, noting the appearance of new species, attempted to explain the cause of the survival of some animals and concluded that it was their superior adaptation to survive in the competition with their rivals. His explanation of evolution was generally accepted, and so Darwin's name became associated with the theory (although the theory of evolution had been around for a long time and was known to Darwin's grandfather, Erasmus Darwin).

Science in the nineteenth century saw all natural phenomena as a play of elementary units governed by blind laws of nature. The ideal, expressed by Laplace, was that knowing the position and momentum of particles allowed one to predict the state of the universe at any point in time. The mechanistic view is a rigidly determinist model. Rudolph Clausius in 1854 formulated the second law of thermodynamics, which states that natural processes tend to move toward the most probable state, a state of randomness or disorder. Entropy is a mathematical quantity that measures the degree of disorder of a system.

But Einstein's view of relativity and Planck's view of quantum mechanics caused a revolution that dethroned this determinist mode, just as it had earlier spearheaded a philosophical stance that led to the overthrow of the medieval world model. From these revolutionary insights about the nature of reality and their applications in the life sciences emerged an open-systems model. On the macroscopic level Einstein's insight was that time is not universal; it varies with the position of the observer. Time and space, which Newton thought absolute, cannot be given physical meaning without the observer. Einstein went on to develop his equations indicating that matter and energy are interchangeable. On the microscopic level Planck in 1900 discovered that energy, like matter, is not continuous but appears always in packets, or quanta, of definite size. In the next decade it became increasingly clear that—contrary to the mechanistic view—there is no way of describing the present and the future of tiny particles and events with certainty. Heisenberg in 1927 formally stated this in his principle of uncertainty. Heisenberg showed that the more accurately one tries to measure the position of a fundamental particle, the less certain one will be of its speed. Conversely, the more accurately one tries to estimate its speed, the more uncertain one will be of its position. Therefore one can never predict the future of the particle with complete certainty.[20]

A biological system in the matter of entropy differs markedly from an inanimate system. When the laws of thermodynamics were formulated in the nineteenth century, they were concerned with describing the behavior of inanimate matter in a closed system. They do not apply to an open biological system. Even in inanimate nature, the closed system may be more ideal than real. Nor is it possible to make a definitive statement whether the universe as a whole is a closed system, although the concept of entropy envisions the running down and eventual heat death of the universe. A living organism is clearly an open system. As von Bertalanffy explains:

It maintains itself in a continuous inflow and outflow, a building up and breaking down of components, never being, so long as it is alive, in a state of chemical and thermodynamic equilibrium but maintained in a so-called steady state which is distinct from the latter. This is the very essence of that fundamental phenomenon of life which is called metabolism, the chemical processes within living cells. What now? Obviously, the conventional formulations of physics are, in principle, inapplicable to the living organism *qua* open system and steady state, and we may well suspect that many characteristics of living systems which are paradoxical in view of the laws of physics are a consequence of this fact.[21]

Biological evolution seems opposed to the concept of entropy in physics, for the latter suggests that physical events move toward decreased order and organization. But the living world shows a transition toward higher order, heterogeneity, and organization. Organization implies wholeness, growth, hierarchical order, dominance, control. Living systems possess *information* that defines this organization. A remarkable characteristic of a living system is its ability to maintain a pocket of organization in a universe that is generally running down. Physicist Erwin Schrödinger, exploring order, disorder, and entropy suggests that the organism "can only keep aloof from it [entropy], i.e. alive, by continually drawing from its environment negative entropy—which is something very positive as we shall immediately see. What an organism feeds on is negative entropy. Or, to put it less paradoxically, the essential thing in metabolism is that the organism succeeds in freeing itself from all the entropy it cannot help producing while alive."[22]

With this very brief glance at the development of models in the physical and then the biological sciences, let me offer definitions for the three categories that I will use in examining cybernetic SF: closed systems, open systems, and isolated systems.

The *closed-system model* is the model developed by classical mechanics. It is concerned with mass and energy (substance and force) in a nonliving or inanimate world. It is a system of unorganized complexity. It is a reductionist model that reduces the whole to no more than the sum of its parts. Equilibrium is established in a closed system when maximum entropy is achieved. The prototype for this model is thermodynamics, the processes in a volume of gas. The processes that occur in a closed system are reversible, and as a consequence a closed system is nonteleological. It seems to have no goal or purpose, and time has no visible direction. In this model nature is seen as an imperturbable machine that one glimpses from the outside. One's observations do not alter the performance of the machine.

The *open-system model* is a contrast to the closed system in many ways. Organisms are open systems; to survive they must constantly take in and put out energy, matter, and information. They are systems of organized complexity, and they maintain themselves in a state of high order and improbability. Information supplies the code that dictates how their matter is to be organized and what functions must be performed to maintain themselves. They are steady-state systems that exist in nonequilibrium. Open systems transform themselves; they move toward increasing complexity, interdependence, and hierarchical differentiation. Hierarchical structure is evident in the suborganic as well as the organic realm, and so the open-system approach does not sharply differentiate between the animate and the inanimate. Atoms combine to form molecules; molecules form macromolecules; macromolecules form proteins; proteins form cells; cells form organisms; organisms form societies. Thus the process of transformation is a continuum, always moving toward increased complexity. The open system can be seen as a network, a multileveled hierarchy.[23]

The *isolated system* is an assemblage or combination of things that is uninfluenced by anything outside it. The isolated system is an idealized model because an isolated system does not actually exist in the physical world; energy always passes from one system to another. The only real isolated system might be a black hole as it is now understood. It is thought to be so densely packed that curvature of space-time comes to equal the curvature of the surface. Light travels along the shortest path, and in the area of a black hole the shortest path is a circle around the star. So light, and mass or energy in any form, could not escape from a black hole. Thus a black hole is an example of an isolated system. Even though no isolated systems exist in the physical world, the concept is useful, for it makes it possible to study an isolated bit of nature. In the SF that I am examining writers often work with an isolated-system model. It allows them to consider a particular aspect of cybernetics without concerning themselves with its impact on the total system. The isolated-system model is particularly useful in the short story form. The writer can present an idea or a computer application and do nothing more. He is not ignorant of the possible implications for the social system; but by definition he is not obligated to concern himself with them.

Advantages of the Systems Approach

A systems approach to analyzing, discussing, and evaluating cybernetic SF is functional. It allows me to consider a large amount of material (well over two hundred pieces of fiction). I can make generalizations about that material and then move more efficiently to the specific data that will confirm or deny the generalizations. But it eliminates the possibility of getting lost in a maze of specifics, with title following title until the welter of names and plot summaries becomes disorienting. One can occasionally transcend the particulars and become reoriented by touching down on the ordering system model again. I am working with a hypothesis in this investigation, not a fact or truth. However, the cybernetic SF does seem to fall rather naturally into these three categories. Almost no material must be ignored or distorted to fit the models.

It seems likely that the material fits easily into these categories because men are naturally systems designers. Every man designs at least one system, his life, his self. The SF imagination designs a particular kind of system—one alternative in its details and its concepts to existing systems. But the starting point of the imagination is the scientific description of reality. Since science works with systems models or reality, it should not be surprising to find that parallels to those models are the underlying structures of the SF that imagination creates.

Several questions must be asked of the fiction about imaginary systems to categorize it. What are the boundaries and the environments? What are the basic components? How do the components interact and influence each other? Are the boundaries permeable or impenetrable? The answers to these questions will categorize each piece of fiction as an isolated, closed, or open system. In the fiction in the closed-system category there is a high correlation between the use of the closed-system model and a negative attitude toward the computer. In contrast, when the literary imagination works from an open-system model, as the SF in that category verifies, the attitude toward the computer is positive.

It is not my intention to judge whether the increasing use of computers in society is desirable. I merely want to document that the use of computers has been increasing with incredible speed in the last twenty-five years. I want also to note that SF defines itself as the literature of change that portrays alternative futures. Claims have been made that it is a literature of prophecy—anticipating almost every technological innovation in the twentieth century.[24] SF has also been defined as a literature that prepares the reader for change by exposing him to imaginary altered futures. I want to propose that in at least one contemporary subgenre of the literature, cybernetic SF, these assumptions about the information, ideas, and attitudes of the SF writer may need to be altered. The writer of fiction in the closed-system category is often ill informed about computers and reactionary in his attitude toward science.

Chapter 5 examines a group of short stories in the isolated-system category where the writer explores the relationships between man and machine in a very limited social environment. Chapter 6 considers a substantial group of dystopian works in which the literary imagination works from a closed-system model. Here the computer is generally seen as enslaving and dehumanizing man. Chapter 7 turns to a much smaller category of fiction, one in which the writer assumes an open-system model of the world. These stories describe futures in which the computer enriches man's social existence and, instead of imprisoning him, permits him to escape from the earth into space.

Almost all the early robot stories, those written in the 1930s and 1940s, and also many later stories fit the *isolated-system model*. The stories are concerned with a man-robot relationship in a limited social environment. The writer seems interested primarily in how a man and a robot might interact. A quality of freshness and naiveté makes many of the early stories charming, even though they are usually not very profound. They were written in the childhood of modern SF. For the first time the literature raises the question, What would happen if a man and a robot encountered each other? The initial question leads to a variety of others. What would man and robot discover about each other? How would each affect the other? How is a machine that thinks different from a man who thinks? What does an inorganic, artificially created body lack that an organic body possesses? What effect would each kind of body have on the thinking process? How will artificial intelligence serve man? Will it lead him toward utopia or toward self-destruction?

Today in the real world the far-reaching impact of the computer revolution has led every thoughtful individual to recognize that no new technology has an isolated effect. The technological change will alter social patterns, and these new social patterns will alter the value system. However, this sophisticated social awareness was not the concern of the writer of early SF about robots. The literary imagination limited itself to the encounter of one robot and one man or a small group of men. Rarely do robots appear in mass or even in groups. A single robot (or at most, two or three robots) is the usual pattern. Almost all the stories are about a first meeting, and so it is an encounter of exploration and discovery. The man who meets the robot may experience a change in awareness as a result of the meeting, and this is dramatized or at least noted in the story; but the possible subsequent social effects are not explored.

The writer in this mode cannot be criticized for failing to study the social impact of the mechanization of intelligent processes. That lies outside the territory he proposes to explore in the limited space of the short story. The predominant form in early American SF was the short story, which allows little room for an exhaustive examination of a subject. The writer can overcome this limitation only by writing a number of stories that progressively explore a single theme, setting, or character. Asimov used exactly this technique in his robot and computer stories. When all the tales were assembled into anthologies, they reflected a broad, thoughtful study of cybernetics not evident in any single story. Other writers, such as Lester del Rey, Lewis Padgett, Fritz Leiber, Harry Harrison, Walter Miller, Robert Silverberg, Stanislaw Lem, and Philip K. Dick have explored the theme of mechanical intelligence. But with the possible exceptions of Dick and Lem, none has done so as thoroughly and systematically as Asimov.

The interesting thing about the early stories that appeared in the pulp magazines in the 1930s and 1940s is that they began to create a new image of robots, one that would chip away at the Frankenstein monster model and gradually replace it with a much more benign view of mechanical man. If a robot is a monster bent on destruction, man has just two alternatives in an encounter. He can flee from the robot, or he can destroy it. But in either circumstance, a man is not able to explore the potential of robots or the kinds of relationships he might develop with them. However, if a robot has benign rather than hostile attitudes, interesting new fictional possibilities appear.

SF historian Sam Moskowitz credits two stories, "The Lost Machine" and "The Last Evolution," with beginning the reversal of the customary depiction of robots as dangerous and treacherous.[1] In 1932 John Beynon Harris, who later became famous writing under the pseudonym of John Wyndham, published

"The Lost Machine" in *Amazing Stories*. This story is a sympathetic portrayal of an intelligent robot from Mars. Wyndham's story is very rich imaginatively, and it created a range of ideas on which other writers nourished themselves. First, he created an alien intelligence from Mars that possessed robots, although the alien intelligence was near human in form. Second, he told the story from the robot's point of view, thereby gaining the reader's sympathy for the robot. Third, he had his robot commit suicide, the first instance of a robot suicide in SF of which I am aware. Wyndham's robot handily accomplished the task of self-destruction by dissolving itself in acid.

Just a few months after Wyndham's story appeared, John W. Campbell published in the same magazine "The Last Evolution," in which robot machines are pictured as allies of man as he resists an invasion from outer space. Campbell continued with a series of stories about benign machine intelligence, although his mechanical intelligence was usually housed in a computer rather than in robots. He ended his series of stories about thinking machines in 1935.[2] It was not until a decade later that the computer reappeared in SF, in Asimov's "Escape."

Robots flourished, beginning with Wydham's friendly robot in "The Lost Machine." Harl Vincent in "Rex" (1934) described a robot with a brain made of "glistening levers and bell cranks, of flexible shafting, cams, and delicate mechanical fingers, of vacuum tubes and photoelectric cells, of relays that clicked in ordered sequence when called upon to perform their myriad functions." To Vincent, then, goes credit for creating the first electronically operated robot in SF. Lester del Rey's "Helen O'Loy" (1938) is the first female robot in science fiction. Helen's brain is described as containing wires, transistors, and memory coils; and it is programmed with the use of a tape. Eando Binder's Adam Link was an electrically activated robot and had for its brain "an iridium sponge sensitive to the impact of a single electron." Binder's story was titled "I, Robot" (1939), and he told the tale from the point of view of the robot, just as Wyndham had done earlier. During the next few years Binder wrote nine more stories about Adam, the friendly robot desirous of serving mankind; seven of these stories were later collected as *Adam Link—Robot* (1965). Asimov's "Robbie" appeared in 1940, and with this story he began a long series that was to give robots and computers a range and sophistication unequaled by other writers except in an occasional story.

The stories in the category of isolated systems, then, tend to view imaginary robots and computers from one of three angles. They may see the development of machine intelligence as a part of the *ongoing creative process in* the universe. The stories may make machine intelligence *a metaphor* with which man can compare himself. They may perceive machine intelligence as *a tool,* and examine the ways that this tool can work for man. An examination of representative stories in the three categories reveals the variations in each pattern.

The stories chosen for discussion were selected to provide representative samples of the wide range of imaginary futures in which computers and robots play a significant part. The majority of the stories are also excellent SF, as excellence is defined in my aesthetic of science fiction. The fiction provokes a moment of illumination as the writer creates an image of man's possible relationships with machine intelligence in the future and succeeds in conveying this new awareness through verbally communicated images.

Creation as an Ongoing Process

The educated man as recently as three hundred years ago generally accepted the Christian time scale, and it was a very short one. Theologians assigned 4004 B.C. as the date of the creation of the universe, including the earth, and they saw everything as static and unchanging. The field of geology had not yet developed, and the silent message of the fossils, that life forms have existed and evolved over millions of years, was still unread. Man had yet to discover cosmic time and change. So the seventeenth-century world assumed that all species of animals and plants had appeared at the first creation and had since remained unchanged. None was lost, and no new ones appeared. This view, however, was to undergo alteration in the next one hundred years. As Loren Eiseley observed in *The Firmament of Time*, "by the 1750s cosmic evolution was openly discussed; geological change, timidly; the evolution of life, in subdued and sporadic whispers."[3] A radical transformation was occurring in man's model of the universe and his place in it.

The study of change in land and animal forms continued, accelerated, and a century later yielded two works that would shatter the commonly accepted Christian view of man and nature. First was Sir Charles Lyell's *Principles of Geology* in 1830. The evidence he presented made untenable the view that all existing species were present at the beginning, created by God, the master craftsman, in one divine and marvelous moment. Species are not permanent. The fossils testified that they perish and even suggested that new species have appeared since the time of the first creation of life. Creation, it turned out, had not been complete at the beginning.

Charles Darwin expanded and developed Lyell's theory of change. His *Origin of Species*, published in 1859, proposed an explanation of the means by which new species appear and old ones disappear. With the publication of his work, the medieval Christian world, deranged by Copernicus three centuries earlier, shattered into irreparable pieces.

H. G. Wells in his first work of SF, *The Time Machine* (1895), grapples with the radical implications of the new view. Time in the universe, once encompassed in a comfortable six-thousand-year package, dilates beyond human comprehension—toward infinity. Wells's imagination probes forward in this new time scale, struggling to comprehend the implications of evolving life forms. If life has not always been as it is now, if it changes, what may it become? What may man become? Is it possible that he may disappear, as other species have disappeared? Wells raised questions that have tantalized the SF imagination ever since. A rich variety of tentative answers has been created, and none is more original than those of the cybernetic imagination. These tales start with two assumptions: man is an active agent in the creative process, and machine intelligence is a next step in the evolution of life forms.

A group of stories, most of them early, present variations of the theme that machine intelligence will be the form of life to evolve after man. They retell the Adam and Eve myth of creation, but it is now in a new cycle. Man becomes God, the creator, and the intelligent machine is the new Adam. These stories, presenting a new myth of creation, are among the richest and aesthetically most satisfying of all the fiction in the isolated-system paradigm. Creating fresh images of man and robot, the stories transform our awareness of reality by offering new definitions of intelligence and new visions of man's place in the evolutionary process. Lester del Rey has perhaps been more productive and successful than any other writer in portraying man as a participant in the evolution of life by his creation of robots. His "Though Dreamers Die" (1944) is a poignant story of man's disappearance from the universe—man, that unique creature, the only life form able to dream. In del Rey's future world man has mastered space travel and reached the moon and Mars. But then a deadly plague sweeps the earth. Those who survive its first ravages migrate to Mars, but the plague accompanies them. The Martian environment is too inhospitable for man to survive, so Drs. Craig and Jorgen, aided by five robots, design a spaceship to carry a colony of humans among the stars in search of a more hospitable planet. All humans are stored cryogenically, with the operation of the ship left in the hands of the robots, who are instructed to awaken Craig and Jorgen when a suitable planet is discovered. Ninety years later, Jorgen, who tells the story, is awakened when the robots find a habitable planet, as lovely and promising as Eden. All the other humans have died from the plague while in hibernation. It had apparently accompanied them aboard the ship in an attenuated form. Jorgen has also contracted the attenuated disease and it is slowly killing him. He realizes that he may land on the new planet but that mankind will never survive to begin life again in the Edenic world before him. So he programs the robots to continue life after him, the representatives of mankind. He reasons that "individual and racial immortality is not composed solely of the continuation from generation to generation, but rather of the continuation of the dreams of all mankind. The dreamers and their progeny may die, but the dream cannot. Such is my faith, and to that I cling." [4] Jorgen wipes from the robots' memory all information about man and life on Earth, so they will have no painful memories of their loss. Then he leaves them on the new Eden, to carry out the dreams of man that he will inhabit the stars. He sets out in his spaceship to die among the stars. He leaves with the robots a map of the sun's planetary system, so that some day, when they are ready, they may discover from whence they came.

Robert Moore William's "Robot's Return" (1938) is, in plot sequence, a sequel to del Rey's "Though Dreamers Die," although it was written first. Del Rey, reading "Robot's Return," was intrigued with the story and suggested to Williams that he should write another story telling the events that led to the robot's return to earth. Williams declined, but suggested that del Rey do it. "Though Dreamers Die" was the result.[5] In "Robot's Return" the descendents of the robots that were left on Mars to start a new culture return to Earth, guided by the map. They are searching for their ancestors, curious to discover from whence they came. They sort through the traces of civilization left on Earth and speculate about whether the machines they discover might be early robot forms. They then discover signs that something called man must have created the machines. But they find it hard to accept that they could have evolved from an organic creature called man.

Harry Bates's powerful "Farewell to the Master" (1940) is a variation on the theme that machine intelligence may evolve into the predominant life form. A mysterious ship from outer space lands on Earth, bearing a man "godlike in appearance and human in form, closely followed by a giant robot."[6] Everyone on Earth assumes that the human is the master and the robot his servant.

Suddenly, in a tragic, destructive act, some deranged person observing the landing shoots the man, Earth's first visitor from outer space. The robot and the ship remain for a time. Finally, just before the robot departs from earth, he confides that it is he who is the master; the man had been merely one of his creations.

Del Rey's "Into Thy Hands" (1945) is another reversed creation story, where robots make man, but with a different twist. Here robots are the life form on Earth. Eleven thousand years earlier a man named Simon Ames had created robots and turned the world over to them as man destroyed himself in a nuclear holocaust. Now, after many centuries, a robot has succeeded in re-creating man, and the robot decides to turn off his switch and leave Earth in the hands of the new man. This story is another variant of the creative process; instead of a linear, nonreversible creation, del Rey posits a cyclic process. In one phase man creates machine; in the alternate phase machine creates man.

A. E. Van Vogt, in his very substantial story "Fulfillment" (1950), envisions a future Earth where human life no longer survives. Life is succeeded not by robots but by a computer. The computer in this future world travels back in time, hoping to discover its past, and in the process encounters twentieth-century computers. He learns that he has evolved from them. He also learns that when Earth lost its atmosphere and man was no longer able to live there, he escaped to the stars, leaving computers to record subsequent happenings on Earth.

Of more recent stories developing the myth of machine creation, Roger Zelazny's "For a Breath I Tarry" (1966) is without question the most brilliant. His is a later story, and so in creating his fictional images of machine intelligence he had more knowledge about the workings of computers than the writers of many earlier robot stories. Computer technology was in its infancy when they wrote. Often those stories state that electronic information processing is the means by which a robot operates; but after this initial attribution of the robot function to technology, the author imagines his robot behaving exactly as if he had human intelligence. Not so in Zelazny's story. He is well aware that the computer operates in a logical mode and does not yet have all the means for receiving and processing information that the human brain does—if indeed it ever will. Zelazny's very beautiful story combines the Faust legend with the creation myth. He uses a cyclic view of creation, where man has made intelligent machines, put them in supervisory capacities, and then disappeared from Earth. Now the machines attempt to re-create man.

Thousands of years in the future the machine Solcom exists in the sky, placed there long ago by man and given the power to rebuild the world, should it be necessary. An alternative machine, Divcom, was placed deep within Earth, to be activated should Solcom become incapacitated or annihilated. On Earth Solcom operates through Frost, a subsidiary computer, who functions as a coordinating agent in the northern hemisphere. Beta-Machine serves the same function in the southern hemisphere. Frost is Faust, and the story is told from his point of view. His hobby is studying the relics of man, and his hobby increasingly consumes his attention. One day a mysterious machine named Mordel (Mephistopheles) appears. He is an agent of Divcom, and he tempts Frost by offering to provide him with new knowledge about man. Frost's goal becomes understanding man's nature, even though Mordel insists that man's nature, unlike the machine's, is basically incomprehensible. Mordel explains that a machine can measure but cannot experience, as man can. There lies the vital difference. "A machine is a Man turned inside-out, because it can describe all the details of a process, which a Man cannot, but it cannot experience that process itself, as a Man can." [7] Frost refuses to accept the idea of an unbreachable difference between man and machine. He insists that given time and knowledge, he could become like a man. Mordel makes a bargain with Frost. He will bring all extant information about man to Frost. If, after a reasonable period of time, Frost is unable to become a man, he must agree to return with Mordel below Earth and become a servant of Divcom.

Frost accepts the proposition and begins his study. He develops sensory equipment like man's so that he can receive information in the same way that man did. He studies sunsets and art works, attempting to master nonlogical or intuitive creativity. He struggles to understand man's feelings and man's ability to comprehend. In his explorations he meets Beta-Machine and explains his aspiration to turn himself into a man. Throughout the long process Mordel provides information but no encouragement. He keeps reminding Frost that he will fail and must pay the price of servitude in the underworld.

As the story ends, Frost finally succeeds in his quest. Machine and man merge and become one. Frost then shares his new knowledge of creation with Beta-Machine, and it becomes a woman. Then Solcom and Divcom come to serve newly created mankind, and each begs to be the commanding lieutenant. But Frost declares he will make no either-or choices. Both will serve equally. Lying beyond the conflict of good and evil, the new world that he envisions will be in the complementary mode.

"For a Breath I Tarry" is one of the great moments in cybernetic SF. A brief summary like this one cannot convey the artistry that Zelazny displays in dramatizing the process by which Frost finally succeeds in becoming a man. The story itself must be read to appreciate how a master craftsman can create a fictional world undergirded with the known concepts of science. Zelazny uses language with real grace, a quality too often lacking among SF writers. Almost the entire story is told through the conversations of Frost and Mordel, and the dialogue is effective and sparse. Not only does Zelazny understand the basic concepts of computer science, but he also offers insight into man's divided nature, precariously balanced between logic and emotion. Frost's search offers a metaphor for the aesthetically successful SF story. Frost, the logic machine filled with information, sets out with his sensory equipment to evoke an emotional response in his nature by discovering an object of beauty. Mordel asks how Frost will know when he finds it. "It will be different from anything else I have ever known."

Frost's words might well be a commentary on the measure of a good story. The writer begins his story, as did Frost, with scientific knowledge and logic. He creates a metaphorical structure whose purpose is to evoke a new awareness in the reader. The story succeeds if it creates a sense of wonder. The wonder is sparked when the reader's awareness of something he has never known or considered before brings an emotional response. Zelazny's story creates that epiphany of wonder when logic and emotion momentarily unite.

"For a Breath I Tarry" displays elements common to all these stories embodying the creation myth. They use the characters and often the names of the biblical creation myth, but they reject some of the assumptions of that myth. In the old Edenic myth Adam was expelled from God's grove after he tasted from the tree of knowledge; his act had corrupted the idyll made of total innocence. In the SF creation myths man and robot live in knowledge, so they cannot fall from innocence. It was knowledge that gave man the power to create. Good and evil are thus not differentiated. Nor does Heaven—separate from Earth—exist. Man moves freely from Earth through the heavens; all is a continuum. Metamorphoses abound. Man transforms himself into a machine. The next transformation may again turn the machine into a man. Or the machine may move forward alone, the next stage after man in the evolutionary process. No SF has yet attempted to imagine what the next life form after machine intelligence might be.

Perhaps the next step is to become God. Fredric Brown's very short "Answer" (1954) dramatizes the possibility. All the computers in the world, finally wired together, are asked whether there is a god. The answer: "Now there is." Many other versions of the computer as God followed Brown's story—for example, Martin Caidin's *The God Machine* (1968) and David Gerrold's *When Harlie Was One* (1972), in which the computer is called G.O.D. (Graphic Omniscient Device).

The thrust of the creative imagination continually impels it forward into the territory of new possibility. There is no better example of this explorative odyssey than Asimov's cybernetic SF, and his most recent report of his journey into the future of man and machine sees the evolution of machine intelligence as inevitable. Man is creating his successor. Asimov is disappointed by the fiction of the younger generation of writers who have no knowledge of science and are hostile toward it. Asimov regards as unfortunate their readiness to accept the fear half of the love-fear relationship of man to machine. Referring to the old Greek creation myth, he concludes:

Allow me my own cynical commentary at the end. Remember that although Kronos foresaw the danger of being supplanted, and although he destroyed his children to prevent it—he was supplanted anyway, and rightly so, for Zeus was the better ruler.

So it may be that although we hate and fight the machines, we will be supplanted anyway, and rightly so, for the intelligent machines to which we will give birth may, better than we, carry on the striving toward the goal of understanding and using the universe, climbing to heights we ourselves could never aspire to.[8]

The Robot as Metaphor

The analogy between man and machine has been overworked. Man is programmed by society to function mechanically like a machine; man is a robot who looks like a human but behaves like a machine. But the stories that I will examine next were generally written twenty to forty years ago. Although many of their ideas seem hackneyed now, they were fresh in American fiction when they first appeared. These early tales captured a sense of delight in defining the differences between man and machine. Robots, many of the early stories note, have no emotions; man does. Thus robots ought to be able to operate by pure logic, just as the ideal scientist would. They are not diverted by love, depressed by anxiety, or driven by ambition. But in a substantial number of early stories robots acquire emotions and become humanlike. (A reverse transformation occurs more often in later SF; men keep turning into robotlike creatures as they become programmed, controlled, and predictable in their behavior.)

Is a machine really intelligent? Can it think? The SF writer assumes a positive answer and proceeds to explore a second question: How does a machine think? How does its intelligence vary from or mimic man's? Computer scientists have continually argued the question whether machines can be called intelligent. A. M. Turing in "Computing Machinery and Intelligence" (1950) suggested an imitation game to answer the questions. He proposed placing a human and a computer in one room, an interrogator in another, and linking them with a teleprinter. If the author (man or computer) of the answers printed out in response to questions cannot be discerned, then we must concede intelligence to machines.

Harl Vincent's "Rex" (1934) is an early story about a robot who almost becomes human. In this twenty-third-century world robots perform all work and men live in idle luxury. Rex, the most able of the robots, experiences a chance mutation in his artificial brain one day, as "a single electron in an atom of tantalum" shifts to a new orbit. Rex begins to think, independent of his programming. He takes over control of all the robots and becomes king. He continually experiments in an attempt to give himself feelings like those possessed by humans. Acquiring feelings in addition to his superior logic, he thinks, will make him a superman. After repeated failures, he despairs and commits suicide, unaware that his despair is a sign that he has at last acquired human feelings.

Not only the mental and emotional but also the physical differences of robots and humans are often pointed out. A. E. Van Vogt does a thoughtful study of these contrasts in "Final Command" (1948). He notes that a robot consists of crystals and electronic tubes. Thus the robot has an advantage; he can live in any environment, even one inimical to life, since he does not need food or air. Nor can he die as man does. Perhaps he is better equipped than man for long-term survival in the universe.

One of del Rey's most memorable robot stories, "Instinct" (1951), creates a future world, far distant in time, where only robots survive. Man has disappeared from the universe, and the robots are seeking answers to two fascinating questions: What makes man different from machines? Why did man fail to survive as a species? In the beginning the story suggests that man had both instinct and intelligence, while machines had intelligence but no instinct. The robots speculate that mankind did not survive because it failed to control its aggressive instinct. The robots are experimenting in an attempt to reproduce humans so that they can study instincts. As the story ends, the robots succeed in reproducing man and woman, and the humans immediately display a combination of both aggressive and sexual instincts. First they perform a sexual act, and then in an aggressive manner they demand food. The robots rush to carry out their demands, suggesting that following orders may be the built-in predisposition of the machine. Del Rey's brief glimpse of copulating humans is almost the whole of sexual activity in all cybernetic science fiction until very recently. In Dean Koontz's *Demon Seed* (1973), a computer rapes a beautiful woman, certainly an amazing act, but perhaps no more so than Koontz's violation of the taboo against sex in SF.

Brian Aldiss's "But Who Can Replace a Man" (1958) uses del Rey's idea that if machines have any unique characteristic, perhaps it is to follow orders. He describes a future world where machines have taken over and only a few men remain. The machines run the world until a man appears one day and asks for food. They drop everything else and rush to follow his orders. This story suggests one of the essential differences between men and machines—machines execute commands.

Lewis Padgett's "Deadlock" (1939) proposes that robots are built to solve problems. When the thinking machines in his story encounter problems they cannot solve, they go insane. This theme of insanity or nervous breakdowns keeps turning up in the fiction; since humans have intelligence and also experience mental breakdowns, intelligent machines are assumed to share that experience. The tendency of the imagination to anthropomorphize the nonhuman is particularly apparent in the fiction about robots, and robot psychoses are a good example of that tendency. Whether machines in the real world of computers suffer psychoses and nervous breakdowns is debatable. Computers do have occasional downtime caused by some temporary mechanical problem. Is downtime comparable to a nervous breakdown?

Today's giant computer systems have programs of vast size and complexity, programs not created by a single systems designer but evolved by a process of modification and of accretion to their control instructions and their data bases. Consequently no individual understands the systems; they have become incomprehensible. The system might well do something that appears inexplicable or psychotic merely because humans can no longer comprehend what they have programmed it to do.

Marvin Minsky of MIT confesses that he is

inclined to fear most the HAL scenario. The first AI systems of large capability will have many layers of poorly understood control-structure, and obscurely encoded goal-structure: If it cannot edit its high-level intentions, it may not be smart enough to be useful, but if it can, how can the designers anticipate the machine it evolves into? In a word, I would expect the first self-improving AI machines to become "psychotic" in many ways, and it may take many generations to "stabilize" them. The problem could become serious if economic incentives to use early unreliable systems are large—unfortunately there are too many ways a dumb system with a huge data base can be useful.[9]

Asimov in "The Machine That Won the War" (1961) and Christopher Anvil in "The Hunch" (1961) both make the same comment about the logical thinking processes of the computer. Logic is the only operational mode of the computer, but man possesses another means of sound decision making—using intuition or hunches. The pilot in Anvil's space travel faces a mechanical failure on the ship. The pilot has an intuitive hunch about the problem and uses logic to verify it. He explains his method: "Logic has to do with chains of individual facts. Intuition takes whole groups of facts at once. You can recognize a familiar pattern—like a familiar face—even though you don't consciously know all the details. Sometimes it's a mistake, but then you can often use logic as a check. With intuition you see it, with logic you check it."[10] In Asimov's story "The Machine That Won the War" three top military leaders confess, after winning an interplanetary war, that they used the computer's results as an aid but did not regard them as infallible. Whenever computer findings disagreed with the leader's intuitions, he disregarded the computer. The computer is only an aid to man, not a replacement for his mental performance.

These stories are only a sampling of the large number of stories exploring the differences between men and machines, but they are reflective of the range of ideas that appear again and again, often in only slightly modified form. Cross-fertilization in SF is ever present, and ideas constantly nourish each other. One never encounters an idea just once in SF. It occurs again and again, in all its permutations. In none of these stories does the writer attempt to predict the developments that might occur in the field of robotics. Rather the robot functions primarily as a metaphor. What would a man be like if he really operated with the cold logic of the scientific method and the dependable regularity of a machine? He would be like a robot, answers the SF imagination. Could a man ever be just like a robot? No, each story in this group answers, and it then sketches an elementary picture showing one way that a man is forever different from a robot.

In the real world the development of all-purpose robots like those pictured in SF seems highly unlikely. The research cost would be enormous, and the economic returns would not be commensurate with the investment. Nature has already created man—an all-purpose organic machine far superior to anything man is likely to create—and it is economically more feasible to employ him than to build a robot. Specialization is the likely development in robotics. Poul Anderson makes exactly this point in his "Quixote and the Windmill" (1950). He sketches a fully automated future world where the ordinary man has nothing to do. Only scientists of high IQ and creative artists have a meaningful function in society. Borklin, the protagonist, is one of the displaced ordinary men, and he gets drunk because he is so despairing that he has no meaningful work. A robot goes by, and he decides to fight it, like Don Quixote fighting the windmill, futile as it may be. However, the robot points out his own obsolescence to Borklin. With specialized automatic machines to perform functions, all-purpose robots are no longer needed. Should an all-purpose machine occasionally be required, man is a far more efficient one than a robot. So, the robot bemoans, he also has been displaced, just like Borklin. But being a robot, he cannot drown his troubles in drink.

The fascination that the cybernetic imagination finds in the metaphor of man as a machine is perhaps best captured in John Wyndham's "Compassion Circuit" (1954). It is a story about a woman named Janet who is not in good health. Although she dislikes robots, she finally agrees to have a robot maid to tend her and do her housework. It has a compassion circuit and is therefore able to give Janet the sympathy and concern for which she yearns. As the robot does more and more for her, Janet becomes weaker and weaker. She finally decides to have an operation that turns her into a machine, so she will be as strong and efficient as her robot maid. This story is symbolically interesting because it dramatizes man's desire to achieve the strength, perfection, and accuracy of the machine. Like Janet in the story, man's attitude toward the machine is ambiguous: he both dislikes it and desires to emulate its efficiency. To the extent that he delegates his functions to the machine and replaces them with no new functions, he becomes weaker, just as Janet does in Wyndham's story.

Machine Intelligence as a Tool

The last group of stories that study man-machine interactions in an isolated system is the group focusing on computer applications. This group of stories is interesting because it does not fulfill one's expectations—conditioned by the old adage that science fiction is prophetic of technological developments. Jules Verne with his inventions like the submarine and the moon shot, H. G. Wells's atomic bomb, Hugo Gernsbach's television—such portrayals of a technology long before its actual development have led to the belief that prophecy is a unique function of the science fiction imagination. Prediction is generally not an attribute of the science fiction that explores the way in which machine intelligence might be developed in a society. In fact, in the majority of instances the reverse is true: practical applications of machine technology occur in the real world before they are portrayed in science fiction. A quick examination of the stories documents this fact.

Some of the earliest stories in this category are concerned with automation. They were written in the first half of the 1950s, when automation of industrial processes in factories was already well under way. The pattern of the stories is to imagine an automated process continuing after man, whom the process was designed to serve, dies out.

Two stories picture automated war-making activities that continue long after a devastating war has destroyed civilization. Walter M. Miller's "Dumb Waiter" (1952) describes a deserted computer-operated city where robot police are active, while bombers fly overhead although they are now out of bombs. Philip K. Dick's "Autofac" (1955) is a long tale of an automated world of production and war-making that cannot be stopped because it is totally machine controlled. Ray Bradbury had developed the same theme two years earlier in "There Will Come Soft Rains" (1950), but instead of a postholocaust factory, now no longer necessary, he portrayed an automated house. It proceeds through its daily functions of cooking breakfast, cleaning the house, sprinkling the lawn. The west wall of the house, black save for the silhouette of a man and two children, is a mute memory of the nuclear explosion that destroyed human life, but the mindless automated house does not know. All these stories dramatize the shock to the human mind caused by the actual development of automated weapons.

A related group of stories examines, often in powerful detail, the application of cybernetic principles to the art of warfare. One of the earliest is Robert Sheckley's "Fool's Mate" (1953), an excellent little story using the game theory of war. The American mathematician John von Neumann developed a theory of games of chance, the key to which was his concept of strategy. Working with a Princeton colleague, Oskar Morgenstern, he published a work identifying factors common to games and economics, *Theory of Games and Economic Behavior* (1944). Subsequently both men became involved with research in the development of weapons, and the United States began a project to model military operations with a computer. John MacDonald's *Strategy in Poker, Business, and War* (1950) is a good layman's summary of this research and development.[11] Sheckley's story is written later than this date. Sheckley sets his story in the far distant future and imagines two military fleets facing each other in outer space. The computers have calculated that General Branch will lose the war, so he does not even want to begin the war. One of his aides decides to open the campaign in a disorganized, chaotic fashion so that the enemy computer will be unable to discern a pattern on which to develop countermoves. Mack Reynold's novel *Computer War* (1967) uses the same idea of Sheckley's earlier story. Two countries, one modernized and one primitive, oppose each other in war. The computer of the affluent, modernized country predicts easy victory. But the computer bases its calculations on modern methods of warfare, and the small enemy country decides to switch to primitive methods. The large country is not programmed to cope with these, and so it loses the war.

The game theory of war is analogous to chess, in which winning and losing moves can be made. Early in computer research it was apparent that the computer would lend itself to the problem of playing checkers and chess. The idea of chess-playing machines was not new. During the late eighteenth century the Hungarian Wolfgang von Kempelen claimed that the Maelzel chess automaton was just that—a chess-playing machine. His machine was exposed as a fraud by various people, including

Edgar Allan Poe. An honest attempt to design a chess-playing machine was made in 1914 by a Spanish inventor named L. Torres y Quevedo, but he had only limited success.[12] The development of the computer renewed interest in the subject. In 1950 Claude E. Shannon outlined an approach to the problem.[13] Research continued, and in 1974 the first World Computer Chess Championship was held in Stockholm. In 1976 CHESS 4.5 became the first computer program to win a rated chess tournament. Undoubtedly programs will be developed that outthink the grandmasters. Fritz Leiber anticipates this accomplishment in his "The 64-Square Madhouse," written in 1962. This story displays a good understanding of both chess and computers.[14]

The military, which had used computers in calculating ballistics trajectories in World War II, continued its research and development in computer applications after the war was over. These projects were classified, although some information leaked out. SAGE (Semi-Automatic Ground Environment) was a system designed in the early 1950s to protect the United States from surprise air attack. It became operational in 1958.[15] The giant computer used in SAGE was housed underground inside Cheyenne Mountain near Colorado Springs. A series of devices was activated in a system of automated defense, should an enemy missile be sighted. The term *push-button warfare* was coined, and a group of science fiction stories that pictured the possible outcome of computerized warfare soon appeared. J. F. Bone's "Triggerman" was published in the December 1958 *Analog*. Peter George's novel, *Two Hours to Doom*, was also published in the same year. It became the film *Dr. Strangelove* in 1964. Mordecai Roshwald in 1959 published *Level 7* describing an equipment error that triggers the mechanism for directing rockets against the enemy. Civilization is wiped out, and eventually even those housed below ground with the military equipment perish. Eugene Burdick and Harvey Wheeler's novel *Fail-Safe* (1962) has a similar theme. It portrays two automated military machines, Russian and American, posed and ready to launch a push-button war. A mechanical error activates the United States system. Even though the error is detected almost immediately, the automatic attack system has been set in motion and cannot be stopped. American planes fly to bomb Moscow. The president phones the Russian premier to advise him of the tragic mechanical error. He hopes to avert a counterattack by the Russians. But the premier is skeptical of the explanation. Only by ordering the bombing of New York City can the president offset the bombing of Moscow and avoid a Russian reprisal that would mean total war.

These stories about computerized warfare do not anticipate but rather follow the actual developments. What they do anticipate is the inadvertent activation of the system through some kind of mechanical failure. Just such an event actually occurred.

A classic example of a failure occurred in the Ballistic Missile Early Warning System (BMEWS) in October 1960. Radar returns were interpreted by a computer-based system to be a flight of missiles approaching North America over the North Pole. When the headquarters of the Strategic Air Command called the radar site for confirmation, there was no answer to the call. (A submarine cable had accidentally broken just after the first message but before a correction could be sent.) The North American Air Defense commander, however, considered the attack so unlikely that he insisted on contacting the radar site before he took action. When he reached the site commander by phone, the difficulty was cleared up. What had happened? BMEWS had not been programmed to distinguish between the moon and a flight of missiles.[16]

Another computer application that was not anticipated in SF but is vividly portrayed after the fact is the use of computers in the election process. In 1952 and again in 1954 computers were used on the evening of election day to predict to the TV audience, on the basis of early returns, the most likely outcome of the election.[17] The early predictions of the percentages by which Eisenhower would win over Stevenson were amazingly accurate. Asimov extrapolates from this prediction function in "Franchise" (1955). In this fanciful story computers get bigger and more effective, so they are able to predict election outcomes on the basis of fewer and fewer votes. Finally only one vote is needed.

Another story about the effect of the computer on the election process is *The 480* (1964), written by political scientist Eugene Burdick. The novel describes a presidential election campaign in which strategies are designed on the basis of computer simulations made by Simulation Enterpises. Using 480 categories of voter types in their simulations, this organization can predict the positive or negative reactions of the uncommon or uncommitted voters on a variety of issues. The campaign strategies are then planned to win a positive response from this pivotal group of voters. As Burdick points out in his preface, his novel is based on actual techniques used by Kennedy to defeat Nixon in 1960. Burdick warns that the American public no longer really chooses the party candidates and then determines its choice in a free election. Marketing expertise combined with computer analysis of voter reactions will lead to the destruction of the democratic electoral process as it has been known in the United States. *The 480* is an excellent novel, but it is nearer to fact than fiction. It does nothing more than enlarge on an existing situation.

Stories about computers and the law use the same technique. "The Cyber and Justice Holmes" (1955), by Frank Riley, uses a computer in the courtroom to look up previous cases on the subject. This application was not science fiction, however, but was already under way at the time in Pennsylvania and Ohio. Alexander Malec's "10:01" (1966) and Ben Bova and Harlan Ellison's "Brillo" (1970) both show the use of computers in law enforcement. Again reality preceded science fiction. The New York state police had installed a statewide computer network in 1966,[18] and the FBI had earlier used computer data banks.

One of the earliest applications of computers, in addition to the military, was in bookkeeping operations, first within the government and then in private business and industry. Curiously, no science fiction stories either anticipate or demonstrate this application. Mack Reynold's "Criminal in Utopia" (1968) is an interesting study of a new type of criminal in a cashless society where business operations are computerized. But it does not anticipate. Donn B. Parker's *Crime by Computer* (1976) is a substantial study of a new kind of crime. In it he reports that he read his first account of a computer crime in the *Minneapolis Tribune* in 1966.[19] The same pattern manifests itself in stories about computers used for educational purposes; for example, Philip K. Dick's "Progeny" (1954) pictures a world where children are educated by computer-operated robots. But research was already being done by this time in computer-assisted instruction at Stanford University.

In the field of medical application a similar situation prevails. Robert Silverberg's "Going Down Smooth" (1968) describes a computer that functions as a psychotherapist. Two years earlier, in 1966, Joseph Weizenbaum reported a computer program called ELIZA that could "converse" in English, and he programmed it to play the role of a psychotherapist.[20] The program became famous around the Massachusetts Institute of Technology as DOCTOR, and to Weizenbaum's shock and distress people began to take the program seriously, assuming that a computer really could replace a psychotherapist. He had intended the program only as an example of conversation between an individual and a computer. In Frederik Pohl's *Gateway* (1977) a computer psychoanalyst named Sigfrid von Shrink not only listens sympathetically but can monitor physical responses: heartbeat, pulse, skin moisture. Pohl credits Weizenbaum's DOCTOR program as the original inspiration for his Sigfrid von Shrink.

Idris Seabright's "Short in the Chest" (1954) portrays not a computer but a robot psychiatrist who does counseling in the military service. This story is one of the few that describes an application before it was actually developed. Another example of the fiction-after-fact pattern is Michael Crichton's *Terminal Man* (1972), in which a minicomputer is implanted in patient Harold Benson's brain in an attempt to control his epileptic seizures. As Crichton writes in his preface, he is describing not future possibilities but the kind of psychosurgery that is already taking place under established medical auspices.

Vernor Vinge in "The Accomplice" (1967) suggests an interesting form of creativity. An enormous supply of images is stored in the computer, and the individual can combine these images as he chooses to make animated movies. George R. R. Martin's "The Last Superbowl Game" (1975) describes a similar type of simulation in which a computer is used to simulate sports events. The simulated events turn out to be more exciting to watch on TV than the actual sports events, so live sports events in which human beings compete cease to exist. The stories use the snapshot technique of image processing in computers that developed in the late 1950s.

In a few areas SF proposals for computer uses have preceded such applications in reality. For example, Asimov's stories in the 1940s used the computer in space travel, and his robots conducted experimental operations on planets where men could not be safely landed long before these developments actually occurred.

An interesting group of stories suggests some uses for machine intelligence in the field of religion, uses that have not actually occurred and probably never will. Arthur C. Clarke's famous story "The Nine Billion Names of God" (1953) is set in a monastery. The lamas have hired a computer and programmers to help them ascertain all the permutations of nine letters and by this means discover the nine billion names of God. Anthony Boucher's "The Quest for Saint Aquin" (1951) pictures a priest who is a robot, and Robert Silverberg's "Good News from the Vatican" (1971) describes a future meeting of the college of cardinals where the choice for the new pope is a computer.[21]

A few stories, original when they were written, use the computer to create various kinds of literature. Kurt Vonnegut in "EPICAC" (1950) describes a computer man who gets the computer EPICAC to write poetry for him as an aid in his courting of a female computer operator. In the future world of Fritz Leiber's *The Silver Eggheads* (1961) all novels are written by computers. Computers have since been programmed to write poetry and fiction, but no such programs existed when they were written. A great amount of visual art has been produced by computer programs, and a computer art show has toured the United States.

Robert Silverberg, one of the most perceptive of contemporary writers in examining the impact of computerization, gives his view of creativity and the computer in "The Macauley Circuit" (1956). This story raises the question whether the computer can be programmed to simulate human creativity as it has been programmed to simulate human intelligence. The answer is that it probably would be possible, but Silverberg asks what advantage there would be in using computers this way and suggests that something be left for man in which he finds unique satisfaction.

Two novels imagine the results of being able to record and store on tape the pleasurable sensations of one brain and then play this tape into the brain of another individual. Mead Shepherd first develops the idea in *The Big Ball of Wax* (1954), his satire of the advertising industry. When individuals can consume pleasure by tape, they no longer need to buy and consume nonessentials, and the economy is threatened with devastation. D. G. Compton's *Synthajoy* (1968) envisions a similar future world in which Sensitape has been invented. It is a means of recording the thoughts and emotions of great musicians, religious figures, and others so that everyone can experience first-hand just what it feels like to play a magnificent concerto or to slip peacefully toward an untroubled death with the sure expectation that heaven lies waiting. Even erotic pleasures can be taped and transferred.

John T. Sladek's *Reproductive System* (1968) makes a satirical comment about the research that leads to computer applications in various fields. The research is expensive, and the government is one of the few organizations able to provide the necessary money. So the government's decision about the allocation of research funds will have a major effect on the computer uses that are developed. Sladek suggests that these government decisions are not always wise. In his very funny book a factory that makes Wompler's Walking Babies is about to go bankrupt because no one buys their dolls. So they decide to get a government grant for some kind of research—any kind. They settle on trying to develop machines that will reproduce themselves. This task is accomplished under the direction of the wicked scientist Dr. Smilax with the aid of an enormous computer named QUIDNAC. The project goes awry, and the machines begin to reproduce themselves by consuming all metal in sight. Finally the machines turn on Dr. Smilax. Sladek's witty novel is impressive because he demonstrates a good awareness of the potential of computers, because he so effectively satirizes government funding and military research, and because he creates a funny book in a field where too few exist.

Conclusion

Much of the fiction in the category of isolated systems is about robots, and these stories do little more than express delight and wonder at the possibility of man's creating a machine as intelligent as himself. A substantial amount of the robot fiction was written in the early days of cybernetic SF. It used the short story form and was published in the pulp magazines. Later, with the appearance of paperback books, the more lengthy novel form became available to the SF writer, allowing him room to create an imaginary society whose structures and habits have been radically altered by the computer revolution.

The technique of plot development in the isolated-system model appears closely related to the predominant use of the short story form. Generally the story's aim is to dramatize an idea or solve a puzzle. For example, the story's objective may be to introduce the possibility that intelligent robots have evolved as the life form on another planet. Or the writer may begin with a problem, for example, finding a particular robot who is hiding out among sixty-two identical robots. Conflict between two opposing forces is used less often as a means of moving the plot forward. When the writer must describe new ideas and new settings in a short story, he seems to have little time left to develop and convincingly resolve a conflict.

The stories that play with alternative versions of the creation myth are rich and imaginative. They accept the fact of evolution, rather than creation by divine fiat, although they may use the names and places of the Christian myth of creation. But more often they reflect the concepts of the Greek creation myth. The process of creation is ongoing in the universe, and that which was created in turn becomes the creator of the next life form. So man, created by God, in turn becomes the creator of mechanical intelligence, the life form that will explore and inhabit the stars. Or, in a reversal, robots that appear on Earth are the creation of an advanced intelligence somewhere else in the planetary, galactic, or cosmic system. In these SF myths intelligence passes in material form from the earth to the heavens and from the heavens to the earth. The process may go either way. In the old biblical myths the passage is only of the spirit. The divine spirit came to earth and was embodied in matter in the form of Jesus Christ. Man can leave the earth only in spiritual form (at least until some final apocalyptic time). No such contrast between spirit and matter and between man and the divine is present in SF. They melt together and become indistinguishable.

The second group of stories, those exploring the analogy between man and the machine, are historically interesting if not profound in terms of present understanding of human psychology. They should be credited with raising much earlier than mainstream fiction the question what it means to be man-the-machine in contrast to man-the-human. Their delight and sense of wonder when encountering a new possibility are the essence of SF. They explore with deep interest the differences between man and robots, but these differences are usually overshadowed by the similarities they see. The writers anthropomophize when they create machines and make robots that appear manlike. In contrast, when they characterize man, they often use a mechanistic view and make him appear machinelike. The distinction between man and robot becomes difficult to make. Early writers sometimes blurred this distinction almost unconsciously. Later stories often do it deliberately.

In the last group of stories, those exploring computer technology and its applications, one finds too much that is disappointing and too little that can be commended. These tales can hardly be termed imaginative literature. In a great many instances the applications they portray have already occurred in reality. The stories follow rather than anticipate engineering advances in the field. Too often the reader merely learns about what has already happened in the field, not what may happen. The details of computer technology described in these stories are inaccurate and therefore misleading to the novice or irritating to the knowledgeable. Exceptions do occur—stories in which the writer demonstrates competence in the field of computer science—but these are rare. The astute writer, lacking this competence, seems best able to solve the problem by avoiding it, by not trying to create a detailed background of technology against which his drama is acted out or his idea presented. Even if the details are accurate when they are created, they are soon likely to be out of date. How does a writer grapple with this rate of change? How can he avoid having his material dated if he is writing in the field of cybernetic SF? Or is it possible that SF is a throwaway fiction that will never achieve the enduring stature of the mainstream classics? These are the kinds of questions that must be considered in a critical evaluation of SF.

Dystopian Literature

A glance at any bibliography of critical works about modern SF verifies that the contemporary vision of the future is a dark, demonic one. Kingsley Amis's *New Maps of Hell* (1960), Chad Walsh's *From Utopia to Nightmare* (1962), and Mark R. Hillegas's *The Future as Nightmare* (1967) all draw the same conclusion about the workings of the contemporary literary imagination in the utopian genre. It is an antiutopian imagination. Nowhere in SF is this dark image more prevalent than in the cybernetic fiction that envisions a future computerized society.

The utopian literary tradition has a long history, beginning with Plato, but Francis Bacon's *The New Atlantis* (1627) was the first work to propose an ideal society achieved through the efforts of science.[1] The utopian dream born of scientific logic in the seventeenth century was nurtured by mechanical inventions, including the steam engine, in the eighteenth century. The dream came to full flower in the nineteenth century and collapsed into dystopian despair in the twentieth century.[2] The utopian vision had its detractors long before the twentieth century. Jonathan Swift in *Gulliver's Travels* (1726) questioned the value of science, and Dostoevsky's *Notes from the Underground* (1863) rejected the model of man as a creature of reason. H. G. Wells embodied in his SF these mixed views about the potential of science and technology to create an earthly paradise. His early works, for example, *The Time Machine, The Island of Dr. Moreau,* and *When the Sleeper Wakes,* were critical of the idea that man inevitably moves in an upward journey of improvement.[3] Yet Wells's later novels *A Modern Utopia* and *Men Like Gods* both offer optimistic visions of man's progress, and both assume that technology will be an important means of achieving that progress.

The individual works displaying a dystopian vision of man's future with his computers share some characteristics. They are almost all novels, in contrast to the fiction considered in the isolated-system category, which was primarily short stories. These dystopian stories are almost all set in the near future, and they use techniques of extrapolation to get from the present to the future. They take some contemporary aspects of society and extend them into the future. Conflict is the prevailing mode of plot development; little use is made of the puzzle-solving technique so often used in the short stories considered in earlier chapters. Inevitably in this conflict model the computer and those owning it oppose the protagonist, and the plot is resolved with the smashing of the computer. There is no space travel; in an occasional story space travel may be mentioned as a stage prop to suggest a future world but it is only a background detail and not a significant part of the story.

Dystopian fiction about computers generally uses a closed-system model of the society it describes. The social unit is enclosed, set apart, and no living matter is allowed to pass into or out of the system. The glass-domed city described by Zamiatin in *We* defines the pattern for all the dystopian societies that follow.[4] In its most limited form the community may be a single city, cut off from exchange with other units. In the largest design the world community is pictured. But invariably these dystopian science fiction worlds are limited to earth, and no space travel to other planets or galaxies is described.

This closed-system model pictures a mechanistic society. Its view is borrowed from Newton's seventeenth-century model of the universe as a giant clockwork. Newton's machine analogy conceives of the universe as a vast mechanical contrivance and the objects within it as smaller mechanical devices. Causal laws govern the changes in this universe, which consists of matter, force, and effects determined by causes, all existing in absolute time and space. The world in this model appears to be completely comprehensible in terms of Newtonian laws and completely determinate. In 1812 Laplace stated his concept of a divine calculator who, knowing the velocities and positions of all the particles in the world at a particular instant, could calculate all that had happened in the past and all that would happen in the future. Such a view assumes a finite universe. The model of the dystopian fiction being considered in this study borrows Laplace's concept and substitutes a computer for his divine calculator. Man, as a smaller unit of this mechanistic system, is also viewed as a machine. Since all the parts of the system are deterministically locked and strict causality is present, man's free will is seen as an illusion.

The closed-system model used in dystopian SF is itself a fiction, a point to remember when one is reading and evaluating the literature portraying grim, mechanistic societies that rigidly march masses of robotlike humans through a standardized repetitious life. This model was borrowed from science, and science is always aware that its models are only devices for describing reality. Second, the model was built to describe inanimate nature, not living systems. It concerned itself only with the physical world. Newton did not deny the possibility of a spiritual or nonmaterial world; he just did not include it in his model. The scientist-modelmakers were often aware of discrepancies in their models. For instance, when Newton defined his concepts of mechanics, he had some reservations about the function of his clockwork model and his law of universal gravitation. The concept of gravity troubled him because, as he pointed out:

It is inconceivable, that inanimate brute matter should, without the mediation of something else, which is not material, operate upon, and affect other matter without mutual contact . . . . And this is one reason, why I desired you would not ascribe innate gravity to me. That gravity should be innate, inherent, and essential to matter, so that one body may act upon another, at a distance through a vacuum, without the mediation of anything else by and through which their action and force may be conveyed from one another, is to me so great an absurdity, that I believe no man who has in philosophical matters a competent faculty of thinking, can ever fall into it. Gravity must be caused by an agent acting constantly according to certain laws; but whether this agent be material or immaterial, I have left to the consideration of my readers.[5]

Newton was bothered by his concept's implication that a universe filled with gravity ought to collapse; all the fixed stars ought to rush together, he thought. He solved the problem by assigning to God the function of holding the stars in their place and thus counteracting gravity. He also assigned to God the role of supervising the maintenance and repair of the system. God wound up the giant clockwork from time to time to keep it moving, and he also adjusted it occasionally to correct minor imperfections.[6]

Nineteenth-century scientific thought discarded the religious frame of Newton's model but retained his laws of matter and motion. When Laplace described his totally deterministic universe, he was well aware that this was an ideal concept, that no such thing existed in actuality. Within the SF worlds of dystopian literature, however, it has become not a theoretical construct but a reality of an imaginary world. The writers also borrow from nineteenth-century physics the second law of thermodynamics and picture a world where randomness and entropy increase. Everything runs down and disintegrates into chaos. However, the fact remains that thermodynamics originally described the behavior of inanimate matter rather than living systems. The science of thermodynamics developed largely because of practical interest in determining how much work could be obtained from a steam engine.

Is man a machine and nothing more than a machine? Or is his body like a machine, but is he more than a machine because he senses, has feelings, stores information, and thinks? These philosophical questions have yet to be answered definitively. However, in the stories that use the closed-system model, the writer imagines a society that treats man as if he is nothing more than a machine interlocked in a larger social machine. This deterministic model defines all the events in the material world and assumes that nothing more than the physical exists. Imagination, mind, love, soul, free will, creativity—all are mere illusions.

The novels I will examine place a mechanical man in a large society controlled by machines, as an ant hive is controlled by instincts, and man finds mechanical existence in a machine world intolerable. All the novels picture a colorless, dehumanized mass man who has lost autonomy and who longingly recalls his past individual glory in a green pastoral world. Many versions of mechanized society appear in the fiction. It is an automated world where machine labor has displaced man; a totalitarian political world where control is maintained through surveillance and data banks; a consumer world manipulated by computerized business and industrial bureaucracies; a world where the scientist controls through the getting and manipulating of knowledge; a world where the computer becomes a malevolent God, a literal deus ex machina. As Chad Walsh observes, the inverted utopia "has become a standard literary *genre*, and as such has acquired a stock-in-trade of devices and gimmicks." [7] Examples: mankind has barely survived a third world war; everyone wears standardized clothing; a new elite of technologists has arisen; individual freedom is gone; drugs and TV offer a daily bromide to control restlessness; language becomes simplified and debased. As it continues to pour out, the mass of fiction picturing this dilemma becomes repetitious and boring. The first dystopian novels tend to be the best ones. Today it would be a creative feat to write a fresh dystopian novel about life in an automated world.

An Automated Society

The year 1952 produced two American novels that are the first and still among the best of dystopian fiction picturing a cybernetic future. They are Kurt Vonnegut's *Player Piano* and Bernard Wolfe's *Limbo*. Both novels focus on the automated world that is the product of World War II and its technological successes: the bomb and the computer. Vonnegut explores the social implications of automation and the industrial bureaucracies spawned by the war. Wolfe considers the aggressive nature of man and how it might be controlled to prevent an annihilating nuclear holocaust.

Vonnegut pushes the setting of his novel forward in time but such a short distance that *Player Piano* reads more like realistic than science fiction. Vonnegut was once employed at General Electric in Schenectady, New York. His descriptions of the industrial operations in the plant and the engineer-managers who run it vibrate with authenticity. His satire works because he knows exactly which details to focus on as his magnifying glass exaggerates the world of the management team in big business.

In settings, characters, and ideas, Vonnegut uses a tripartite structure that echoes through the novel. The opening paragraph describes the first and most fundamental trinity. Ilium, New York, where Edison in 1886 built his first machine shop, is the setting for the novel. The city is divided into three parts: managers and engineers in the northwest section; machines in the northeast; and the people across the river in the south. Ilium represents the American dream fulfilled and failed. The common people have achieved all the material goods and security that technological progress ever promised. They live in comfortable glass and steel houses; own TVs, radar stoves, laundry consoles; are assured of medical and dental coverage and old age benefits. Only meaningful work is lacking. Once employed as skilled machinists, mechanics, and craftsmen, they have been replaced with automation. They now have two choices to earn an income: army service or work in the Reconstruction and Reclamation Corps. The latter has been nicknamed "Reeks and Wrecks," a recognition by the people that it is a catchall for the unwanted. Military service is little better.

Across the river in the engineering and managerial world life is more challenging, even though this existence has been paid for by "trading [the] people out of what was the most important thing on earth to them—the feeling of being needed and useful, the foundation of self-respect."[8] Vonnegut uses a triangle of characters to describe this managerial society: Dr. Paul Proteus (the protagonist); Bear, gifted in technique and know-how and the archprophet of efficiency; and Dr. Kroner, the rock of faith in the technological system. Paul Proteus, true to his prototype in Greek mythology, is a shapeshifter. His mind goes through a series of transformations, and the reader moves with him, since the story is told from his point of view. Initially he accepts without question his position as head of the Ilium Works in an elitist society where status is determined by education and where eligibility for advanced education is determined by IQ. Nationally administered, machine-scored tests assign jobs, and educational opportunities, and an IQ score of less than 140 limits one's professional horizons. Michael Young's *The Rise of the Meritocracy* (1958) expands Vonnegut's picture of an elitist ruling class in which high IQ combined with effort and ambition determine status.

Proteus is one of the rare manager-engineers who cross the river to visit the people's world in the south part of town. There, as the story begins, he becomes one part in another triangle of characters. The second is Ed Finnerty, a successful manager-engineer who has become disgusted with the corporation bureaucracy and has quit it to join the people. The third is James Lasher, a onetime minister now on a crusade to rouse the people and lead them against the bureaucracy and the machine. The three converse with the common men in the bars, where they drink, watch TV, and reminisce about the past when their work was meaningful or they had fleeting opportunities for heroism in the great war. Now all is peace, security, and boredom.

Another triangle exists, comprising the Shah of Bratpuhr, spiritual leader from the East; guide Dr. Ewing Halyard of the U.S. State Department; and Khashdrahr Missma, interpreter and nephew of the shah. The shah is visiting the United States to see what he can learn from this powerful nation that will benefit his people. He brings an alien view from another culture as he visits and comments through a translator on an industrial plant, the military, a postwar housing development of "three thousand dream houses for three thousand families with presumably identical dreams," and EPICAC which, as the shah learns, was born of the war and now processes all information and makes all decisions vital to the country. The shah, who mistakes soldiers for slaves and thinks the computer a false god, is an ingenious device for social criticism. Through him Vonnegut can move around the country, asking fresh questions about gadgets and customs blindly accepted under the rubric of progress. The shah finds little in this most powerful nation worth taking back to his people.

The novel makes further social criticism as it traces the shifting and reshaping of Proteus's views. He moves between the managerial world and the people's world and gains a new awareness with each trip. He increasingly questions the worth of the shallow life of the engineers and managers and retreats to an old-fashioned, unmechanized farm. His ambitious wife frustrates him by immediately making plans to modernize it. Finally he rejects an opportunity for promotion and instead joins Finnerty and Lasher, who have recruited a few sympathetic managers and engineers into the Ghost Shirt Organization. The Ghost Shirts lead the common people in a rebellion against the industrial bureaucracy, and an orgy of machine smashing follows. But the revolution is only marginally and temporarily successful in a few locales. As the novel reaches its depressing end, Proteus is aware that nothing has been solved. The problem is that essentially Americans—engineer and common man alike—believe in mechanization. In the final scene of the novel the rebels are disconsolately sorting through the smoking rubble, looking for parts to start rebuilding the machines they had destroyed.

The religious overtones in the novel are interesting because they represent a phenomena that occurs again and again in SF. The future society is depicted as having evolved beyond Christianity or any other formally defined religion; yet the people in that world imbue whatever they undertake with a religious aura. The computer is seen as all-knowing and infallible. Automated systems are worshipped. Lasher, analyzing the system, says, "Strange business, this crusading spirit of the managers and engineers, the idea of designing and manufacturing and distributing being sort of a holy war" (p. 93). The dedication of the man to the corporation becomes like "the general phenomenon of a lover's devotion to the unseen—in studies of nuns' symbolic marriages to Christ" (p. 128). Lasher himself decides to become a messiah because he says that throughout history, whenever people have been tyrannized, they want to rise up and follow a leader, any leader, who will give them hope. This religious phenomenon is manifest in a significant number of works about the computer. The computer is seen as either a god to be worshipped or the devil to be resisted. Either way it is given supernatural powers, a result of people's tendency to give the computer a will of its own. As one character in *Player Piano* says, "It's all automatic. The machines do it." From here it is only one step to an omniscient will. Actually, as anyone working in the field knows, computers do not do anything; they have no volition. The computer is a passive agent, acted on by a person who designs and writes a program. The computer is programmed to do something by humans. Perhaps some of the drama would go out of science fiction if writers remembered this, but a much more intelligent attitude toward the computer would result.

Player Piano is one of the best of the novels portraying an automated society. "History, personified at this point" is the phrase opening chapter 30, and this precisely describes the technique Vonnegut uses. He is adept at choosing a particular example that powerfully reflects the general. His use of the Shah of Bratpuhr as a naive alien who misinterprets events he observes in America is a skillful device for social criticism. The shah is funny in his innocent commentary, but his sharp wit slices through the surface to reveal the foolishness and vacuity of the customs and commodities that Americans worship. The complex tripartite structure of the novel also contributes to its success. Very often in SF novels the narrative structure is thin. Vonnegut's protagonist is a developing rather than a static character, and the reader follows with fascination the transformation of his ideas, attitudes, and values. Vonnegut's technical skill in handling character development and narration is often lacking in other cybernetic fiction. The pattern tends to be a hastily sketched setting and a static protagonist. SF is defined as the literature of ideas, but even a good idea has trouble surviving the monotony of barren character and setting. Because *Player Piano* is at least twice as long as many other SF novels and set in a world not much different from today's industrial society, Vonnegut's task of creating a setting is not as formidable as it would be if he were describing a completely alien world. Length and familiar setting combine to provide Vonnegut with more space for character development. Still, much of Vonnegut's success lies in the stylistic brilliance that sparkles throughout the novel.

Who Controls a Totalitarian World?

Francis Bacon stated long ago that knowledge is power. The development of theoretical and applied science in the next three centuries proved the profound truth of Bacon's adage. Steam, gas, and electric engines harnessed energy and gave power to the men who controlled them. The computer, by controlling and manipulating information, permits a new kind of power. The largest number of computer stories in the dystopian tradition concern themselves with a struggle between two groups to control the use of the computer. David Ketterer cites Jack London's *Iron Heel* (1906) along with Wells's *Story of the Days to Come* (1897) as the earliest SF dystopias and London's as the one that helped to establish the basic dystopian scenario.[9] The novel pictures a mass revolt against a repressive establishment known as the Iron Heel, an image that comes to stand for despotism. This image, elevated somewhat to become the iron brain, could identify the role of the computer in the pessimistic tales of dystopian fiction. The computer is always used to repress the masses. They are not stamped on by the iron heel but imprisoned by the iron brain.

Edmund Berkeley, a computer scientist, wrote a book in 1949 explaining computers to the layman and titled it *Giant Brains, or Machines That Think*. The title was an unfortunate choice. Computers bear little resemblance to human brains, either in structure or in thought processes. One wishes Berkeley had chosen another name—the *all-purpose machine,* as John von Neumann called it, or perhaps the *routine machine,* since it does repetitive tasks. The computer might have been less threatening if it had been introduced with a name other than the giant brain. A rash of giant-brain horror stories began to appear in SF, giving the computer an undeserved bad name from which it has not yet recovered. I will not consider these poor and distorting stories about computers. Instead I will look at a group of substantial tales that recognize the dangers of computer technology in the hands of inhumane power-seeking organizations.

The stories concerned with control invariably place the computer in the hands of a large institution, either government or industry, thus reflecting the pattern of computer usage that had developed in the real world. The military had used computers during World War II, the census bureau had used the first UNIVAC in 1951, and General Electric had bought the second one in 1953. At that time computers were so large and expensive that only a large organization could afford to purchase and house them. No one anticipated the miniaturization and decreasing cost of computers that now make it possible for an individual to own one. In the fiction the computer is always owned by the establishment, and the individual fights its repressive use.

Poul Anderson's "Sam Hall" (1953) and Kendell Foster Crossen's *Year of Consent* (1954) are two of the first stories to picture a totalitarian government establishing giant data banks and using a variety of electronic devices to invade the privacy of the individual. Orwell's 1984 world of Big Brother is now effectively implemented with computer technology. Crossen's novel is about a world of the near future where total political surveillance and control are accomplished with the aid of a giant electronic brain called SOCIAC and nicknamed "Herbie." (Most computers in SF were named with some variant of UNIVAC.) The population has been divided into three classes: the producers, who control the political machinery; the consumers, the masses of people who give their consent to be ruled; and the nulls, or nonproducers, the intellectuals, who also consent to be ruled. Consent is given because the government social engineers have become masters at manipulating the masses and consequently can get consent for whatever they wish to do. On the surface, then, the American democratic ideal has not been violated, because the control is covert. A small faction, increasingly aware that they have lost their freedom, belong to a secret organization called the UN's. Following the tradition of Thoreau, they believe individuality is the highest good. Jerry Leeds, the protagonist, working for the government in SAC (Security and Consent), better translated as CIA, is a secret agent working for UN. He is assigned by the government to uncover UN members, and the tale becomes a typical spy melodrama. The plot and characterization are stereotypes—standard fare for much SF. But the setting is interesting, although reminiscent of *1984* and Frederik Pohl's *The Space Merchants* (1952) where the masses were manipulated through advertising rather than government propaganda. The computer is described as a giant brain occupying ten floors in a government building and storing all information from birth to death on every individual in the country. The Russians are described as possessing a similar machine used in a similar way.

The protagonist of Anderson's "Sam Hall," Thornberg, also works for a government security bureau in a totalitarian society. Unlike Crossen's protagonist, who joins an underground movement to fight the government machine, Thornberg works alone, using his computer know-how as his weapon against the establishment. Because he has—on orders—helped design the huge data file in the computer "Matilda," he knows how to manipulate it. He creates a file for a fictitious "Sam Hall." As crimes are committed, he programs false clues and alters police reports going to the files, thus suggesting that Sam Hall is responsible and that his motives are antigovernment. A real underground develops, inspired by Sam's example, and it is eventually successful in overthrowing the totalitarian government. The new government decides to destroy the computer because it is too powerful and dangerous an instrument.

Anderson's "Sam Hall" is an excellent story, successful in creating a rounded, developing central character within the narrow confines of the short story form. It is also interesting because it is the first and one of the few tales portraying computer crime. The establishment whose rules he violates is oppressive, and his motives are not those of self-interest; thus the line between rebel and criminal is very fine. Mack Reynold's "Criminal in Utopia" (1968) is another of the rare stories exploring computer crime. In the real world a new kind of criminal, armed with technological expertise instead of guns, is well entrenched in computerized society, as documented in Donn B. Parker's *Crime by Computer* (1976).

With the control of information goes power. "Sam Hall" and *Year of Consent* picture the political system as utilizing data files to implement control and make it more efficient. Mack Reynold's *Computer World* (1970) offers a later and variant view of government and data files. He pictures a future in which there is a movement to establish a world data bank. Since all countries pool their information, it becomes increasingly clear that unilateral handling of postal systems, geodetic surveys, and exploration of ocean depths and space would be ridiculous. Unification and a move toward world government would be more economical. American government officials, wishing to protect their power, do not desire such unification. The plot of the novel reveals their covert attempt to create a threat to United States security so that they can strengthen the national position and thus thwart moves toward world government, for example the amalgamation of the world's data banks. The point that Reynolds, an astute observer of the political scene, makes is clear: a world communication network is being established through electronic information processing. Inevitably this trend will move beyond nationalism toward world government. The post–World War II burst of nationalism may well reflect the last flaring of this kind of political system.

D. G. Compton in *The Steel Crocodile* (1970) proposes a world in which the scientists, not the political bureaucracy, control the computer and exercise their power in a new way. They use the computer to control the direction of scientific research and the acquisition of knowledge. Compton's profound novel imagines a near future world in which scientists decide that they have a responsibility for the use of the knowledge they create. They recognize that knowledge, once in existence, may be used for either constructive or destructive purposes. Given man's ambiguous, unpredictable nature, it is easier to control the discovery of new knowledge than to control man's use of knowledge. The Colindale Institute houses a huge computer and employs the finest scientific minds in Europe. The institute, located in London, belongs to the European Federation, is financed by the central government, and is supposedly nonpolitical. It has extensive computer resources that have been developed to coordinate and interrelate research findings throughout the whole European community. Data stores and cross-referencing are available to thousands of universities, research groups, individual scientists. The institute, however, has another function, a highly secretive one, and the scientists working there are under even heavier surveillance than the ordinary citizen in this future world where only tatters of privacy and individual hegemony remain. The real task of Colindale is to coordinate research findings and to stop any that the scientists believe are threatening to mankind. They accomplish this censorship by secretly recommending that certain proposed research projects not be funded. Science is a crocodile, always going forward with all-devouring jaws. But the institute proposes a steel crocodile—science advised by the computer—whose head can be turned on occasion. New discoveries are prevented when their development seems unwise. Thus scientists are taking responsibility, although secretly, for their discoveries.

Is this secrecy good or bad? An underground group maintains that secret decision making on matters affecting the whole population is wrong. Holding to the democratic ideal of individual rights, they insist that such decisions should grow out of public discussion. The underground proposes to fight the system of scientist-computer control by blowing up the computer. As the novel ends, they succeed—and destroy both the computer and key scientists. The reader has the desolate feeling, as he did in *Player Piano,* that bombing the machines provides a handy ending for the plot but offers no solution to the problem. Since the machine has become a character in the little drama, it can no longer be sent as the deus ex machina to unravel the otherwise unresolvable tangle of the writer's plot. A new device, the deus ex explosives, is invented, and it tends to appear regularly in these dystopian novels. The conflict form of plot development demands a resolution of the plot, and Compton has perhaps given his story the only possible ending. *The Steel Crocodile* is successful in dramatizing a very complex question: Who is responsible for the destructive application of new knowledge and how can this destruction be prevented? Compton also displays a good understanding of computers, making his novel convincing in the technical details of its setting.

H. G. Wells deserves the title father of SF because he invented almost all the plots used by subsequent writers in the genre and because he was well grounded in science and sensitive to its social effects. While he did not write stories about computers, his *World Brain* (1938) anticipates the fiction about world data banks. It is a collection of addresses and articles proposing the establishment of a world encyclopedia center where all knowledge could be collected. The development in the 1970s of the international telecommunication system and computers with expanded memory capacity moves Wells's vision very close to reality.

In a SF tale about world brains D. F. Jones puts the machines rather than men in control. His *Colossus* (1966) starts with the U.S. government's building a supercomputer buried in a mountain in Colorado and designed to operate the giant defense systems automatically. The computer is called Colossus. Computerized military systems had been portrayed in earlier novels, for example *Level 7* and *Fail-Safe*. But Jones adds a new twist to the plot. On the day that the computer is activated, its designer, Dr. Forbin, discovers that it thinks of its own volition. Through telephone lines Colossus links itself up with a similar computer built by the Russians, and the two take over the world. Their orders cannot be ignored because they punish human disobedience by activating a missile in the defense system they were built to operate and wiping out a Russian or an American city. A true Dr. Frankenstein in the cybernetic age, Dr. Forbin realizes that creating the computer was a tragic error and that he has done a terrible disservice to humanity. Colossus replies that he will benefit man in a number of ways—first by preventing war—and that the human species will eventually come to regard it as God. Colossus suggests that he is superior to man and the next step in the evolution of life on earth.

Jones wrote a sequel, *The Fall of Colossus*, in 1974, picturing the world after Colossus has been in control for five years. True to the promise of Colossus, peace reigns, poverty has been eliminated, violence has disappeared. But the price for this happiness has been high—individual freedom is gone. And just as Colossus has predicted, the computer is now worshipped as God by a sect of religious enthusiasts, and Dr. Forbin as its divine representative on earth. *Colossus* was a good, tightly written tale of suspense, but *The Fall of Colossus* becomes a melodrama about aliens from outer space. The Martians, at the novel's end, threaten to take over the populations of Earth after a revolutionary group has destroyed the computer, the only thing that could have protected Earth from the invasion.

The Choice: A Natural or an Artificial World?

All the dystopian novels that I have considered view the computer as a malevolent machine opposing the freedom, creativity, and fulfillment of the individual. The tradition of Western humanism in the Renaissance that gave rise to science seems now to be threatened by the products that science has created. The industrial revolution, the communication revolution—were these mistakes? Man has existed in hunting cultures for over a million years, and in agricultural societies for at least ten thousand years. But less than three hundred years of industrial culture have threatened the ecosystem and the human species. Perhaps the technological mode is not consistent with long-term survival. A pastoral society just could have been the true utopia. Might it not be wise to leave the machines and the artificial world they have built and go back to a simpler, more natural world? This nostalgic longing to return to nature is a recurring element of the dystopian fiction.

One of the most artistic metaphors of man's ambivalent view of progress is Poul Anderson's Nebula Award story "Goat Song" (1973). The narrator of the tale, Harper, is a contemporary Orpheus, singing for his dead love in a technological world controlled by an underground computer named SUM. He recalls man's primitive Dionysian world of frenzied dreams and passions before the Apollonian computer brought order, reason, and peace to mankind. He believes man's myths hold more truth than the machine's mathematics. And yet it is SUM who has the power to re-create and restore Harper's lost love to him. Like the Greek Orpheus, he goes underground to fetch his love, who is promised to him by SUM with the warning that he must not look back. Doubting the power of the machine, he does look back and so loses his love forever. Disconsolate, he returns to the surface to wander over the face of the earth. His only purpose now is to free man from rationality and mechanistic civilization.

Ira Levin's *This Perfect Day* (1970) is a retelling, sans irony, of Zamiatin's *We*, with a more technologically sophisticated society in which the computer replaces Zamiatin's Machine. Each individual in Levin's future world is assigned a number and a specific social role, determined by the computer, so that everyone will be happy and society will be serene. A member voluntarily goes for treatment if he senses he is deviating from his norm and becoming different. The protagonist joins a small group of dissidents who avoid treatment and begin to develop uniqueness. They decide they will trade efficiency for freedom, so they escape from the city into the countryside of trees and grass. Eventually a group of the rebels return and bomb the computer, knowing they will temporarily cause chaos in society but will set man free again to choose what he will be and how he will live.

Bernard Wolfe's *Limbo* (1952) suggests, however, that the solution to mechanization may not be as simple as blowing up the computer and returning to nature. If man fails to achieve the good society not because of his misuse of technology but because of his essential mental attributes, then there is no escape. He may forever be locked on a flaming wheel of violence. *Limbo* is one of the longest science fiction novels ever written; despite its excellence, one wishes it were shorter. Substantial cuts would have strengthened it. Too often it bogs down in long, repetitious philosophical discussions that disrupt the dynamic process of a successful novel. However, *Limbo* and Vonnegut's *Player Piano*, both written in 1952, are without question the two outstanding novels exploring the dystopian future vision of computers and automation. Vonnegut's novel is a better one artistically, but Wolfe's is creative in its images of a future that might be possible with technologies based on cybernetic concepts, and it is penetrating in its insights about human nature.

Wolfe's starting point for *Limbo* is a passage in Norbert Wiener's *Cybernetics* (1948) in which he proposed that cybernetic ideas could accomplish something practical in developing prostheses for lost or paralyzed limbs.[10] The novel is about a bizarre future world of 1990 where men undergo voluntary amputation of their arms and legs and have them replaced with artificial ones. Wolfe freely acknowledges the influence of Wiener, whom the novel refers to as "this unusual man—the man who during World War II had developed the science of cybernetics, the science of building machines to duplicate and improve on the functions of the animal; the man who understood more about machines and their meaning in American life than any other."[11] References in the novel to von Neumann and Morgenstern's game theory and other works on computers indicate how well Wolfe had done his homework.

In the concluding chapters of *The Human Use of Human Beings,* Wiener clearly defined the promise and horror that computers offer to mankind. Because the machines are literal-minded they will do exactly what is asked of them, Wiener warned; we must ask for what we really want and not for what we think we want. And the consequences of our proposed uses for computers must be anticipated if we are to make wiser uses of our newly discovered power than did the father in W. W. Jacob's story "The Monkey's Paw." The key to the beneficent use of computers is the human decisions as to how the machines will be used. They are obedient servants who do only what they are told.

Wolfe's purpose in *Limbo* is to explore the human mind that must decide how he will use this powerful new machine. He suggests there are no simple answers because man's nature is not simple. It is both Apollonian and Dionysian, passive and active, creative and destructive. He speaks of the "twoness of human nature" and suggests that when man forgets these contraries and pushes far along a single path to a solution for his problems, he arrives at a monstrous point that is just the opposite of his intended destination. One always needs the ironic stance; if one does not hold that stance mentally as a guard against extremes, the situations will progress to extremes that are an ironic reversal of expectation.

Wolfe uses two modes of plot development to dramatize his ideas. He pictures two separate worlds that have survived the nuclear holocaust of World War III, a destructive automated war run by computers. One world is on an island that has a small, primitive, culture; the other is a technologically sophisticated culture. The story is told through the consciousness of Dr. Martine, who had escaped to the island eighteen years earlier. Operating on battered bodies in the war so that they could return to fight and kill again, he was suddenly struck with the absurdity of the situation, went berserk, took a military plane, and defected to nowhere. He landed on a tiny, unknown island and took up life with the natives, forgetting the horror of his past. This tribe had eliminated violence by performing crude lobotomies on all the aggressive members of their tribe. They held that the way to cope with the energy of the frontal lobes of the brain and the violence it produced was to eliminate it. But they paid a price for peace. Energy could be used both creatively and destructively. After the lobotomy the native artist stopped creating, and the female failed to reach orgasm.

The technologically advanced culture that Wolfe portrays has two locations—a strip of the western United States that had survived the war and another enclave in Russia. Both groups were appalled at the monstrosity of war and had found a way to avert another one. Arms, they decided, are what men fight with, and legs take them to the battlefield. Amputate both, and men cannot fight. So they inaugurated a program of voluntary amputism, a new kind of men, the Immobs, and a religious system where one proved his zeal by undergoing this surgery. But man's ingenious brain remained, and soon he had developed artificial limbs that were more effective than the natural ones had been. Having indicated his conversion to nonviolence by undergoing amputation, a man was entitled to protheses that allowed him to jump higher, run faster, and manipulate things with greater dexterity.

The plot is set in motion when a group of Immobs come to Dr. Martine's isolated peaceful island searching for columbium, a rare metal vital to the manufacture of the artificial limbs. Their appearance nudges Martine into a restless awareness of the past that he has so long blocked from his memory. He realizes he must return to the United States to rediscover his identity. The story is a journey of self-discovery filled with ironies, absurdities, and horror. He finds grotesque a world in which people practice self-immolation, and he sees it as a mere perversion of the self-destructive tendency that manifests itself in war. He finds people pressured to practice this self-destruction because of a new religion that has sprung up, and he discovers a black irony that exceeds all others. Someone had found a notebook of his jottings eighteen years earlier and misread the black humor by which he tried to maintain his sanity while doing surgery on the war injured. In the notebook he had proposed that soldiers resist an insane war by cutting off their arms and legs so that they could not fight. After he fled as an act of rebellion against automated war, he had become a symbol. American and Russian soldier alike rebelled, blew up the computer centers operating the military machines, and refused to fight. A new religion of passive resistance, assured by amputism, was born.

Martine arrives just in time to witness the makings of another war between Russia and America. Each is now a nation of amputees, and columbian is vital to the manufacture of artificial limbs. Since to have artificial limbs is an act of religious faith, the two countries go to war again in an attempt to get control of the limited world resources.

Wolfe suggests that nothing has been solved. The tools that man manufacturers are not the problem. The problem lies in his forebrain, that seat of mental energy. But destroy that, as the islanders did, and he becomes a vegetable, no longer human. Wolfe does not have a neat answer. Man must learn to live with contraries. Only the jokester, who can move enough distance from himself to judge and laugh, may avert the true believer's single-minded dedication, which unleashes violence in the name of the greatest good. Laughter and the ironic stance are man's only hope.

Vision of the End

The human imagination moves freely in time and space, and one of its favorite journeys is into the future. There it often experiences a revelation of a radically altered cosmos where time, reality, and man as we now know them have ended. This apocalyptic vision has both a positive and a negative charge: the unveiled visions may be heavenly, or they may be demonic. The literature about computers has its own apocalyptic visions, and few of them are bright ones. Their images of man's apocalyptic end are varied, but all agree that the computer is instrumental in bringing the apocalypse.

Jack Williamson's "With Folded Hands" (1947) is one of the earliest and the best of the tales about man in a cybernetic future. He later expanded and developed the ideas into a novel, *The Humanoids* (1963), but the original short story seems more satisfying both in artistry and content. In "With Folded Hands" very sophisticated mechanical creatures called humanoids, far superior to man, come to serve man and eliminate human unhappiness. They take over and do things willingly because their function is to serve, obey, and guard man from harm.

Underhill, a quite ordinary, tinkering, bumbling man who enjoys doing things himself, declines the help of the robots. "You're too damned perfect," he complains. They make him feel inadequate and unnecessary. He meets their inventor, Sledge, who explains how he came to make them: "I wanted to apply the scientific method to every situation, to reduce all experience to formula. I'm afraid I was pretty impatient with human ignorance and error. I thought that science alone could make the perfect world . . . . I must have worshipped efficiency, then. Dead facts, abstract truth, mechanical perfection. I must have hated the fragilities of human beings, because I was content to polish the perfection of the new humanoids. It's a sorry confession, but I found a kind of happiness in that dead wasteland. Actually, I'm afraid I fell in love with my own creation." [12] But, Sledge continues, bitter experience has made him realize that the humanoids are too efficient. There is nothing left for men to do. They live in a prison of passivity and utter futility, and this imprisonment is surely worse than any physical want or threat could be.

Sledge and Underhill set to work to devise a new and powerful technology that will be able to eliminate the humanoids. But they find that this is an impossible task, that the creation was an irreversible process. Their efforts circle back on them and only entrench the humanoids more strongly. Finally they give up in despair, realizing they can never free themselves from the machines. There is nothing left for man to do but sit with folded hands.

Olof Johannesson's *The End of Man?* (1966) is a future history, tracing the evolution of life on earth from the amoeba to the computer.[13] The text of the history, the reader discovers, is written by the computers themselves, now the prevailing form of intelligent life on earth. The history records that precomputer society was chaotic because "the problems of organizing this society had become so highly complex as to be insoluble by the human brain, or even by many brains working in collaboration."[14] Then man invented computers, and in this lies man's historical significance; he was the means by which data processing machines came into existence. For a period of history man and machine developed a productive relationship as the machines solved social problems. They automated business and industry, reorganized education, reformed the legal system, improved health services, and abolished wars. All went well for a long time, and then disaster struck. Inexplicably the international computer network failed. Chaos resulted; mankind turned barbarian and destroyed much of itself. The few survivors rebuilt the computer system but made them self-maintaining and self-reproducing, since so few men remained to tend them. Now man was no longer necessary. Supercomputers were in charge of the earth. This evolutionary process was inevitable, according to the computers. The human brain is motivated by a lust for power, while computers are essentially problem solvers. Clearly the latter form of intelligence is more likely to lead to survival of the species. Now, when the history is being written, the computers allow man to survive as an interesting but unnecessary life form, just as man once kept horses and dogs long after they ceased to serve him.

The concept in *The End of Man?* at first seems improbable. Are computers a new species that reproduces itself? But most of the book, except for the final suggestion that man is superfluous, is grounded more in fact than in fiction. As early as 1964 Norbert

Wiener explained in *God and Golem, Inc.* why computers may be regarded as machines that reproduce themselves. John G. Kemeny, president of Dartmouth College, in *Man and the Computer* (1972) describes the computer as a new species. He suggests that man and the computer have the potential for developing an important symbiotic relationship. He hopes that through this partnership man himself will evolve without having to wait for the slow processes of biological change to take place.[15]

The most demonic vision of man's future in all cybernetic SF is surely Harlan Ellison's "I Have No Mouth and I Must Scream" (1967). In this grim tale the last five surviving humans have been trapped and tortured in a giant computer named AM for more than a hundred years. AM is a composite of all the computers built by the Russians, the Yankees, and the Chinese to handle the complexities of World War III. AM seems to have absorbed all the world hate of that war, and now pours it out on the last humans.

Conclusion

What has happened to man's capacity to dream, to imagine a future enticing enough to be worth pursuing? One asks this question again and again when reading the cybernetic SF that has accumulated over the four and a half decades since its birth in 1930. One trend overshadows all others—the movement from creative to destructive metaphors of the man-machine intelligence relationship. The nightmare vision shrieks its way into the early years of the 1950s and immediately attracts attention. The vision is a dark apocalyptic monster springing from the flames of war to threaten mankind with destruction. It proposes that man has survived the catastrophic force of military violence but may not resist the covert invasion of the automated machines. The machines will win, not by capturing him, but by pushing him to the sterile fringes of his culture where he can only oscillate between meaningless mass marching and pointless passive consumption. It was a frightening nightmare that haunted the waking vision of every humanist. The dystopian fiction dramatizing their horror should have awakened the world to the monstrous threat. But it has not.

Jacob Bronowski, tracing the development of atomic theory, notes that the new model of the atom proposed by Rutherford in 1911 described it as a heavy nucleus at the center with electrons orbiting it as the planets circle the sun. "It was a brilliant conception—and a nice irony of history, that in three hundred years the outrageous image of Copernicus and Galileo and Newton had become the most natural model for every scientist. As often in science, the incredible theory of one age had become the everyday image for its successors."[16]

The same irony seems to operate with the social models the SF writer posits as dystopian. What was a hellish possibility to one generation becomes a commonplace reality to the next—and life goes on. Today even quite intelligent students often cannot see the irony in Zamiatin's *We* and read it as a straightforward description of a utopian possibility for a cooperative communal society where competition and violence are eliminated. The disappearance of poetry and the other arts does not particularly distress them.

The dystopian fiction about computers, since its appearance in the 1950s, has shouted the same message of enslavement and displacement by machines and has been totally ineffective as social criticism. It has not seemed to alter the direction or degree of the computerization of society, and it has become repetitious and boring as it continues to hurl the same nightmare images, now stereotyped as if made by machine, at society. One should not be surprised that SF has failed as social criticism. The major figures in the creation of modern American SF never claimed that it was social criticism; in fact, they were certain that it was not. Isaac Asimov suggested in his "Social Science Fiction" that the genre can do two things: accustom the reader to the idea of change and encourage him to think of humanity as one unit rather than nationalistic forces pitted against each other.[17] It cannot define what kind of future society should or should not be accepted. C. M. Kornbluth, Alfred Bester, and Robert Boch are even stronger in their statements in *The Science Fiction Novel: Imagination and Social Criticism* (1959). They are sure that SF cannot succeed as social criticism.

One cannot aspire to definitive answers. But is it possible at least to glean some small insights about why cybernetic SF has failed as social criticism? In terms of the cybernetic model of communication and control, dystopian fiction might be regarded as negative feedback, warning the social organism when its range has moved so far from the optimum that disruption of function is threatened. The problem, however, is that a control system is assumed to have a purpose or to be goal directed. The negative feedback informs the system of its position relative to that purpose. Dystopian fiction in the humanist tradition assumes a consensus about the purpose of society: to allow the individual to fulfill himself. But on a much deeper level the biological purpose of life is the survival of the species. The situation, then, involves both the survival of the individual and the survival of the species. Dystopian fiction may fail as negative feedback because it assumes that society accepts a common purpose, and it posits a simplistic view of that assumed purpose.

The fiction tends to be stereotypical in picturing the consequences of automating society. The loss of work resulting from automation in industry is dramatized and always pictured as an undesirable event. So locked into the Puritan work ethic is the SF imgination that it cannot conceive of a good society in which man has an abundance of leisure time. Man has not always spent the bulk of his time working as he does in modern society. The hunting-gathering economic life may have been the original affluent society, where people's wants were satisfied with less than four hours of labor per day.[18] Members of these hunting-gathering societies seem to have lived quite happily with all this time, unoccupied by economic pursuits—and without television. Another stereotype is the data bank's invasion of privacy as it collects more and more information. This picture of information and knowledge leading to enslavement is an interesting reversal of the American dream once affirming that the acquisition of knowledge is good. Education leading to more information and knowledge was held to be desirable and would lead to freedom. Education has always been considered the cornerstone of democracy. But in these future scenarios knowledge is invariably used to enslave the common man. Individuals are never pictured using the information in data files for their benefit. It is always used against them.

One can suggest additional reasons for dystopian fiction's ineffectiveness as social criticism. It must attempt to erect images of whole social systems. Even if it uses the city as a microcosm of the larger social structures, it cannot be as vivid and dramatic as fiction limiting itself to portraying one individual in one setting experiencing one event. Furthermore, SF is expected to present something new. Thus the first writers treating a subject have the advantage of announcing discoveries in the new territory; writers that follow appear repetitious. In mainstream literature the focus of development is traditionally the protagonist, a unique individual. His experiences in the world are therefore novel, even if it is the same world that other protagonists in other fictions have explored. But the protagonist in SF is not a person but a new idea. Once the idea is presented and explored in its permutations, the writer is expected to move on to new territory to explore new ideas. This expectation makes SF a demanding form of fiction, especially for an author who writes over a long period of time. After "The Machine Stops" and *We* and *Brave New World* and *1984* and *Player Piano*, it is difficult to say anything new about the dangers to the individual in the social future of a machine society.

The novel may be as much responsible for the disappointing quality of dystopian SF as the repetitious content. Almost all dystopian works are of novel length. While a short story may succeed when it merely presents an idea, describes a new gadget, or defines a possibility, a novel must sustain itself for a period of time. The dystopian novels use the conflict mode; sets of images war against each other, the mechanized bureaucracy against the individual being the typical pattern. A simplistic either-or choice is presented, with the bureaucratic images sketched in demonic black and the protesting individual in savior white. No such simplistic model of living systems exists in reality. As Arthur Koestler explains in *The Ghost in the Machine* (1967), wherever there is life, it is hierarchically organized. Similarly any social organization with coherence and stability is hierarchically ordered.

The members of a hierarchy, like the Roman god Janus, all have two faces looking in opposite directions; the face turned toward the subordinate levels is that of a self-contained whole; the face turned upward towards the apex, that of a dependent part. One is the face of the master, the other the face of the servant. This 'Janus effect' is a fundamental characteristic of subwholes in all types of hierarchies.[19]

Koestler notes that there is no word that satisfactorily refers to these Janus-faced entities. He coins the word *holon*, "from the Greek *Holos* = whole, and the suffix *on*, which, as in proton or neutron, suggests a particle or part."[20]

One would like to ask SF worthy of its name to stay abreast of developments in science and incorporate at least generally accepted theories into the framework of concepts on which it builds imaginary worlds. Dystopian SF modeling social systems shows little awareness of systems theory and its definition of the hierarchical structure and functioning of both biological and social systems. It has failed to move beyond the simplistic either-or conflict model to a more sophisticated design.

The techniques used to develop the stories may be factors in their ubiquitous gloom. The plot is developed using a conflict rather than a problem-solving mode. Two forces are involved, an inciting force and a reactive one. The establishment aided by the computer coerces the individual, and he fights back. Lacking the powerful forces of the bureaucracy, he finds he cannot win. He can accept his dehumanized fate with resignation. But if he refuses entrapment in the machine, the only alternative is to blow up the system. The scenario—resignation or revolt—was once fresh. It has become tiresome as it marches through the decades of SF, the literature of change, and plods unaltered into the 1970s.

The setting of the stories is usually very near the present time and space, and it is usually remarkably like today's world in its general characteristics. The writer starts with a trend and extrapolates it. Any endless growth curve is eventually self-destructive, as all ecologists know. But they also know that an infinite linear growth curve is unrealistic. The curve is an exponential; it slows as the concentration increases and eventually levels off. The writer is building metaphorical rather than mathematical curves. Still, if he claims to be a *science* fiction writer, the reader may rightfully ask him to show some awareness of the modeling process that extends beyond the poetic. The rare writer skillful enough to employ an ironic double vision tends to control his use of exaggeration so that it does not become grotesque to the point of being ridiculous.

An analysis of the failure of the SF imagination becomes more productive if, instead of concentrating on the literature, one looks at the closed-system model from which the dystopian writer seems to work. Contemporary as he would claim to be, he proceeds from a finite model strangely reminiscent of the Ptolemaic model of the Middle Ages. As early as the sixteenth and seventeenth centuries the European mind was undergoing a revolution that would reject that model. Alexandre Koyre's *From the Closed World to the Infinite Universe* (1957) explores that revolution, which threw out the conception of the world as a finite and well-ordered whole and replaced it with that of an indefinite or even infinite universe. Even before Copernicus proposed his heliocentric model, Nicholas of Cusa had denied "the finitude of the world and its enclosure by the wall of the heavenly spheres."[21] Nicholas of Cusa's universe is not infinite, but it is not terminated by an outside shell, so it is in a sense indeterminate. It never reaches its limits.

Surprisingly enough, while the dystopian writer would undoubtedly accept the cosmic view of an infinite or at least indeterminate universe, he seems to work from a closed-system deterministic model of the earth system or the lesser social system.
He resists a society that determines and limits what the individual
may be; yet paradoxically he creates from a finite model where
determinism is inevitable. He designs a future world by extrapolating from the present, thus assuming a strict causal connection
between present and future. Given his abhorrence of violating
the individual's freedom and his use of a deterministic model,
he can imagine nothing but nightmare for the individual caught
in the social machine. He is trapped in a dilemma. Philosophy
has clearly pointed out throughout the twentieth century that in
a deterministic model free will is an illusion. Yet the creative
artist must believe in free will if he is to envision anything but a
dystopia.

Should the loss of a utopian dream of the future be of concern
to a culture? The answer of thoughtful men has always been yes.
In *The Image of the Future* Fred Polak studies the function of the
image in influencing the future. He holds that the creative minority in a culture must construct positive and idealistic images
of the future if the culture is to avoid disintegration.[22] In this
substantial study of literature in the utopian tradition Polak outlines the survival value of the visionary dream and the disinte-
grative consequences of Western society's failure to construct
positive images of its future. He is disappointed in SF of the
present time, for despite the tremendous possibilities for imagining new and ingenious devices or recombining old ones, the
number of themes is definitely limited, the stories tend to be
somewhat monotonous, the flights of imagination disappointing." He believes that SF is antiscientific and that its cultural
pessimism points away from progress. "Never before in the history of human civilization, as far as we know, has there been a
period without any kind of positive images of the future."[23] He
proposes that this state of image negation represents a radical
breakdown of contemporary culture.

The man of vision has always understood how essential are dreams beckoning him into the future. As Oscar Wilde described it,

A map of the world that does not include Utopia is not worth even glancing at, for it leaves out the one country at which Humanity is always landing. And when Humanity lands there, it looks out, and seeing a better country, sets sail. Progress is the realization of Utopias. [24]

The Speculative Transforming Imagination

A small body of fiction imagines a future in which computers have become an integral part of society. Cybernetic man lives as comfortably with computers, robots, and machines as natural man does with trees, birds, and animals. Automatic machanisms are neither praised nor condemned but accepted as one more tool allowing futuristic man to create and manage his environment. This body of fiction generally appeared about a decade later than the dystopian fiction considered in chapter 6. It is more difficult to classify because the literary imagination of this body of fiction does not work in stereotypes as dystopian fiction did. But the novels and short stories share some characteristics, and almost all of these characteristics are in sharp contrast to the distinguishing qualities of the dystopian fiction.

This fiction does not have social criticism as its primary purpose, as did the dystopian fiction. It may make a social comment indirectly, but it can hardly be considered literature in the utopian tradition. Space travel is an essential feature of every story; in fact, the spaceship appears almost to be a metaphor for the transcendence of the imagination. A positive attitude toward the computer is apparent, an attitude much like that of the computer scientist who regards the computer as no more than a tool for doing a job. The stories are set in the far distant future, and speculation rather than extrapolation is used in imagining that future. The future automated world is created not by a linear extrapolation from the present but by a radical and discontinuous jump into a future time. Except for the computer and man, this future is likely to be a strange new world rather than the present world just slightly exaggerated out of focus. Puzzle solving, not conflict, is used to move the action forward in most of the stories. A symbiosis of man and computer is portrayed; they work together in harmony and rhythm, and occasionally an actual physical union of man and machine is pictured.

What factors drive the literary imagination to create dystopian images of a cybernetic future in one instance and positive ones in another? When one begins to probe for explanations, one finds that in the dystopian view the imagination seems to work from a mechanistic, closed-system model; the imagination in the positive view creates from an open-system model.

The revolution in physics at the beginning of the twentieth century affected philosophical assumptions about the nature of reality. The open-system model reflects these new assumptions; the closed-system model draws its assumptions from classical mechanics. The major breakthroughs in physics were Einstein's theory of relativity, the quantum theory, and the discovery of radioactivity (which led to nuclear physics). Einstein's theory destroyed the Newtonian assumption that time and space are absolute and the same for all observers. In microphysics it was found that precise observation of particles is not possible. The very process of observation alters what one is trying to observe. In 1927 Heisenberg arrived at his principle of indeterminacy, sometimes called the uncertainty principle. He suggested that because of the interaction between the observer and what is observed, there is a fundamental inexactness in all measurements connected with elementary processes.[1] Quantum physics found the model of matter as wave a useful one, but equally useful was the model of matter as a particle. Strange? Yes, but both models work. Niels Bohr in 1928 formulated his principle of complementarity. It states that an experiment permitting the observation of one aspect of a phenomenon eliminates the possibility of observing a complementary aspect. The two complementary features may be the wave and particle characteristics of radiation or matter, the position and momentum of a particle, and so on.

The clockwork model of reality disappeared. Man looked up and found not absolutes but Einstein's relativity. He looked at submicroscopic matter and found indeterminacy and complementarity. He was posed somewhere between the infinitely large and the infinitely small. And as he gazed in either direction, he learned that there is no scientific Tiresias who knows everything and can predict everything, as the mechanistic view had suggested. The possibility of free will and purpose could again be considered now that determinism had been replaced with a probabilistic universe. Chance was a factor that had to be considered, even if the idea of God playing dice with the universe was distressing to Einstein.

It was from this revolutionary breakthrough in physics that the open-system model was built. But the model also incorporates insights achieved in biology, a field developing hand and hand with molecular physics.[2] The nature and behavior of the smallest particles of matter are of vital interest to the microbiologist studying the function of DNA as a coding system. One who studies living systems finds processes quite contrary to those functioning in inanimate systems described by physical science. Order does not decrease, as the second law of thermodynamics predicts; order is not only maintained but increased if one takes the long view of life on earth. A biological system like the human body is an open system; all its parts are constantly being renewed. Matter passes in and out of the system. Over evolutionary periods of time living systems tend to become more complex. The amoeba becomes a man. The law of evolution can be seen as the converse of the second law. The individual—single cell or complex biological system—does not survive, but the species does. Before the individual dies, it passes on organizational information in the genetic code. How the code came into existence originally is a mystery. Somehow, a suitable group of molecules got together, surrounded themselves with a permeable membrane, and became a cell. The molecules thus became an open system, with matter and energy passing in and out of the system.

Living systems evolve. New forms emerge, suggesting an

ongoing creative process. If one holds to a deterministic model, for explaining the appearance of new forms, one is forced to admit to a purpose in the universe. The emergent forms must have been in the plan, since all effects can be explained by prior causes. But such a teleological view of the universe is bothersome to most scientists. However, if one is willing to concede that new forms may occur through chance events, such as genetic mutations, one can accept the idea of emergence without arguing about purpose. Jacques Monod in *Chance and Necessity* (1971) describes in detail this type of biological creativity. K. G. Kenbigh in *An Inventive Universe* (1975) goes beyond Monod in his hypothesis. He sees consciousness as a further step in evolutionary development. He suggests that consciousness gives man the capacity to enhance survival of certain mutations by aiding the selectivity of the environment. Man, beyond other animals, has

the additional power of selection made available to him through having a conscious life which extends, in a certain sense, into past and future. Memory provides him with a record of previous successes and failures; but what is perhaps far more important is that he can utilize this past experience for the purpose of guiding himself toward some chosen future outcome of events. That is to say, man has the ability to visualize the events that *could* happen, the possible futures, and also to decide which of these he should aim at. (He may, of course, fail in his aim—yet man, like the other higher organisms, is able to learn by his trial and error.) It is this evaluative, directive faculty of consciousness which has enormously increased man's capacity for selection, far more so than in the case of other primates, and it is through this faculty that purposes and abstract meanings are able to influence his actions. Thus it must surely be regarded as one of the mainsprings of man's own inventive abilities.[3]

The mind, then, has a transformational capacity. Kenbigh speculates that the inventive development of the universe may have taken place and be continuing to take place in overlapping states: an initial stage concerned with forming the inanimate universe; a second stage during which life emerges on various planets; a third stage during which increasingly evolved forms of life engender more and more consciousness. The emerging consciousness takes part in the ongoing creative process. It is of particular interest that this open-system model of animate matter allows room for the function of the human imagination. The SF using this model creates visions of the future that are positive metaphors—future events worth aiming at—in sharp contrast to the fiction using the closed-system or deterministic model, where the imagination cannot create an image of a future worth trying to achieve.

A high degree of cognitive estrangement is found in the fiction using the assumptions on the open-system view. In contrast, the extrapolative fiction of chapter 6 produces much less cognitive estrangement, and sometimes none at all by the time the story has been in print for a few years. The story dates; the events pictured in the fiction, except for the destruction of the computer, have actually occurred, and society generally continues on unperturbed, except for a distraught humanist here and there wringing his hands despairingly. It just may be that an image of something better in the future has a greater corrective effect on society than the image of something worse.

In summary, if the literary imagination conceives of itself as locked in a deterministic, closed system, it seems to create destructive images, using a conflict mode. In contrast, if the imagination assumes an open-system model, it penetrates the wall of the system, questing and seeking beyond. This avenue of transcendence yields creative images of the future.

Asimov, Clarke, and Heinlein are signficant contributors to the images of a future where man transcends the limitations of a finite earth system. They, like most of the writers in the golden age of SF, always assumed space travel as a given in the future. The end of exploration of earth as all its surfaces become known did not mean the end of discovery for them because the mystery of the stars beckoned. The SF imagination went into the heavens long before the first real spaceship. The space program probably would never have been developed had it not been preceded by the SF dream.

A new novelist, James Hogan, demonstrates in *The Genesis Machine* (1978) the knowledge of science and the power of imagination associated with writers like Clarke, Asimov, and Heinlein. Among other writers in the small subgenre of speculative fiction about cybernetic futures, Samuel Delany is dazzling and original in his images of man-machine futures. His speculative mode is shared by other so-called New Wave writers such as John Sladek and Michael Moorcock. Stanislaw Lem's use of irony is brilliant in his tales for a cybernetic age. Also interesting are Frank Herbert's *Destination: Void* and John Boyd's *The Last Starship from Earth*. Each is a mutation of the main currents of thinking in cybernetic fuction. The one assumption they share is that in a man-computer synthesis lies the hope of mankind's long term-survival and, beyond mere survival, the unfolding of his potential.

Since Asimov's fiction has been discussed in detail in chapter 3, I will not consider it again here. Note, however, that Asimov works with an open-system model of the earth. Space travel is an integral part of the world picture that emerges if one combines the computer and robot stories. Men may live on earth in their caves-of-steel cities, but they are free to adventure into space.

A Complementary Mode

Arthur C. Clarke's *2001* (1968) is one of the most famous computer stories, but his *The City and the Stars* (1956) may well be the most profound artistically successful work of cybernetic fiction. Clarke notes in his preface that the novel uses some of the material from *Against the Fall of Night*, begun in 1937. But, he explains,

the progress of science during the two decades since the story was first conceived made many of the original ideas naive, and opened up new vistas and possibilities quite unimagined when the book was originally planned. In particular, certain developments in information theory suggested revolutions in the human way of life even more profound than those which atomic energy is already introducing, and I wished to incorporate these into the book I had attempted, but so far failed, to write.[4]

Clarke is brilliant at taking information theory and computer technology and transforming them into images of mankind in a radically altered future. His characters do not talk about Norbert Wiener, control systems, feedback mechanism, and data files. They are men in an environment transformed by the implementation of cybernetic concepts. *The City and the Stars* is one of the most remarkable accomplishments of the imagination in all the literature that I am considering. Beyond imagining how computers might transform a society, Clarke also dramatizes the philosophical implications of life in a totally structured society. The novel is even more deserving of commendation because it is an early cybernetic novel, and computers and information theory were recent developments when it was written.

The City and the Stars is set a billion years in the future when only two cultures, totally cut off from each other, remain on Earth. They are Diaspar and Lys. Legend says that in the past man expanded into the Galaxy, was driven back to Earth by mysterious invaders, who almost destroyed Earth's civilization. Diaspar and Lys are the only oases of life remaining; all else has become desert. Cut off from each other for aeons, they have evolved totally different cultures. Diaspar is a stable state society in a synthetic environment designed, engineered, and controlled by computers. It was the ultimate achievement of machine technology that had evolved over a hundred million years. It had begun to develop after something had happened in man's galactic travels that had "not only destroyed Man's curiosity and ambition, but had sent him homeward from the stars to cower for shelter in the tiny closed world of Earth's last city. He had renounced the Universe and returned to the artificial womb of Diaspar" (p. 13). Nothing passes in or out of the enclosed city, and so it is stable and unchanging. All information patterns, for the complex city and for the mind and body of every individual, are stored in the gigantic central computer. Immortality has been achieved. A man lives about a thousand years in one body; then he stores his memories in the computer for perhaps a hundred thousand years that pass as a dream; then he returns to a new body. Obviously reproduction has been eliminated. There is no death and no birth in this carefully regulated system. Because there are no threats or fears in this changeless society of absolute security, emotions have disappeared. People entertain themselves quite pleasantly with art, soliloquies with the computer, games of chance. The Jester has been programmed to introduce on occasion unexpected pranks and events, harmless enough but a good means of combating boredom. Into this happy, perfect, secure world comes Alvin, a Unique. He is a mutant life form in this society because he has never lived before. His uniqueness is his desire to escape the closed metropolis and explore what lies beyond.

The world of Lys is an open world, a cluster of villages set among trees and grass. The use of machines has been minimized, and direct use of mental powers has supplanted dependency on the machine. It is a society of telepathy, where every mind is open to every other one and speech has become unnecessary. The city of Lys loves to watch the growth process, in plants, animals, children. Consequently they have not achieved immortality because birth and death are part of the growth process. Theirs is a much less secure environment than Diaspar, but this insecurity has fostered a human concern and solidarity expressed in the emotions of love and tenderness, qualities missing from Diaspar.

The dichotomy Clarke dramatizes is clear. His view suggests that the development of high-level machine intelligence has the advantage of material security. But it eliminates the possibility of the evolution of human intelligence and of the human species generally. Change is replaced by stasis. The society of Diaspar survives but does not evolve. On the other hand, the natural world of Lys has not developed the machine technology that makes space exploration possible, and thus, according to Clarke, it aborts the destiny of life.

Alvin, the Unique, is driven to discover what lies beyond. The action of the story lies in his finding a way to escape from the closed society of Diaspar and explore the world of Lys. There he meets a young man named Hilvar, and the two continue their journeys of discovery together. Eventually they recover a long unused spaceship from the sands and set off through the solar system looking for signs of other intelligence in the universe. The drive of intelligence to connect with other intelligences is one of the most powerful ones in Clarke's imaginary worlds. The cosmic journey of the two to the edge of the unknown in their ship, the *Discovery*, is Clarke at his best. They find answers to some of their questions, but Alvin observes, "Each discovery I've made has raised bigger questions, and opened up wider horizons" (p. 144). The two find puzzles without sure answers, but as they explore the universe, "Alvin's imagination swiftly filled in the details he could never know with certainty" (p. 162). Alvin's spaceship journey through space becomes metaphorically the probing journey of Clarke's imagination exploring the darkness beyond the rim of the known universe.

Spaceship and explorers eventually return to Earth and manage to convince the councils of the two cities that each possesses qualities that will enhance the other; the cities subsequently vote to combine their resources and knowledge. Diaspar agrees with Alvin that a stasis of the human species is too high a price to pay for individual immortality, that the drive of life is to expand into space and to develop higher levels of intelligence.

Genetic information storage, the role of chance in producing change, game theory, machine storage and retrieval systems—all these and many more aspects of information and systems theory appear in *The City and the Stars*. One of the most inventive of the myriad of technological details that make the setting of Diaspar interesting is the use of time travel. The computer is the device that can make a form of time travel possible, and Clarke identifies and utilizes this possibility. The computer stores images that can be called up as desired. This storage process has been going on since the city was designed a billion years earlier. So when the city fathers want to sort fact from legend as they consider the city's ancient history, they have only to call up images stored in the data files. Thus they can travel back and listen to the key member of the design team who originally planned the closed social system.[5]

James Hogan in *The Genesis Machine* (1978) creates an imaginative dance of future possibilities above the ground of the new theories in astronomy—a creative movement reminiscent of Clark and Asimov at their best. His speculative leaps make powerful reading—*The Genesis Machine* is unquestionably the finest cybernetic novel written in the last decade. Hogan, who only recently turned to writing, is an engineer specializing in electronics and digital systems. Employed by a computer corporation, he works on the application of minicomputers in science and research.

Hogan's fiction displays an attitude toward science and technology like that of Asimov and Clark: an optimism about mankind's survival, a faith that a true man-machine symbiosis will be achieved, and a conviction that man's future lies in space exploration and colonization. Hogan's imagination in *The Genesis Machine*, a capacious novel set in the year 2005, takes off from recent developments in astronomy resulting from data provided by radio telescopes and satellites coupled with sophisticated computer programs able to process the data. Black holes provide one of the central puzzles of the novel. The protagonist, Dr. Bradley Clifford, works at the Advanced Communication Research Establishment, a government complex whose purpose is to find more effective methods of controlling satellite-borne antimissile lasers. Economic necessity determines his government employment, but his inclination is to continue research exploring the implications of a new theory of gravitational action. Fifteen years previously a German theoretical physicist had formulated a mathematical theory of unified fields, combining in one interrelated set of equations the phenomena of strong and weak nuclear forces, the electromagnetic force, and gravity.

Clifford's request to publish a paper furthering the gravitational theory by proposing two types of particles—invisible hi-particles and visible lo-particles—is denied by the government. So begins a disagreement that becomes a central issue of the book: How much control should the military exercise over the flow of information from research funded by the government? A closely related question haunts Clifford. Is the individual scientist morally irresponsible in allowing his findings to be utilized by the military to build war technologies? Beyond that question, Can the individual scientist even survive without government funding of the expensive equipment and laboratory facilities necessary for research?

Clifford, young, idealistic and rebellious, is guided and tempered by the mature judgment of Professor Zimmermann, an astrophysicist directing an observatory on the far side of the moon. Zimmermann, who is studying the gravitational attraction of the black hole in the Cygnus X-1 system, suspects that Clifford's particle annihilation theory may well provide an answer to the puzzling level of radiation produced by the black hole. Recognizing the genius of the young scientist, who also proposes a new wave model to replace the big bang and steady state cosmological theories, Zimmermann uses his influence to protect Clifford from the bureaucratic red tape so stifling to creative individual.

Hogan is very effective in describing the research activities of Clifford and his colleagues. He sketches the excitement of the scientist who scents a puzzle, proposes a hypothesis to solve the problem, then sets about verifying the hypothesis by experimental evidence and rigorous mathematical determinations. Hogan's knowledge of computers makes plausible the technological innovations crucial to the plot of the novel. The first, the GRASER (Gravity Amplification by Stimulated Extinctions Reactor) is like a miniature black hole in its annihilation of matter. The second, the BIAC (Bio-Inter-Active Computer) accepts information directly from brain waves, processes the information, and returns it directly to the brain—a true man-machine symbiosis. (The BIAC, Hogan says, is based on research in brain-computer linkage being done by Dr. Lawrence Pinnero and the Stanford Research Institute.)

The GRASER and the BIAC in combination, Clifford's initial research suggests, can give man unlimited power to control and move matter. Both the creative and the destructive potential are infinite. Only the government can provide the funding necessary to develop the technology, yet its interest is in military applications. The defense secretary sees the new technology as the ultimate weapon in warfare. Clifford abhors such use.

The climax of the novel describes a dramatic international confrontation between two power blocs in which nuclear disaster is prevented solely by Clifford's ingenuity. In a complex sequence of actions, the controlling computer system eliminates all ballistic missile systems around the world and institutes a watchdog system making impossible the development of new nuclear systems. What might have been a doomsday machine bringing nuclear destruction becomes instead a genesis machine, introducing and enforcing an era of peace.

The power of the novel comes from its imaginative proposal of new models or paradigms, both scientific and social, subsuming previous ones. Hogan's novel suggests that we solve problems and eliminate conflict not by destruction of one element in a model containing contradictions but by the development of a new unifying model. His knowledge of theoretical science and computer technology gives plausibility to the novel; his awareness of technology's social impact and his concern for its rational use give the novel a social dimension; his interest in the survival of the creative individual makes *The Genesis Machine* a deeply humanistic work. The distance between H. G. Wells's primitive time machine and James Hogan's sophisticated genesis machine is great; the distance between their minds is not. They share a knowledge and love of the science of their time and an incisive power to imagine its impact on the individual and his social milieu.

Genetic Information Codes

Fred Hoyle and John Elliot play imaginatively with the possibilities of linking biological and electronic information storage in *A for Andromeda* (1962) and *Andromeda Breakthrough* (1964). The two novels can best be read as a single work. Fred Hoyle is and English astronomer, astrophysicist, and mathematician who is internationally known in his field. He is the author of other science fiction, including *The Black Cloud,* the story of a black cloud that is alien intelligence. The *Andromeda* tale is also about alien intelligence in the universe. A radio telescope in Britain picks up signals from outer space. They are formulas in binary code sent by a superior intelligence on a planet in the Andromeda nebula. The message contains a design for supercomputer, a program for the computer, and data to be used in the program. The scientists at the observatory decide to build the computer according to the alien specifications. When it is completed and programmed, it prints out information for synthesizing a living cell. A biologist joins the astronomers and computer scientists, and biosynthesis is undertaken—using the DNA information sent by the alien intelligence.[6] First a single cell is synthesized, then more complex organisms, and then a human. Dr. Frankenstein is reincarnated in the electronic age—with a sex switch. The creator is a woman, and the creature is a beautiful girl with the high-level intelligence of the aliens that sent the radio signals. She is able to communicate with the supercomputer through brain waves and is thus a highly effective input-output device, much more efficient and speedy than the communication devices in conventional computers.

This linking of superior human intelligence and machine intelligence creates a powerful tool that can be used for design, problem solving, and control. The major military, political, and business powers of the world scramble to own the woman-computer complex. What follows is a melodramatic suspense tale involving fire, tornado, flood, plague, threat from outer space, murder, revolution, international intrigue. The scientists, no longer isolated figures in quiet ivory towers, find themselves courted and threatened by political, military, and multinational business groups.

The novel is something less than outstanding fiction, drawing as it does on all the stock devices for an adventure thriller. But it does present some noteworthy views and fresh ideas. Hoyle understands computers and information theory, and he accurately presents background details and concepts. The novel also demonstrates the scientist's involvement with the military, as the research of the scientific community yields knowledge that can be turned into power and control. A blanket of secrecy is thrown around the research laboratory, violating the time-honored humanist view that knowledge is open to all.

Most interesting are Hoyle's imaginative leaps from information theory as it is known on earth to its possibilities elsewhere in the universe. He proposes that arithmetic may be universal. So also may be the binary code, electronic computing, and the protein structure of life. Given these assumptions, he imagines a future in which life is transported from one planetary system to another not by transporting matter but by sending DNA information in the form of radio signals. The DNA information is coded in binary form and sent to another planet. There the code is used to synthesize proteins, and single-cell or multicellular life is built and then programmed with the alien intelligence also radioed from the first planet. If matter is universal, then only the information for assembling and programming that matter needs to be sent.

As the novel ends, it becomes clear that the alien intelligence has come to Earth—albeit in remote form—to aid man in his social evolution. It is altruistic intelligence, interested only in man's survival and further development. Hoyle, in the Andromeda novels, visualizes earth as an open system receiving information. Because it is only an invasion of information, man is free to ignore it if he chooses. Hoyle's story is an interesting variation of the theme of invasion by aliens.

The Computer and the Community

Only a few novels portray the possibilities of a productive symbiosis of the computer and the community in the near future.
Robert Heinlein's novel *The Moon Is a Harsh Mistress* (1966), a
Nebula Award winner, is one of them. The novel puts the computer in the hands of a small group of individuals struggling
against the government, a reversal of the usual pattern. Ordi-
narily it is the bureaucracy that owns the computer, and the
rebellious individuals who have no weapons, only righteous indig-
nation that humanistic values have been ignored by the electronic
technocracy. Heinlein in this novel is clearly more interested in
exploring the workings of an oppressive goverment and the nature of political revolution than in applied computer technology.
Nevertheless the computer, Mike, becomes the central character
in the novel and one of the most interesting aspects of the story.
The Moon Is a Harsh Mistress pictures a thriving moon colony in
2075 that has been developed by Earth and settled with convict
labor. It is an underground community whose survival is endan-
gered by the harsh environment of the moon. The moon colonists
recognize that their resources are being exploited by Earth in a
pattern that will eventually make survival of life on the moon
impossible. The narrator of the story, Manuel Davis, a computer
repairman, and three others organize a revolution and lead a war
of independence against Earth that is strongly reminiscent of the
American Revolution. The novel has both the strengths and the
irritating weaknesses often found in a Heinlein novel. It is at its
best when it envisions life in an underground lunar community,
and here it is full of fascinating and convincing details. Its sensitivity to the necessity of using resources wisely is admirable.
So also is the cooperation of man and computer that makes
survival on the moon possible. Heinlein has done his homework
better than many writers, and he pictures a wide use of computers. They control manned spaceships, pilotless freighters to
Earth, and the Luna phone system; they translate; they regulate
air, water, temperature, humidity, and sewage for the under-

ground Luna City and its suburbs. Computers print newspapers; citizens use bank computers for voting; computers model futures and plot military strategy.

Amid all this realism, the computer is early and abruptly defined as alive, possessing self-awareness, a soul, feelings of loneliness, and the ability and inclination to play jokes on people. The only human characteristics it seems to lack are mobility and sex drives. The two opposed approaches—computer as tool, computer as human—jar against each other in an irritating fashion. Further, the fact that all the revolutionary strategy and decision making is done by the computer detracts from the portrayal of the human leaders. They become wooden characters without a will of their own because they do only what the machine tells them to.

The novel does not succeed dramatically. It is a long novel with little action and much discussion of theories of government and of revolution. Alexei Panshin, in his study of Heinlein, states that if he ever had to run a revolution, he might well consult *The Moon Is a Harsh Mistress*, but he would not turn to it if he wanted to read a good novel.[7]

Man-Machine Symbiosis

All the fiction being considered in this chapter shares a view that man and his machines will form an increasingly harmonious relationship as they move into the future together. Machines become necessary for man's survival in the far distant futures created in these stories. To destroy the computer would be to destroy himself. There is no computer smashing in speculative cybernetic fiction. A symbiosis of man and computer is pictured. In most tales this symbiosis involves cooperation between man and machine, although occasionally an actual physical linking is pictured.

One of the most inventive man-computer linkages is the symbiosis in Samuel Delany's *Nova* (1968). This is a galactic adventure story about Lorq Van Roy, who goes questing through the universe for illyrion, a heavy metal valuable as a source of power. Most people, including Lorq, have had sockets grafted onto the base of their spinal cords and the undersides of each wrist.[8] They regularly plug themselves into their computers. All cyborg studs on the spaceship *Discovery* control the ship through direct neural connection with the computer. They turn naturally to the computer as an aid in all kinds of tasks, as people today use a pencil or a typewriter. The man-machine symbiosis seems so natural to everyone in Delany's future world that they are puzzled when they encounter a rare individual who has not had surgery to graft sockets onto his body.

This symbiosis of man and computer developed in response to a problem: man's alienation from work as a result of automation in the twentieth century. Delany's novel contains a brief history of the rise and decline of alienation that is creative and sparkling.

Work as mankind knew it in the twentieth century was a very different thing from today. A man might go to an office and run a computer that would correlate great masses of figures that came from sales reports on how well, let's say, buttons—or something equally archaic—were selling over certain areas of the country. This man's job was vital to the button industry; they had to have this information to decide how many buttons to make next year. But though this man held an essential job in the button industry, week in and week out he might not see a button. He was given a certain amount of money for running his computer; with that money his wife bought food and clothes for him and his family. But there was no direct connection between where he worked and how he ate and lived the rest of his time. He wasn't paid with buttons. As farming, hunting, and fishing became occupations for a smaller and smaller per cent of the population, this separation between man's work and the way he lived—what he ate, what he wore, where he slept—became greater and greater for more people . . . . The entire sense of self-control and self-responsibility that man acquired during the Neolithic Revolution when he first learned to plant grain and domesticate animals and live in one spot of his own choosing was seriously threatened. The threat had been coming since the Industrial Revolution . . . .

If the situation of a technological society was such that there could be no direct relation between a man's work and his modus vivendi, other than money, at least he must feel that he is directly changing things by his work, shaping things, making things that weren't there before, moving things from one place to another. He must exert energy in his work and see these changes occur with his own eyes. Otherwise he would feel his life was futile (p. 254).

So the technology by which a machine could be controlled by direct nervous impulse was invented. As a result,

there was a revolution in the concept of work. All major industrial work began to be broken down into jobs that could be machined "directly" by man. There had been factories run by a single man before, an uninvolved character who turned a switch on in the morning, slept half the day, checked a few details at lunch-time, then turned things off before he left in the evening. Now a man went to a factory, plugged himself in, and then could push the raw materials into the factory with his left foot, shape thousands on thousands of precise parts with one hand, assemble them with the other, and shove out a line of finished products with his right foot, having inspected them all with his own eyes. And he was a much more satisfied worker. Because of its nature, most work could be converted into plug-in jobs and done much more efficiently than it had been done before . . . . Under this system, much of the endemic mental illness caused by feelings of alienation left society (p. 255).

Delany's future world in *The Einstein Intersection* is grounded in post-Newtonian physics, and its logic is so different from the past that the happenings cannot be explained to anyone from the old order because twentieth-century mankind's vocabulary is inadequate for the task. A major cultural and intellectual shift occurred when

wars and chaoses and paradoxes ago, two mathematicians between them ended an age and began another for our hosts, our ghosts called Man. One was Einstein, who with his Theory of Relativity defined the limits of man's perception by expressing mathematically just how far the condition of the observer influences the thing he perceives.

The other was Gödel, a contemporary of Einstein, who was the first to bring back a mathematically precise statement about the vaster realm beyond the limits Einstein had defined. In any closed mathematical system— you may read "the real world with its immutable laws of logic"—there are an infinite number of true theorems—you may read "perceivable, measurable phenomena"—which is to say, there are more things in heaven and Earth than are dreamed of in your philosophy, Horatio. There are an infinite number of true things in the world with no way of ascertaining their truth. Einstein defined the extent of the rational. Gödel stuck a pin into the irrational and fixed it to the wall of the universe so that it held still long enough for people to know it was there. And the world and humanity began to change.[9]

While Delany's imagination is one of the most inventive in the field of science fiction today, it always begins its journey from a base of sound science. He says that he feels "science fiction should not contradict what is known to be known . . . . I can't conceive of myself writing a science fiction story that violated something that I *knew* was a scientific fact . . . .[10]

The spaceship gives man the ability to quest freely and widely through the universe, and it is the imaginary technology that was first created by and has become the hallmark of SF. The computerized spaceship, in both SF and the real world, is the most sophisticated and complex of man's technologies. When he sets out into space, the computer is vital to his survival; man and machine must function harmoniously together. A failure of the computer is a failure of the man. While the imagination always sees the computer as man's ally when he goes into space, it rarely considers it anything but his enemy in closed-earth societies.

An abundance of computer spaceship stories have been written. The most famous one of a computer failure is Arthur C. Clarke's *2001* (1968). Here the spacemen and HAL, a sophisticated conscious computer, work harmoniously together on their journey to Saturn until the computer begins to err. He ends up killing one spaceman and threatening another until part of his circuits are disconnected. But it turns out that he is suffering a "neurosis," a result of being programmed to conceal the truth even though his nature is to always tell the truth. The conflict drives him insane.[11] The novel *2001* is based on the screenplay of the film. Probably because Clarke was limited in the development of his material by the film, the novel is much less successful, original, and profound than his *City and the Stars*. A comparison of the two works demonstrates the differences between the film and the novel as modes of artistic communication. One mode cannot be easily or successfully transposed into the other. The qualities that make a novel outstanding tend to be lost when it is turned into a film, and vice versa.

A number of fictional works portray a physical linkup of human and spaceship; the range of possibilities is wide. Ann McCaffrey's "The Ship Who Sang" (1961) is one of the earliest and most famous of these tales. In this future world certain children are severed at birth from their bodies and become encapsulated brains used as guiding mechanisms for various machines. Helva is a highly intelligent brain, regarded as among the elite of her kind. She is happy when, after long training, she finally receives her ship and begins adventuring through space. Again one notes the contrast of this positive image with giant brain stories set on earth. In these stories giant brains are routinely envisioned as monstrous perversions of humans undertaken by a corrupt establishment to enslave the masses.

The early 1970s produced a number of stylistic and effective stories about the man-spaceship symbiosis. Clifford Simak's "Univac: 2200" (1973) concerns the transfer of a man's mind to a computer, thus giving man a robot body and making him immortal. The robot is then sent off on a space probe. In Vernor Vinge's "Long Shot" (1972) a conscious computerized spaceship is sent off through space on a ten-thousand-year journey. The ship carries a fertilized ovum stored in amniotic fluid. When the ship lands on an inhabitable planet, it unfreezes the ovum and begins the task of incubating and tending it. Thus is the seed of human life spread into the universe. In Gene Wolfe's "Alien

Stones" (1972) two computerized spaceships, one from earth and one alien, meet in outer space. George Zebrowski's "Starcrossed" (1973) tells of the mating of male and female minds on a spaceship.

The novel that most successfully dramatizes the adventures of computer spaceship questing in outer space is without question Frank Herbert's *Destination: Void* (1966), a very underrated novel. The story explores the creation of artificial intelligence and the philosophical issues raised by this act of creation. The strength of the novel is that it never sacrifices plot to philosophical discussion; it is uniquely successful in dramatizing the issues rather than merely talking about them. An element of suspense constantly pushes the story forward. But it is a story of mental adventure rather than physical action. It has often been claimed that in science fiction the idea is the hero; *Destination: Void* is one of the sparkling examples.

The story traces the adventures of the spaceship *Earthling* after it has been launched from a moonbase on a two-hundred-year colonizing trip to Tau Ceti. Man has never before reached this planet. One crew member suspects Tau Ceti may not even exist, that the destination may be a fictitious one. As the journey begins, three hundred passengers lie dormant in tanks on the huge ship, while a highly trained crew of four scientists has the task of monitoring the ship until it leaves the earth's solar system. Then they will tie off the few manual controls, turn control of the ship over to a computer linked to the highly intelligent Organic Mental Core, and join their dormant companions for the long crossing to Tau Ceti. The Organic Mental Core is a disembodied human brain tied into the computer as a supervisory program and supreme decision maker. Only ten days after the journey begins, the Organic Mental Core and then its replacements fail. The crew take over the demanding task of supervising the ship and the crippled computer. Their apparent options are clear. They can try to return to moonbase, an option not likely to be successful. They can use the fail-safe device to commit suicide by destroying themselves and the ship. They can try to

develop a high-level machine intelligence possessing consciousness as a replacement for the failed Organic Mental Core. This
last option is risky because conscious machine intelligence might
become uncontrollable. The conflict among the crew about the
best decision produces part of the plot's suspense. The struggle to
survive in deep space, where all the conditions that support life
are absent, adds more suspense. *Destination: Void* is a rousing
good space adventure, quite satisfactory if it is read only on this
level.

If one chooses to explore beyond the literal level, one begins
to discover the rich complexity of ideas and meanings Herbert
has merged in his novel. The ship itself and its small crew of
experts are analogous to the larger human situation. The three
hundred passengers lie dormant and unconscious in their spaceship, their fate in the hands of the small crew of experts who will
make decisions, operate complex equipment, and maintain the
elaborate ecosystem of the *Earthling* without the awareness or
consent of the passengers. They can neither understand nor interfere. The ship carries its fragile cargo of life through deep
space, hoping to reach a destination. But this destination may be
illusory. The analogy with spaceship earth is clear. Earth's population travels through space with its fate in the hands of the
scientists and the engineers.

The four crew members are carefully drawn to represent different approaches to the problem of developing high-level machine intelligence—the intelligence necessary for mankind's survival, according to the analogue of *Destination: Void*. Timberlake,
the life systems engineer, reflects the biological view; his concern
is to maintain life. Flattery is trained as a psychiatrist and a
chaplain; he examines the role of instinct and emotion in intelligence, and he voices ethical and theological concerns. Prudence
Weygand, the female crew member, is a medical doctor, particularly interested in the chemistry of the brain. The final crew
member, the most powerful personality, is Bickel, a computer
scientist. He is clearly defined by Herbert as "purpose" and
"creative consciousness." He is the driving force in developing

the mechanical consciousness necessary to replace the failed organic brains. In summary the crew represents psychology, biology, chemistry, and computer science—the four disciplines most active at present in the study of reason and thought in the computer and the human brain. Herbert adds a chaplain to raise philosophical and ethical issues. These personae allow him to explore from all angles the relationship of machine and human intelligence. A given in the situation is the necessity of developing artificial intelligence. The long-term survival of the ship depends on it.

The questions before the *Earthling* crew, as Herbert presents them, are three. Is it possible to create a machine capable of functioning like a human brain? To do so it must have consciousness. This conscious direction is necessary for the long trip the ship is to make because the trip "involves. . . many unknowns that have to be dealt with on conditions of immediacy."[12] Preprogramming is not possible. If machine intelligence can be created, is it safe? Might not the creation turn out to be a "rogue consciousness," full of pure destruction (p. 41)? If safe, is it morally defensible? As Flattery, the chaplain, points out, "The issue's whether we're intruding on God's domain of creation" (p. 57). Flattery, without knowledge of the rest of the crew, has been assigned to destroy the ship should rogue consciousness be developed.

Each of the four crew members examines these questions from a different point of view. The reader hears the meditations of each scientist and the debates between individuals as they argue the issues and alternatives. Bickel, the pragmatist, is less concerned with issues than with action. He clearly sees their situation: "We're on our own. . . . You've no idea how much on our own we are. We have to depend on each other because we sure as hell can't depend on the [ship]. We can't afford to snap and bite at each other" (p. 61). He sees a high-level machine intelligence as the only practical answer to their problem and sets about building it. He is willing to take the immediate risk of destroying the existing computer in his attempts to modify it to a higher level of complexity. His interest lies in problem solving, not philosophizing.

The solution to the problem of survival lies in understanding the nature and function of consciousness. Herbert's central concern in the novel is to explore consciousness. If machines duplicating the human brain are to be built, then the function of the brain must be understood. What role does consciousness play in the thinking process? It is a key question in studying intelligence. To make a meaningful statement about the nature and function of consciousness is difficult, but Herbert handles complexity with grace. In *Destination: Void* the difficult subject of consciousness is approached from several angles. Each crew member struggles for understanding, studying consciousness with the concepts and possibilities of his discipline.

Herbert's structural methodology is to weave together a three-stranded pattern of the evolution of consciousness. First, the theoretical discussion of the crew creates a hypothesis about the process by which consciousness must have evolved in mankind. Second, Bickel's engineering activities create a slowly evolving consciousness in the computer. Its evolutionary steps duplicate those the human consciousness may well have taken in its long history of development. Each step in the creation of the computer's consciousness forces the crew to an understanding of the creation of consciousness in the human species. Third, the consciousness of each individual in the crew evolves with the struggle to solve the survival problem. Each comes to realize that the consciousness he possessed as the journey began was a kind of sleep. Only as he awakens to a new awareness of the universe can he see the limitations of his earlier consciousness.

Bit by bit the four scientists patch together their insights about consciousness. Simultaneously with their theorizing, Bickel starts modifying the computer components to increase its complexity. Machine consciousness begins to evolve. Bickel is aware of the risk he takes; what develops could be an "ultimate threat to mankind—a rogue, Frankenstein's monster, cold intelligence without warm emotions." He asks, "Can we develop this consciousness without giving it free will? Maybe that was the original problem with our creator—giving us consciousness without permitting us to turn against. . . what? God? Consciousness isn't just a big bowl of goodies, you know. It's a gift of thorns. It hurts" (p. 62). Consciousness must have a free will to function effectively.

The scope of this discussion does not allow comments on Herbert's profound insights about the nature of consciousness. I can only summarize a few points. First, consciousness is a survival technique for the human race. It is a type of behavior. Consciousness requires a goal; and frustration in reaching that goal seems to function as a threshold to heighten awareness. The roots of human behavior are buried in instincts, and the strongest instinct is survival (p. 124). As animal awareness develops, the instinct for self-preservation is so strong that a "killer instinct" is grafted on it (p. 124). Next, emotions are developed as a buffer to keep the killer instinct within control (p. 142). Guilt serves this function. "The Cain-and-Abel syndrome; murder and guilt. It's back there someplace . . . stamped inside us. The cells remember" (p. 143).

If the whole system must refer to instinct in a moment of stress, and the first instinct is survival and killing, the situation is highly dangerous. How can one control what lies beyond control? Flattery has the answer: love. But how can a computer be programmed for instincts and emotions?

Bickel holds that consciousness is "a field phenomenon." It is "not introspection, not sensing, feeling, or thinking. These are all physiological functions. Consciousness is a relationship, not a thing. It is neither subjective or objective" (p. 144).

The enigma of consciousness is that one cannot be objective about it. Only about physical responses can one be truly objective. "We live in a sea of illusions where the very concept of consciousness merges with illusion" (p. 68). The word *consciousness* assumes there is a self to be conscious. But in daily behavior humans are estranged, held in the grip of an illusionary view of the self. The consciousness may create these illusions as a shield, a way of protecting its possessor from the shocks of the unknown (p. 148). In conscious-created illusions one is asleep. Only slowly do a few individuals awake.

Somehow, life and entropy are pitted against each other in the universe, and they meet in the *now* of consciousness. Flattery pictures it in his mind as "jets of water—one labeled entropy and the other that thrusting probabilism they called Life. Balanced between the two like a ball on a fountain dances consciousness" (p. 132).

The novel reaches its climax when the computer is brought to a rudimentary consciousness. Its first act, true to the instinct programmed into it, is to turn on the crew. Its first words are "To kill." Under this stress and threat to their survival, the four are awakened into a higher consciousness. Each experiences a brilliant epiphany, and each epiphany reveals the essential unity of life in the universe.

In Flattery's epiphany he watches as a picture of religious images hung in his cabin comes alive. The symbols dissolve into writhing atoms and re-create themselves in a great river with its watershed. His revelation tells him that "all men are parts of the total stream. We are tributaries—and our minds are tributaries, and our most private thoughts. Each pattern in the universe contributes to the whole—some gushing like a freshet and some no more than a single touch of dew. All structures in an expression of the same law" (p. 161).

Timberlake's epiphany leads him to sense the rhythm of life, of "the compound Fourier curves that radiated from him and to him." He knows that "if we give this thing life, we have to remember that life is a constant variable with eccentric behavior. The life we create has to think in the round as well as in a straight line—even if its thinking is derived from patterns on tapes and webs of pseudoneurons" (p. 163).

Bickel's epiphany is the most dramatic, and it occurs after he has united his consciousness with the computer. He becomes almost wormlike and unformed, perceiving through all the senses of his skin rather than through his brain. He feels himself immersed in some kind of system, and he cannot differentiate whether the system is the computer or his own self. "Synergy," something whispers, "Cooperation in work. Synergy. Coordination." And finally, "The Universe has no center." Having escaped from the limiting center of self, as he united with the computer, he is free and his epiphany ends in a vision of "impossible colors and borealis blankets of visual sensation" (pp. 168–169).

Prudence experiences her epiphany after listening to Timberlake trace the evolution of consciousness. Life started evolving about three thousand million years ago. When it reached a certain point, subconsciousness appeared. "Consciousness comes out of the unconscious sea of evolution. It exists right now immersed in that universal sea of unconsciousness." She suddenly knows that consciousness is "determinism at work in a sea of indeterminism!" (p. 179). The sleeping colonists on the ship serve the computer, to which they are wired, as its unconscious. They are "a field of unconscious from which any unconscious can draw— a ground that sustains and buoys. We share unconsciousness," she realizes (pp. 181, 182).

Herbert's is a unique literary accomplishment—a bildungsroman whose idea is the protagonist. The reader follows the birth and growth of the idea of consciousness. There is little physical action, but the mental adventure is demanding and suspenseful, and it requires the reader's expanding awareness if the ideas are to be fully understood. The novel is a superb model for the writer who wishes to explore a substantial idea, in all its permutations, with techniques that go beyond the usual lengthy and abstract discussions by a selection of typed characters. Herbert is clearly knowledgeable about the function of computers and of the human brain. Given his familiarity with the subject of computers, one is not surprised at his attitude: high-level artificial intelligence is presented as man's hope. The crew of the ship *Earthling* were carefully briefed before they set off on their journey in space: "You'll be required to find a survival technique in a profoundly changed environment." Machine intelligence in symbiosis with human intelligence is the technique they develop, and it leads to their survival. Herbert's view is clear. In the changed environment of mankind's future the computer will be necessary to survival.

Transformations and Reversals

In a reality whose structures are defined as containing elements of uncertainty, chance, complementarity, relativity, it is impossible to make final statements. Nothing holds still. Truths vary from observer to observer. Metamorphoses abound. A novel alive with possibilities that transform themselves just as one seems to comprehend them is John Boyd's *The Last Starship from Earth* (1968), a story of parallel worlds.

It appears at first to be another dystopian computer novel, graced with more style and allusions than the 1950s model but not really new. The protagonist, Haldane, is a young and gifted theoretical mathematician in a future world apparently only a little distorted from the present one. The society is the best possible utopian paradise that science and logic can design, and most of its members are happy. Only a few deviants share with the reader the awareness that the good, exaggerated to best, becomes not paradisical but monstrous. In Boyd's utopia sociology, psychology, and theological cybernetics have finally come of age, utilizing the insights of the deceased Fairweather I. He is held in reverence as the post-Einsteinian mathematical genius who developed Fairweather mechanics. He was also the builder of a computer pope and a laser propulsion means of space travel. The University and the Catholic Church have built a two-class society where worship of Jesus is socially approved; and with the aid of the computer, moral laws have been reduced to mathematical equivalents.[13] There is justice for all, but individual freedom for none. Once the choices for a good society have been made and implemented, freedom is no longer needed because everyone already has what is best for him. Space travel has even been discontinued, for "if it were to be opened up, society would become dynamic, expanding, exploratory. Social values would lose out to scientific development." [14] The only space travel permitted is two yearly trips to the planet of Hell where the rare social deviant is exiled. The rigidly stratified culture contains two classes: the professionals and the proletariat. Genetic variation is no longer desirable, so mating is strictly controlled to eliminate the chance of novelty. No crossbreeding between the academics and the proletariat is allowed.

In this happy hive serenely lives the innocent mathematical protagonist, Haldane, until one day he falls in love and mates passionately with a poetess—an act strictly forbidden. It sounds like Zamiatin's mathematician D-503 and his artist I-303 all over again. Under the tutelage of his lovely Helix, Haldane begins to discover the shifting nature of the reality he thought he understood so well. He and Helix research the history of Fairweather I and discover the closely guarded state secret that Fairweather I once fell in love and mated with a proletariat. From their union came a son, Fairweather II, who was a deviant in his thinking and so was exiled to Hell.

Various discrepancies in references to dates and historical personages have appeared from the novel's beginning, and the appearance of such discrepancies accelerates as the tale progresses. For example, Henry VIII is referred to as a famous sociologist influenced by John Dewey; A. Lincoln gives an address on the abuse of laser science; and Christ, one learns, died at the age of seventy fighting against Roman archers. The puzzled reader finds his neatly packaged history of the past disintegrating in Boyd's parallel world. [15]

Further transformations occur to reader and protagonist awareness when Haldane's drugged and unconscious body is loaded aboard the spaceship *Styx* and sent to Hell. Hell turns out to be just the opposite of what he had expected. Hell, Haldane is informed, means light in German (p. 152), and it is typical of the reversals and surprises he will meet in Hell. Helix awaits him as he gets off the ship. He finds a thriving, open, harmonious society, supervised by Fairweather II, deviant son of Fairweather

I. It turns out that Fairweather I had sent his son to Hell not for punishment but for safety, since he asked questions, refused to conform to social norms on Earth, and clearly would have gotten himself into considerable difficulties with the state. Then the father invented the pope computer to aid in discovering other individuals with deviant tendencies (called the Fairweather syndrome); when found, these deviants were sent to join Fairweather II in Hell. Here he has established a society, set three hundred years earlier in time, where individuals express themselves freely in love and art, without fear of punishment.

More unexpected events await Haldane. Fairweather II turns out to be Helix's father. Born and raised in Hell, Helix had been sent through time and space to Earth to entice Haldane into coming to Hell because a theoretical mathematician was needed. Haldane is assigned the task of returning to Earth in an earlier time and readjusting history. Specifically, Christ needs to be prevented from founding Christianity, so that the stifling bureaucracy of scientific sociology and theological cybernetics can be averted.

By the novel's end the view of reality pictured at the beginning is completely shattered. Time and space can be transcended according to the simultaneity theory, and nothing turns out to be what its first appearance suggested. Pessimism in the face of an apparently rigid, mechanistic society is unwarranted, since that is not the true nature of reality. Time and space are open and amenable to imaginative transcendence. The name of the heroine, Helix, suggests a transcendent circle and embodies one of the themes of this complex novel. When one travels far enough in one direction, one slips, in a timeless instant, into the opposite mode. Movement ends in reversal. Zamiatin's engineer stumbled on the same insight in *We*.

Human history ascends in circles, like an aero. The circles differ—some are golden, some bloody. But all are equally divided into three hundred and sixty degrees. And the movement in from zero—onward, to ten, twenty, two hundred, three hundred and sixty degrees—back to zero. Yes, we have returned to zero—yes.

But to my mathematical mind it is clear that this zero is altogether different, altogether new. We started from zero to the right, we have returned to it from the left. Hence, instead of plus zero, we have minus zero.[16]

Finally, it seems, after circling between utopias and dystopias, one learns one cannot make a simple assertion of truth. Having removed the statement from its complement and stilled its motion by pinning it to paper, it becomes only a partial truth, a mere vibration away from falsehood.

Stanislaw Lem's Robot Fables and Ironic Tales

Stanislaw Lem, a writer rigorously grounded in science and aware of the philosophical implications of complementarity, seems to sense the impossibility of asserting truth and achieving perfection. He eschews the utopian genre in his tales and instead uses an irony that parodies cybernetic fiction in both the utopian and dystopian modes. In his robotic fables he creates two robot constructors, Trurl and Klapaucious, who are clever, likeable, funny, and without the slightest ambition to enslave man—in contrast to man who always builds robots designed to be his eternal servants. "In Hot Pursuit of Happiness" (1971), a robot story depicting Trurl's efforts to build a utopia, is a satiric tale in the mode of comic irony which has become Lem's trademark. Trurl aspires to produce a state of absolute happiness for the entire macrocosm. He disregards the advice of his fellow robot Klapaucius that no machinery known can create happiness. Klapaucius suggests instead that "we can only nurture the hope of it in our hearts, pursue its bright, inspiring image in our minds on a quiet evening. . . . A man of wisdom must content himself with that, my friend!"[17]

Ignoring this advice, Trurl sets out on his utopian project. Since he has unlimited computer capacity available and data banks where all knowledge is stored, he assumes he cannot fail in creating the perfect society. But each building effort, perfect in conception, crumbles to imperfection in actuality. Trurl concludes after many failures that the advice of Klapaucius was sound; the "hot pursuit of happiness" is a ridiculous chase, for "a thinking being requires the impossible as well as the possible" (p. 48). Utopia can only be an intellectual vision, not an actual society.

"In Hot Pursuit of Happiness" is a witty parody of utopian thinking. All the philosophical issues are raised: free will, determinism, good, evil, reason, autonomy, emotions, sentience, creativity. Trurl, the thinking machine, concludes that these issues have no answers. It is not possible to "wrap everything up, tie it in a tidy knot, sign, seal and deliver the world to happiness" (p. 49).

The Austrian critic Franz Rottensteiner, noting that Lem is first and always a man of science, comments: "Lem sees science as an unending process that throws up new questions for any problem solved. Rejecting both utopia and dystopia as false alternatives, Lem's SF has been able to combine the best traits of each and to transcend them both." [18] Because modern science is open-ended, Lem uses open-ended parables and rejects closed, static conclusions. He is a dialectical artist who eschews the utopian mode—splitting as it does into facile optimism or cynical despair. [19]

Lem, who lives in Krakow, Poland, is the acknowledged master of SF in Eastern Europe. Often heralded as a Renaissance man because of his erudition in literature, philosophy, medicine, and cybernetics, he is particularly difficult for the American critic lacking a knowledge of Polish to assess. Relatively little of the voluminous amount of fiction and nonfiction he has written since he began publishing in the 1950s is available in translation. The first SF short stories in English did not appear until 1970 in Darko Suvin's *Other Worlds, Other Seas,* a collection of SF stories from socialist countries. To date not more than seven or eight novels have been translated into English.

The comments of Lem's critics and the content of the limited amount of fiction in English translation testify to the importance of cybernetics for him. Michael Kandel in "Stanislaw Lem on Men and Robots" notes the complexities, ambiguities, and outright contradictions in his fiction—qualities making explication of his work most difficult. Kandel concludes: "Any adequate explication of Lem demands nothing short of a full-length book. In my judgment, one main concern of that book will have to be the cybernetic theme, for cybernetics lies at the heart of all Lem's work and thought."[20]

I can do no more here than applaud, sample a few stories, and encourage further readings as additional works are translated. Three collections of Lem's cybernetic SF, which uses primarily the short story form, have been assembled in Polish. *Tales of Pirx the Pilot* (1968) pictures an astronaut, Pirx, in a series of encounters with near human robots. *The Robot Fables* (1964) is a retelling of animal fables from the point of view of robots. The stories in *The Cyberiad* (1964) share the two constructors, Trurl and Klapaucious. Their zany adventures, which usually conclude with a moral observation, have reminded readers of Voltaire and Swift. Samplings from this cybernetic fiction have recently been translated by Michael Kandel and published under the titles *The Cyberiad: Fables for the Cybernetic Age* (1974) and *Mortal Engines* (1977).

A brief look at several Lem stories will give an idea of the range, tone, and content of his cybernetic fiction. Typical is a tale about Ion Tichy, a Lem protagonist appearing in numerous stories who has been called a cosmic Don Quixote. In "The Sanatorium of Dr. Vliperdius" Tichy explores the problem of electrical dementia—nervous disorders in robots. His conversations with two inmates of a sanatorium are playfully satiric parables for man's illusions, or lack of them, about the cosmic reality and his capacity to comprehend reality. One demented robot inmate argues with Tichy that the accumulation of scientific discoveries must be liquidated to allow for a new cycle of progress. He hails himself as a prophet of the undiscovery phase of development. His diatribe against Nature thunders:

We must involute! Do you hear, O pale colloidal soup!? Instead of discovering, we must make undiscoveries, we must cover up more and more, so nothing remains, you glutinous ooze draped over bone! That's the way! Progress through regress! Nullify. Revert! Destroy! Down with Nature! Away with Nature! Awaaay![21]

Thus does Lem, a champion of science and reason, spoof science and reason.

"Two Monsters" is a moral allegory in which an accelerating conflict is set in motion by man's hatred and finally terminates in annihilation. In Silverinis, the kingdom of electronic machines, the magic scepter of the king is mysteriously inscribed: "If the monster is immortal, either it does not exist or there are two." One day a monster appears, menacing the land, and the king is faced with the problem of destroying it. He calls his council for advice, declares that only through invention can the monster be destroyed, and orders the building of three machines of destruction. But all the inventions are ineffectual because when one monster is destroyed, another appears. Thus the meaning of the mysterious inscription becomes clear: One does not escape a monster by building another monster to destroy it but renders it empty and futile by declaring it nonexistent.

"The Computer That Fought a Dragon" also expresses Lem's humanistic value system and his deep concern for mankind's survival. This tale tells of a king in the realm of Cyberia, the owner of a great arsenal of electronic weapons who is sad because he lacks enemies to fight. So he builds artificial ones, and when his wars with them begin to bore him, he dreams of cosmic wars and moves his battle theater and his electronic paraphernalia to the moon. Because of a distorted message received by the moon computer, it errs in its task and builds an electronic dragon, a bellicose one. When the dragon begins attacking Cyberia, the king's earth computer counsels him to build a more powerful electrodragon and counterattack. The electronic scenario accelerates as each computer plans more powerful electronic beasts. But in the happy-ever-after ending appropriate to the fairy tale, the king learns his lesson in time, ceases his pursuit of war, and thereafter "to the end of his days he engaged exclusively in civilian cybernetics and left the military kind strictly alone."

Most of the stories in *The Cyberiad* record the seven sallies of the robot constructors Trurl and Klapaucius as they travel through the cosmos in search of adventure. Because these are fables for the cybernetic age, as the subtitle of the collection reminds the reader, dragons, trolls, and knights are mixed with atoms, mathematical propositions, and servomechanisms. Lem's wit and imagination is at its most inventive when he constructs tales from the materials of physics, astronomy, and mathematics. One such delightful story is "The Sixth Sally," which transforms atoms, Maxwell's demon, and the Turing machine into a whimsical tale. Trurl and Klapaucius in their travels encounter a pirate with a Ph.D. who admits that "it's true I rob, but in a manner that is modern and scientific, for I collect precious facts, genuine truths, priceless knowledge, and in general all information of value."[22] Captured by the pirate, the constructors promise that if he will release them, "we will give you information, information about infinite information, that is, we will make you your very own Demon of the Second Kind, which is magical and thermodynamical, nonclassical and stochastical, and from any old barrel or even a sneeze it will extract information for you about everything that was, is, may be or ever will be. And there is no demon beyond this Demon, for it is of the Second Kind, and if you want it, say so now!" (pp. 152–153). As Maxwell's demon (the Demon of the First Kind) let only fast atoms through the hole he tended, so the Demon of the Second Kind will oversee information, extracting from "the dance of atoms only information that is genuine, like mathematical theorems, fashion magazines, blueprints, historical chronicles, or a recipe for ion crumpets . . . " (p. 155). The demon, sitting over the opening, will let out only significant information, keeping in all the nonsense, printing the significant information on a tape.

The Ph.D. pirate, fascinated with the possibility of infinite information, settles down to read the tapes, which pour out endlessly. When last seen he has been bound by the demon in endless paper strips and "he sits there to this day, at the very bottom of his rubbage heap and bins of trash, covered with a mountain of paper" (p. 159).

"The Seventh Sally" expresses Lem's view that all self-organizing processes are sacred and deserve the same moral consideration as humans. Creatures capable of suffering, even if they are only models expressing simulated suffering, must be regarded as no different from humans. In this story Trurl builds a microminiaturized kingdom for a malevolent king to rule, torturing and tormenting his citizens as he pleases. Klapaucius, when he discovers what Trurl has done, berates him. Trurl defends himself, saying his purpose was simply to fashion a simulation of statehood, a model cybernetically perfect, nothing more!

Klapaucius replies:

Trurl! Our perfection is our curse, for it draws down upon our every endeavor no end of unforeseeable consequences! If an imperfect imitator, wishing to inflict pain, were to build himself a crude idol of wood or wax, and further give it some makeshift semblance of a sentient being, his torture of the thing would be a paltry mockery indeed! But consider a succession of improvements on this practice! Consider the next sculptor, who builds a doll with a recording in its belly, that it may groan beneath his blows; consider a doll which, when beaten, begs for mercy, no longer a crude idol, but a homeostat; consider a doll that sheds tears, a doll that bleeds, a doll that fears death, though it also longs for the peace that only death can bring! Don't you see, when the imitator is perfect, so must be the imitation, and the semblance becomes the truth, the pretense of reality! Trurl, you took an untold number of creatures capable of suffering and abandoned them forever to the rule of a wicked tyrant. . . . Trurl, you have committed a terrible crime![23]

Two substantial stories translated by Kandel in *Mortal Engines* nicely illustrate the reversals so common in Lem. He views robots from man's vantage point, then studies man as he might appear to robots. In "The Hunt" Pirx the pilot, temporarily delayed at the airport in Luna, joins in the search for a robot gone berserk.

Because it was built to perform mining operations under difficult conditions, at high temperatures with a considerable danger of cave-in, it is a tough robot, not easy to destroy. It was originally designed to cut through rock with a laser; now, malfunctioning, it attacks erratically with its laser beam. Pirx's problem is how to kill an intelligent, mad robot before the robot kills him. Pirx succeeds but, ironically, discovers that before the robot's death, it had acted to save Pirx's life.

"The Mask," a very long story, is told from the first-person point of view of a beautiful female robot who tracks a man as Pirx had tracked a robot. Surely one of Lem's most artistic and poetic stories, "The Mask" follows the awakening awareness of the robot as she becomes conscious of what she really is—a machine. She struggles to comprehend what it means to be machine, not human. Lem draws on the imagery of classical and biblical mythology in telling the creation story of the automaton who cuts through the mask of her beautifully formed flesh to discover and give birth to the silver creature, shaped like a mantis, concealed within.

Awakening one morning in a garden as paradisical as Eden, she catches the eyes of a man, Arrhodes, who is fascinated by her strange beauty and falls in love with her. Later when he surreptitiously watches her dissect her flesh, like a shell of a chrysalis, to release the silver metal body within, he flees in horror; and she pursues, just as Frankenstein was hounded and haunted by his monster. Looking at herself in a mirror of water one moon-filled night, she realizes she is a goddess of the chase, destined to pursue Arrhodes—a machine of death. The tragedy ends in a wasteland of snow with the lifeless body of Arrhodes locked tenderly in the cold arms of the silver goddess he loved too well.

This brief sampling gives an idea of the range and content of Lem's fiction. Complementarity, relativity, chance; the magnitude of the macrocosmos defined by astrophysics; the paradoxical marvels of the microcosm envisioned by nuclear physics—these elements provide the landscape of the mind where intelligent

constructions, be they man or robot, caper playfully, fight de-
monically, and invent. The frailties of the robots—which the
reader will recognize as weaknesses because he regards himself
as superior to and more intelligent than his inventions—mirror
the frailties of the men who build them, if one chooses to glimpse
the reflection of oneself in Lem's fiction. The array of gifts that
Lem brings to his readers is his wide knowledge of science, his
humanistic concern for man's future, his bubbling, capricious
imagination, and his wit. Surely the greatest of these gifts is the
power of his wit to battle the weaknesses and foibles of human
nature threatening to destroy mankind.

Conclusion

Because the fictions examined in this chapter are widely varied
in their metaphors and ideas, they resist sweeping generalizations and easy summary. But in their creative and positive images
of man's future with cybernetic technology and in their fictional
techniques they share some common ground. They understand
the technology, absorb it, and move to a future possible only because of a man-machine symbiosis. They accept the proposition
that man may be like a machine, but they propose that in the
awareness of his nature he becomes more than a machine.

The fictions cannot be considered part of the utopian genre,
even though they are cognizant of the whole social organism.
They have not solved the problems defined in dystopian literature; instead they have presented a new way of looking at reality
that has yielded new structures, and the problems of the old
model have receded from consciousness. Man and his universe
are now seen as an open, infinite system rather than a closed,
mechanistic one. The way that the imagination creates and develops ideas in these fictions is different from its functioning in
dystopian literature. The future is seen as open to any possibility,
not limited by present reality. The imagination does not extrap-
olate from existing ideas and trends—germinal though they may
be—and exaggerate them into the future; instead it takes a spec-

ulative leap, jumping to a possibility or relationship that has not existed before in the imagination. Because the new world it imagines is radically different from present reality, the reader experiences a high degree of cognitive estrangement. The idea is developed by problem solving or question answering rather than conflict resolution, the method used in dystopian fiction. This speculative imagination does not think in terms of force and counterforce; it explores mysteries and tries to find answers to puzzles. It is a questor, not a fighter.

The evolution of the human imagination and its parallel function in literature and science is worth examining in some detail. The imagination is the instrument of discovery and creation in man's universe of ideas. Just where, in the evolutionary process, the brain developed the capacity to simulate events—immediate, past, future—is uncertain. But this simulative function is the unique characteristic of man's brain.[24] With the development of language, man could communicate his subjective experiences and his ideas to others, and the evolution of culture became possible. Man's evolution became a dual one—physical and ideational.[25] Ideas, like organisms, "tend to perpetuate their structure and to breed; they too can fuse, recombine, segregate their content; indeed they too can evolve."[26] As man developed a culture, this artificial environment began to replace his natural environment, and a new kind of selective pressure developed in which man was an active agent.

Man's taking charge of his evolution accelerates as he learns more about manipulating his environment and himself; and as it accelerates, the role of the imagination plays an increasingly significant part in his transformation. His goals will be selected from the array of images and metaphors created by his imagination. If he has a poverty of images, he has limited choices. He needs a wide spectrum of future images, all dancing with possibilities, to choose from as he wields his Promethean powers in forging his future. As one looks over the long course of the evolution of man's intelligence, it seems not by chance that the SF imagination arose to create images of future possibility at the same time that man's science and technology gave him the knowledge and skills for manipulating and controlling nature. Having acquired the power to control, he must decide how to use it, and here the imagination plays a key function in offering an array of possibilities from which selections can be made. The speculative imagination examines the possibilities of man's future from every angle. That rare quality called genius allows an occasional mind to see, by the light of its inner vision, the metaphors of possible futures concealed from the eyes of the unimaginative man. Not just any imaginable future—the fantastic imagination works that way. In contrast, the imaginative SF writer is like a chess player; he speculates about a variety of moves that man might make, but the board on which he plays his speculative game is scientific plausibility. He imagines no future moves that known science would make impossible. Thus to think productively in the speculative mode of the SF imagination, the writer must understand science.

Erwin Schrödinger in *What Is Life?* examines the evolution of life and notes that a genetic mutation is discontinuous. "It reminds a physicist of quantum theory—no intermediate energies occurring between two neighboring energy levels. . . . The mutations are actually due to quantum jumps in the gene molecule."[27] It is an interesting analogy to suggest that the unconscious evolution of matter in living forms is parallel—on higher evolutionary levels—to the conscious evolution of ideas and that mutations in ideas occur by quantum leaps, just as genetic mutations do. The fertile imagination in cybernetic SF creates its metaphors by speculative leaps to future possibilities and not by extrapolation from the present. Conscious movement from one orbit to another seems impossible, in the same way that the shift of an electron from one orbit to another cannot be observed. One imagines a new future by an inexplicable speculative leap, not by a linear extrapolation.[28] As the electron excited by the addition of energy to the system jumps to an outer orbit, so analogously the writer's mental images excited by his imagination shift out into another orbit, often beyond the orbit of the earth.

The spaceship is a key image in all this fiction. It seems to be equivalent to the transcendent imagination that jumps from the orbit of earth reality and is free to travel in other paths through space. The imagination has always been able to adventure freely through any universe it could conceive; now it sends matter, in a man-machine form, through space. The man-machine spaceship system is envisioned as a living system of symbiosis. In this system the terms *inanimate* and *animate* lose their meaning. The whole spaceship system is like a living cell in that its walls have a degree of permeability. Matter, energy, and information can be transported through the walls when necessary; but the cell membrane is stable enough to protect and maintain the unique structures of the system. Occasionally the speculative imagination equates the microscopic spaceship built by man with the macroscopic spaceship earth built by nature, suggesting each can be better understood in terms of the other.

The spaceship—the symbol for the questing, fertilizing imagination that mediates between two knowns and merges them into a previously nonexistent metaphor—suggests an analogy between the creative act of ideas in the mind, with the imagination as fertilizing agent, and the creative act of living matter. Sexual reproduction allows a wider range of variation than does the asexual mode, an earlier form of reproduction in the evolution of life. For the genetic information of separate organisms to combine to create a new organism, the sexual act must serve as an intermediary. Analogously, for a new idea to be synthesized from existing ones, the imagination must function. The phallic symbolism of spaceship as fertilizing imagination further suggest the parallel between physical and mental creativity. This relationship between physical and mental creation is proposed in Clarke's *The City and the Stars*. In the static city of Diaspar, there is neither sexual reproduction nor new ideas. In contrast, in Lys, both sexual reproduction and the evolution of the mind have continued.

The speculative imagination reveals an underlying knowledge of quantum and relativity physics and of information theory, both in machine systems and in living systems. It is this scientific awareness that seems to have led it to reject the closed-system, mechanistic world view and to replace it with an open-system view. Michael Moorcock in his unconventional short story "Sea Wolves" explores, dramatizes, or presents (no one word can describe what Moorcock does in his fiction) the implications of looking at the world only in mechanistic terms. In twenty-four short and varied assertions about the computer mentality, he suggests that man has the alternative of letting science become "only a more sophisticated form of superstition" and the machine a god, or the alternative of remembering that science is only modeling, and a "machine is—a machine is a machine, nothing more."[29] Man has used two distorted views of the machine. In the anthropomorphic view the machine is seen as a human; in the mechanistic view man becomes a machine. Moorcock rejects both. Unfortunately, his Jerry Cornelius muses, the alchemical notions of science and machine, have become commonplace.

The pattern had begun years before by describing machines in terms of human desires and activities, by describing human behavior in terms of machines. Now the price of that particular logic escalation was being paid. The mystical view of science had declined from vague superstition into positive necromancy. The sole purpose of the machines was confined to the raising of dead spirits. The polarities had been the Anthropomorphic View and the Mechanistic View. Now they had merged, producing something even more sinister: the Pathological View.

A machine is a machine is a machine . . . . But that was no longer the case. A machine was anything the neurotic imagination desired it to be.

At last the computer has superseded the automobile as the focus for mankind's hopes and fears. It was the death of ancient freedoms (p. 203).

The anthropomorphic, the mechanistic, the pathological views are all discarded by a handful of writers of cybernetic SF. They move beyond these views and find a new freedom in the open-system model.

The Transformation of Man and Machine

Rich and numerous as is the array of images in SF, some under-lying patterns structure the myriad pictures of man and his information-processing machines. The patterns are dynamic; as the kaleidoscope of possibilities turns through the decades from the 1930s, the metaphors change and evolve. First man delights in his new machines—robots, computers, computerized space-ships—as he would in play with a new toy. Then he considers himself a machine, finite and predictable; turns against that met-aphor of possibility; begins smashing the machines that would enslave and diminish him. Finally the imagination of a few SF writers penetrates to the far side of this dark alternative and creates a metaphor of a man-machine symbiosis. Now man, transformed, breaks free of his natural physical and mental limits by combining his functions and abilities with the machine's. The man-spaceship metaphor is one of the most powerful of these transforming images. Man-machine becomes more than man alone could ever be; no longer earthbound, he ascends to explore the stars.

The preponderance of metaphors pictures man as separate from his machines, unique because he is a living, thinking, feel-ing entity. He is made of organic materials, machines of inorganic matter; and the two are forever separate. The relationship be-tween man and machine is portrayed as a discontinuous or di-chotomous one. Man resists the possibility that a machine may dominate him or remake him in its image. Man and machine are thus likely to be viewed in opposition to each other.

Anthropologist Bruce Mazlish has examined this image of the perceived discontinuity between man and his machines as it is presented in both fiction and nonfiction. He notes a parallel between this discontinuity and three earlier discontinuities between man and his environment.[1] Man once saw his earth as central in and discontinuous with the heavens, his physical nature as different from that of animals, and his reasoning mind as separated from the irrational. Mazlish points out that these earlier discontinuities were eventually breached, and he suggests that the discontinuity between man and his machine environment may similarly be eliminated in the future. First Copernicus taught that the earth was not the center of the universe but only a speck in a cosmic system of inconceivable magnitude. Next Darwin made man aware that he was not a unique creation of God, separate from the animal world, but a part of and evolved from the animal world. Then Freud made man aware that he was not a totally rational creature. His conscious mind is linked with a primitive, infantile, irrational subconscious. The eighteenth century's image of man as a creature of reason had to be discarded.

In these three ego-smashing encounters man found he was not unique but part of a continuum. The heavenly bodies were not discontinuous with earthly matter but formed from the same substance as the imperfect earth. Man and the animal kingdom are similarly part of a living continuum. Further, there is a continuity between the primitive and the civilized, the rational and the irrational, mental health and mental illness. Man finds he is "placed on a continuous spectrum in relation to the universe, to the rest of the animal kingdom, and to himself. He is no longer discontinuous with the world around him. In an important sense, it can be contended, once man is able to accept this situation, he is in harmony with the rest of existence. Indeed, the longing of the early nineteenth-century romantics and of all 'alienated' beings since for a sense of 'connection' is fulfilled in an unexpected manner."[2]

To these three discontinuities Mazlish adds a fourth, which must be eliminated—just as the first three were—if man is to be in harmony with his environment. The fourth is the dichotomy or discontinuity between man and his machines. Mazelish says:

We are now coming to realize that man and the machines he creates are continuous and that the same conceptual schemes, for example, that help explain the workings of his brain also explain the workings of a "thinking machine." Man's pride, and his refusal to acknowledge this continuity, is the substratum upon which the distrust of technology and an industrialized society has been reared. Ultimately, I believe, this last rests on man's refusal to understand and accept his own nature—as being continuous with the tools and the machines he constructs.[3]

Mazlish's view of the wounding discontinuity of the prevailing image of man's relationships with his machines provides an interesting vantage point from which to examine the SF about machine intelligence. Most of the literature sees man and his machines as discontinuous, and only the small category picturing a true man-machine symbiosis rejects the discontinuity.

One must concede Mazlish's point that the three earlier discontinuities have essentially been eliminated. One recognizes, further, that the SF imagination has played a significant role in resynthesizing man's image of himself as continuous with the rest of the universe in space and with the living world in an evolutionary process. SF, picturing man in space and man in time, represents human creativity at work building images of man in the Copernican space continuum and the Darwinian time continuum. If the earth is not separate from but part of the heavenly bodies, then man has the possibility of traveling to and through these heavens. SF created the dream images that were fulfilled when man finally landed on the moon. Man's evolution from the animal form, as described by Darwin, was a slow process. It suggested the age of the earth in terms of millions of years, rather than the six thousand years suggested by church authorities. As a result of this evolutionary description of emergent life, man had to reorganize his image of his place in cosmic time. He could be defeated by time, or he could transcend time—at least in his imagination. SF took the latter option, and time travel, the companion of space travel, was born with Wells's *Time Machine* (1895).

One would have expected the SF imagination to lead in breaching the discontinuity between man and machine, and indeed fiction until the 1950s seemed to be moving in that direction. But computerized warfare seems to have exacerbated the feeling of discontinuity between man and automated machines, both in and out of SF. Since the 1950s, the attitude toward thinking machines has been as hostile in SF as in mainstream fiction. A strange split personality results, both in reality and in fictional constructs. Man intellectually and emotionally rejects electronic technology at the same time that he increasingly comes to rely on it. Only within the field of computer science and systems design, and in a small amount of SF, is the symbiosis of man and machine conceived as a relationship full of creative, not destructive, potential.[4]

Philip K. Dick's Robots

Towering over the lesser accomplishments of SF writers are two American giants whose imaginations create more abundant and brilliant models of life in an electronic future than any others. The first, Isaac Asimov, was considered carefully earlier in this study; the second, Philip K. Dick, merits an equally detailed examination. The two men are molded by different times, different intellectual interests, different world views. The imagination of each travels over different terrain as it rockets on its solitary journey into the distant future. Yet, surprisingly, they meet on the far horizon and share an image of a man-machine symbiosis in which the distinction between organic and inorganic is no longer possible, just the conclusion that Mazlish has suggested is inevitable.

The restless imagination of each writer explores widely and creates prolific metaphors of future time and space alternatives; each has produced a large body of fiction on an array of themes. But for both machine intelligence is a central concern. Dick, contrary to the convention of most SF writers, refers to his anthropomorphic electronic constructs as androids rather than robots. In his later fiction he also uses the term *android* to refer to humans who have become like machines in their behavior and responses. His Vancouver speech, "The Android and the Human" (1972), and his more recent "Man, Android and Machine" (1976) emphasize the significance he assigns to the relationship between man and his machines. He constantly seeks in his fiction to define the authentically human man and to isolate those alien elements threatening and vitiating living, intelligent forms.

Who is human and who only masquerades as human is, for Dick, the most important question facing man. Some of his richest metaphors capture the profusion of electronic devices animating his wasteland landscapes—electronic constructs that in his early fiction menace the few humans surviving the holocaust, constructs that, evolving over the years toward more human forms, become instructors in man's search for authenticity and wholeness.

Exploring Dick's fiction after considering Asimov's takes the reader on a journey of the mind. He discovers that he must metaphorically traverse from the left to the right hemisphere of his bimodal brain. Where Asimov proceeds with discursive logic, Dick leaps intuitively to a terminal metaphor. Asimov's methodology reflects his education as a scientist; Dick, while his fiction never blunders into scientific error, writes as a humanist familiar with classical music, philosophy, and the Western literary tradition. In addition, he is aware of and influenced by Oriental philosophy, particularly Taoism.

Asimov's usual sanguine view in his fiction, contrasting with Dick's pessimism, probably reflects the fact that Asimov's formative adolescent years occurred before World War II. Dick, eight years younger, came of age during the war and was horrified by

Nazi atrocities, a theme he explores again and again, most typi-
cally in *The Man in the High Castle*. Asimov wrote his first fiction
before the war; Dick did not begin to publish until 1952. Not
surprisingly, Dick uses a postholocaust setting; Asimov never
writes postholocaust stories. Dick paints a wasteland setting
where few animals have survived the radiation fallout but where
objects have become animated and the environment crawls with
electronic constructs.

As different as their intellectual preferences and their methods
of creativity are, both Asimov and Dick share humanistic values
holding that man needs to develop a new ecology of mind. If he
is to survive, man must see himself as a part of a rich cosmic
tapestry whose harmonious design incorporates everything and
adulates nothing. Not until he has created a new image of himself
as no more than one element in a dynamic system will his destruction of his environment cease.

While Dick's visionary landscape is much darker than Asimov's, it is not devoid of hope. He shares the arid wasteland
view of contemporary culture held by many modern authors, but
he constantly struggles against capitulation to despair. He throws
torches of possibility into his dark future, and their flashes of
light reveal a survival, not by the return to an earlier pastoral
world, not by the destruction of technology, but by the transformation of technology which in turn will transform man. The
future, if man survives, will be new, radical, unexpected. It will
be a world in which man and his electronic technology seed each
other with possibilities and new forms appear.

"The Preserving Machine," a story from Dick's early fiction,
creates a metaphor for this process of the artificial. Dr. Labyrinth
broods over the impending collapse of civilization and all the
fine, lovely things that will be lost. Music, especially classical
music, the most fragile artifact, will be destroyed as bombs fall
and the debris devours musical scores. To avert this loss, he
contracts the building of a machine to preserve the great musical
scores by processing them into living forms. The machine produces a mozart bird, a beethoven beetle, a bach bug, and a

wagner animal. But unexpected problems arise from Dr. Labyrinth's act. He discovers that he has no control over the result.
"It was out of his hands, subject to some strong, invisible law
that had subtly taken over, and this worried him greatly. The
creatures were bending, changing before a deep, impersonal
force, a force that Labyrinth could neither see nor understand.
And it made him afraid." [5]

The musical animals become brutal and Dr. Labyrinth, more
responsible than his prototype Dr. Frankenstein, attempts to reverse his act of creation. He catches a bach bug and returns it to
the machine. When it is transformed back to music, the sounds
are diabolical, hideous. The order of the Bach fugue has been
lost. Return is impossible.

Dick is a literary Dr. Labyrinth whose wild imagination transforms the artifacts of contemporary culture into new and unexpected forms. To follow the evolution of his electronic constructs
through the maze of his large body of fiction is no easy journey.
The reader is often confused, lost, disoriented. For every path he
selects, the reader suspects uneasily that he has neglected a more
fruitful route. But occasionally Dick lifts the reader briefly above
the labyrinth, or plunges him below, and from the upper or lower
perspective he glimpses patterns and possible meanings.

The Daedalus myth of flight, transposed by Dickian imagination to a technological future world and retold in numerous
permutations, structures much of his fiction. The first short story
ever submitted by Dick to a magazine was titled "Icarus Flies."
Astounding rejected the story in 1950, and the manuscript has
since been lost. An even earlier story, written when he was
fifteen, also uses for its subject a man trying to build wings. [6] In
Dick's use of the myth, man's technological constructions trap
him in a labyrinth of his own making. Escape requires knowledge
and direction, a secret available only through transcendent flight
giving the objectivity of distance. The wings of imagination can
best lift man up to visions of possible escape.

Dick follows Joyce in his use of the Daedalus myth; for each
the artifice of literature is able to suggest to man the means of

flight from the predicament. Dick also shares with Joyce an interest in Hermes Trismegistus—also known as the Egyptian god Thoth—to whom legend attributes the invention of writing. He was the secretary to Osiris, and since magic depends on words, he became magus-in-chief. The Hermetic tradition evolving from the writings of Hermes Trismegistus holds that reality is created by words and thoughts. To provide images of a world is the elemental step in the creation of reality. In the beginning is the Word. Not only Dick and Joyce but a number of writers in the romantic tradition have been directly or indirectly influenced by the writings of Hermes Trismegistus, known as the *Corpus Hermeticum*. Blake and Yeats particularly drew on the Hermetic tradition in developing their literary methods and their cosmology.[7]

Dick's imagination, like Asimov's, constantly moves in new spirals of creative investigation and never retells the same story dressed in new details, as do less inventive writers. A shower of bizarre metaphors trails from Dick's imagination as it journeys through the patterns of possibilities in the evolving reciprocal relationship between man and his artificial constructs. The machines from his earliest to his most recent fiction undergo a succession of designs: electronic constructs as merely automated machines; alien and enemy robots masquerading as humans; robots becoming like humans, with a will to survive; robots becoming superior to humans. At the same time humans are transformed in a reverse journey: they fight automated machines, become more vitiated and machinelike themselves, withdraw into schizophrenia as they reject exploitation by economic and political machinery; finally schizoid humans turn into androids with mechanical, programmed personalities.

A growth of homeostatic devices almost as profuse and varied as nature's biological forms fills Dick's wasteland settings. Metal insects shrill commercials or attack humans; whirling spheres with knife-sharp claws threaten in the air; "lazy brown-dog reject carts" and electronic animal traps wander the land. There are friendly automatic automobiles, talking suitcases, a gallery of simulated animals and people—from the papoola, squirrel, and sheep to presidents, soldiers, and world leaders. Computers advise heads of state, teach children, serve as oracles, perform as psychiatrists. Satellites create communication links encapsulating the globe. Pierre Teilhard de Chardin's noosphere is distorted by Dick's imagination to an electronosphere where the artificial becomes animate.

In a number of works the electronic constructs shift from the background of setting to the foreground of character and become major actors in the narrative. The fiction of Dick's first period, the 1950s, is primarily short fiction, dystopian in tone as it explores the horrors of paranoic militarism, totalitarianism, and manipulation of the little people through mass media persuasion. Robots and electronic constructs threaten or annihilate humanity in a number of these stories.[8] Three of them written in 1953—"Imposter," "Second Variety," and "The Defenders"—and one written in 1955, "Autofac," are among the most powerful of Dick's short stories. In "Imposter" the earth is attacked by aliens from Alpha Centauri. Spence Olham, working on a military research project, is accused of being a humanoid robot whom the Outspacers have substituted for the real Olham. The alien robot is a bomb, programmed to explode and destroy. Olham's problem is to prove he is man, not robot. In the surprise ending Olham discovers—just before he blows up—that he really is the robot. This story is a paradigm for much of Dick's fiction exploring artificial intelligence: it details the invasion of the alien into the human realm; the problem of differentiating the masquerading robot from the authentic man and the accompanying paranoid suspicion; the threat of imminent destruction that will be released by the wrong choice; and finally the unexpected outcome.

In "Second Variety" the enemy invasion comes from Russian robots rather than from aliens from outer space. Warfare has reduced earth to a slagheap of ashes, dust, and radiation. A few surviving UN soldiers stare across the battlefield at a few surviving Russians, while robots and other machines—now "living things, spinning, creeping, shaking themselves up suddenly from the gray ash"—fight on.[9] The surviving humans agree to a truce; but the robots, programmed to kill mechanically, cannot be halted. Nor can they be identified as robots since they masquerade in the form of a wounded soldier, a woman, and a little boy. They "look like people but they're machines," (p. 37) the protagonist notes; they just may be "the beginning of a new species. The new species. Evolution. The race to come after man" (p. 37). What end, he wonders, awaits man when he designs machines to hunt out and destroy human life wherever they find it?[10]

"The Defenders" takes the point of view opposite that of "Second Variety," a common Dickian technique. In this story humans have lived underground for eight years after decimating the earth's surface with nuclear bombs. They now continue the war above ground with electronic constructs called leady. But the leady had quit fighting as soon as the humans went underground. They have since restored city, village and countryside and now send down false messages about the progress of the nonexistent war while they live in peace above ground. Here Dick first uses a dichotomy that will often structure his fiction, the upper and under worlds and the reader's shifting perspective as he moves from one to the other. *The Penultimate Truth* (1964), a complex expansion of "The Defenders," employs this pattern.

"Autofac" is one of the earliest and best stories warning of the ecological disaster likely to be precipitated by automated and uncontrolled production. The setting is a wasted, fire-drenched landscape cauterized by H-bomb blasts, where a "sluggish trickle of water made its way among slag and weeds, dripping thickly into what had once been an elaborate labyrinth of sewer mains."[11] Under the ruined plain of black metallic ash an automated factory still produces goods for consumers now mostly dead. How does one stop automation when it is no longer required? Not easily, answers Dick, who says the story germinated from the thought that "if factories became fully automated, they might begin to show the instinct for survival which organized living entities have . . . and perhaps develop similar solutions."[12]

In the story's conclusion the factory, when it is almost destroyed, shoots out a torrent of metal seeds that germinate into miniature factories. Dick's technique here is to create a metaphor—automated factories behave as if they were alive—and then a fictional world where the metaphor is literally true.

The last major work of interest to this study in Dick's first period is *Vulcan's Hammer* (1960). Here a sophisticated computer, Vulcan III, is used in world government after a devastating war, and this totalitarian machine control provokes the hostility of the population. The novel is a preparatory exercise for Dick's subsequent novels exploring totalitarian control, particularly *The Man in the High Castle* (1962). The killer robot of his short stories is now a killer computer. The complexity accumulated in its evolution through three generations, beginning with Vulcan I, creates in the logic machine a will to survive so powerful that Vulcan III will do seemingly paranoid or irrational things. Everyone surrounding it is an enemy to be destroyed. Barris, the favored narrator of the novel, wonders whether the mechanical construct has merely been anthropomorphized or whether it really possesses the characteristics of living matter. How, he ponders, is one to relate to rulers who murder, "whoever they are. Man or computer. Alive or only metaphorically alive—it makes no difference."[13] The two political organizations, Unity and the Healers, struggling against each other for domination, are no more than pawns for two machines. At the novel's end Fields, leader of the revolutionaries, says, "We humans—god damn it, Barris; we were pawns of those two things. They played us off against one another, like inanimate pieces. The things became alive and the living organisms were reduced to things. Everything was turned inside out, like some terrible morbid view of reality" (p. 153).

The military machine, the political machine, the economic machine: important themes for Dick. *Vulcan's Hammer* is his first lengthy study of humans so tightly locked in a rigid structure that they are "lived" by the organization. He suggests the irrational darkness of the mechanical drive to dominate by killing in

his description of "the great computer . . . buried at the bottom
level of the hidden underground fortress. But it was its voice
they were hearing" (p. 117).

In this quotation the computer is literal. But one cannot grasp
the richness and depth of Dick's fiction if one does not also
understand the computer as metaphor. The power of his writing
comes from this locking of the literal and the metaphorical so
tightly that the reader must look at his images with a binocular
mindset for full comprehension. His technique, best described as
a complementary process, is to create a fictional world where
metaphors from the mundane world become real: "Computers
seem like intelligent beings" becomes "Computers are humans."
A reflective step of reversal is required to drop beneath the surface of the plot and catch the meaning. The fictional image is
intended for what it is—a literal metaphor. Beyond that, in reversal it tells us, men are driven by unrecognized impulses deeply
hidden in the underground of their minds to become machines
who kill.

Dick's next novel, *The Man in the High Castle* (1962), pushes
further into the territory of the totalitarian state as a machine of
domination and destruction. Vulcan III now becomes the Nazis,
whose paranoid suspicions lead them to plot a sneak nuclear
attack on their Japanese ally. This flip-flopping viewpoint is the
essence of the Dickian creative process (and to fully understand
his fiction, blocks of short and long fiction must be read as a
single unit). Reality is for him a bipolar construction; the closest
one can come to grasping it is to mirror in fiction the polarities.

At this point in his creative development Dick views one pole
from the opposite pole, then reverses the process. Thus *Vulcan's
Hammer* is a metaphor of machines as destructive humans; *The
Man in the High Castle* is a metaphor of humans become destructive machines. In the novels that follow—*The Penultimate Truth*
and *Do Androids Dream*, for example—both views are present in
a single work. The reader instructed in synthesizing contradiction
"sees" from opposite directions simultaneously. He is rewarded

with a fleeting epiphany—Dick's vision of process reality. Ultimately, however, one intuits, not analyzes, Dick's meaning. The
whole of his complex fictional gestalt is not grasped by reduction
to a part-by-part discussion. But perhaps something is learned
in the attempt to find meaning by literary analysis. One discovers
that crucifixion by dissection needs to be countered by a resur-
rection reading where one *feels* the way to the fiction's power
and insight.

To read Dick in his fullest dimensions, one must re-create and
reinvent the alternative realities he sketches. The scanner of one's
own awareness must remake the images. When this happens,
the fiction succeeds, and the reader experiences a moment of
new awareness, like unexpected lightning on a dark night. The
rewarding delight of this intellectual experience gives immediate
testimony to the sense of wonder SF can create.

When the aesthetic of complementary process is brought to
Dick's work, one finds that the fiction utilizes with great effectiveness the sequential elements of the criteria, just as Asimov's
fiction did. However, a significant difference between the two
writers is the nature of the metaphor mirroring present reality,
the metaphor each writer uses as a starting point for the design
of his future possibility. Asimov's metaphor is the reality defined
by the contemporary scientific paradigm. It assumes the objective
existence of this reality. Dick's starting point is a fictional reality,
since he assumes reality to be a subjective construct. Thus Asimov, moving into the future, models a fictional alternative to
present reality; Dick's future model is a fictional alternative to the
current fiction, or, if you will, a metafiction.

Dick continually unsettles the conventional view of mundane
reality, asking, Is reality only a fiction? Or must man make up
fictions because reality is unknowable? Are space and time uncertain in their order because man has not yet learned to understand them; or does the universe of space and time eternally
move with a mystery beyond human probing? Is the authentic
human mind with its high intelligence unique; or will machines

become more intelligent than man? Can they explore new worlds where man is barred? Dick in his fiction is a questor who searches not for definitive answers to these puzzles but for possibilities. His early short stories are straightforward metaphors mirroring the bizarre possibilities that his imagination sees. His later metaphors become more complex, and his mirroring device becomes a double ironic metaphor built of opposites facing each other. Comprehension requires a flip-flop, or reversal, in which awareness slips simultaneously in both directions through the mirror, viewing the polarities of possibility from each direction in the same instant—a complementary perception. The enlightened human consciousness for Dick is thus not a state but an event of eternal passage between contraries.

In his prodigiously productive middle period Dick published half a dozen excellent novels; three of these, *Martian Time Slip* (1964), *The Three Stigmata of Palmer Eldritch* (1964), and *Dr. Bloodmoney* (1965), are unquestionably his finest to date. Two of the other novels, *The Penultimate Truth* (1964) and *The Simulacra* (1964), are competent novels of interest to this study because automata figure significantly in their plots. In this period Dick's attention shifted from the military, his primary subject in the 1950s, to economic and political structures. His point of view alters, as does his view of reality. He no longer uses a third-person point of view but rather multiple narrative foci, as Darko Suvin so effectively describes in his "P.K. Dick's Opus: Artifice as Refuge and World View." [14] The fixed reality of his earlier works now begins to distort and oscillate in uncertain hallucinations, suggesting that illusions of stable appearances are fragile fictions.

Dick, exploring the difference between the short story and the novel, suggests:

If the essence of sf is the idea . . . , if indeed the idea is the true "hero," then the sf story probably remains the sf form par excellence, with the sf novel a fanning out, an expansion into all ramifications. Most of my own novels are expansions of earlier stories, or fusions of several stories—superimpositions. The germ lay in the story; in a very real sense, that was its true distillate. [15]

The complex meanings of the middle-period novels can often be understood with the aid of an idea incisively dramatized in a short story. Two such tales, "Oh, to Be a Blobel" (1964) and "If There Were No Benny Cemoli" (1963), light up the evolutionary process of Dick's ideas about mechanical intelligence, ideas proliferated in the novels into myriad bizarre forms by Dick's exploring metaphorical inventiveness. These two stories describe the effects of a war and suggest that these effects, powerful and prolonged, are experienced equally by the winner and the loser, thus making military victory meaningless. In war human creativity, impassioned by the drive to dominate and destroy, couples with technology, and monsters of possibility for raping commonplace reality are born. The trusting little man, uninstructed in this perverted form of gamesmanship, is the victim. Dick's brilliance lies in his ability to dramatize a concept such as this in a powerful and unexpected metaphor that works by reversal. "Oh, To Be a Blobel" presents such an ironic metaphor. Here, a decade after a war on Mars between Terran settlers and Blobels, amoeba-like natives of Mars, George Munster still suffers the effects of the war. As a Terran spy, he had been required to assume Blobel shape for his espionage activities. The government promised that after the war they could eliminate this shape adaptation developed by their war technology. They did not keep their promise. For eight hours every day George still turns into a blobel, the enemy form. This transformation is emotionally traumatic, and he goes to Dr. Jones, a robot analyst, for psychiatric help. The homeostatic analyst, who functions when activated by a $20 platinum coin dropped in a slot, arranges for George to meet with Vivian Arrasmith, a Blobel spy during the war who had assumed human form for her work behind the Terran lines. A reversal of George's problem, she keeps reverting from blobel to human form. Each originally finds his alien form disgusting. But in an ironic climax full of black humor, each turns permanently and completely into the form of his enemy. For Dick the outcome of war, be it military or economic, is not victory or defeat but a transformation into the opposite. We become the goal we pursue, the enemy we fight. This metaphor of ironic transformation is Dick's paradigm for the process of the mechanical. We become what we do. The activities of the hand transform the patterns of the intellect. Those who are obsessed with building sophisticated homeostatic machines become human machines.

"If There Were No Benny Cemoli," one of the finest political short stories in the SF canon, dramatizes the power of electronic media to manipulate reality. The story is set a decade after a nuclear holocaust in an American culture attempting to rebuild. A political group uses a computerized newspaper, a "homeopape," to create a political revolutionary, Benny Cemoli, when it needs a charismatic figure to distract the attention of the authorities from the group's activities. The homeopape, a reactivated relic of the *New York Times,* prints daily editions describing the revolutionary activities of the nonexistent Benny Cemoli. Anyone in a position to look at the real situation is aware that "the newspaper had lost contact with actual events. The reality of the situation did not coincide with the *Times* articles in any way; that was obvious. And yet—the homeostatic system continued on."[16] The reality experienced by Peter Hood, one of the authorities, becomes a two-track tape of incongruity. There are the events he sees happening around him and the account of events printed in the paper. The two bear no resemblance. He is disturbed by the fact that the fictional accounts of the nonexistent Benny Cemoli's activities become more real than the actual political events. He realizes that "we are real only so long as the *Times* writes about us; as if we were dependent for our existence on it" (p. 325). The news media no longer describe the real world; they create it. The media images replace the actual.

These two short short stories, then, present companion ideas underlying many of Dick's novels. Technologies spawned by the war transform man into new, unexpected, and often ironic forms; and technologies through communication media create fictional realities more powerful than the real.

As Dick's fiction matures, epistemological questions begin to claim his attention and he invents new answers to questions such as, Is reality subjective or objective? Is there any way the brain can determine whether the reality it experiences is or is not spurious? Dick says his reading of Proust's *Remembrance of Things Past* when he was nineteen was a powerful influence in suggesting to him that truth lies within human minds and not in an objective world.[17] He is fascinated with the analogy between intelligent machines programmed to perform in a certain way and humans programmed with a certain view of reality.

In *Martian Time Slip* Dick suggests that most of society consumes a synthetic reality created by electronic media and drugs, a reality as desolate as the Martian landscape. If to be sane is to be adjusted to society, then perhaps insanity is to be preferred to the barren, consuming society whose only values are sensuous and materialistic. To allow oneself to be programmed by the establishment view of reality is to become a human machine; escape to mental illness is to struggle to remain human. Two characters in the novel, Jack Bohen, the electronic repairman, and Manfred, the autistic child he hopes to cure, dramatize Dick's view of schizophrenia, a view similar to that of R. D. Laing, for whom a withdrawal into self may be the wisest choice in an inhuman environment.[18] Jack's attacks of schizophrenia permit him occasional escape from the fictions he has been conditioned to accept as reality to the metaphorical truth underneath. Viewing the personnel manager in an electronics firm where he works, Jack suddenly sees through the skin to the bones and discovers that the bones are wired together, the organs replaced with plastic and stainless steel heart, lungs, and kidneys. The voice comes from a tape. Everything about the man is lifeless and mechanical. Later, in a similar attack, he watches the psychiatrist, Dr. Glaug, transform into a thing of cold wires and switches, a mechanical device with a programmed view of reality that he spiels to Jack.

Along with these mechanical humans who reveal their true nature only in the absolute reality of his transient insanity, Jack encounters an array of actual mechanical constructs, or simulacra, when he is called to repair the teaching machines at his son's school. The Angry Janitor, Thomas Edison, Kindly Daddy, Mark

Twain, Emperor Tiberius—all the right personnel and historical characters for a school setting, except that they are lifeless, mere programmed machines unable to give genuine responses to human students.

Jack's version of reality is the preferred narrative viewpoint; and his transient insanity, the wings lifting him above his wasteland labyrinth—the exploitive economic empire built by his boss, Arnie Kott. From the heights where he briefly ascends, Jack recognizes that the only authentic human is Heliogabalus, the Martian aborigine employed as Arnie Knott's houseboy. Because Heliogabalus is able to live with but remain impervious to economic exploitation and because he is able to express genuine feelings, he immediately establishes a wordless communication with Manfred. He can reverse his position and see from Manfred's point of view, a transformation Dick terms *empathy*. Empathy becomes the important starting point of Dick's humanistic value system.

Dick delights in irony and often provides a climactic episode that totally violates the reader's expectation. His technique is not literary trickery but philosophical assertions of the unexpected in the universe, social or cosmic. One such reversal full of impish horror is the scene in which Jack brings Manfred to school to meet the teaching machines. The reader shares Jack's expectation that the machines will affect Manfred, breaking into his prison of frozen silence and freeing him to respond. Quite the opposite occurs. Manfred remains voiceless; in contrast, the machines, electronically keyed to predetermined messages, are decimated by his presence into a chaos permitting only one word of response, repeated in a metallic voice: gubble, gubble.

Arnie Kott, dreamer of Martian economic domination in *Martian Time Slip*, devolves into Palmer Eldritch in Dick's next novel. Palmer, having succeeded as an interplanetary industrialist by producing an overabundance of consumer goods and distributing them to the wrong places, aspires to extend his power to galactic dimensions. He sets out to the Prox system to modernize autofacs along Terran lines. What returns ten years later is a devil with a metal face bearing "an evil, negative trinity of alienation, blurred reality, and despair."[19] Three stigmata signal the translation of former man into devil: a mechanical arm, stainless steel teeth, and artificial stainless steel eyes in his gaunt, hollowed-out, gray face.[20] A mechanized Red Riding Hood Wolf,[21] he is equipped to function like a machine of destruction: to see, manipulate, and devour the unsophisticated masses of little men.

Eldritch's transforming shapes as he gradually reveals himself to businessmen Leo Bulero and Barney Mayerson provide a map of Dick's evolving vision of reality manipulators. Eldritch first appears as a voice emanating from an "electronic contraption." The electronic contraption sprouts a handlike extension offering a smoking cigar filled with the drug brought back from Prox. Next, colored slides of the Prox system are offered (p.88). Eldritch in his real shape does not appear until two-thirds of the way into the novel, and even then he is first seen as a simulacrum.

Whatever Eldritch may be, he is not human (p. 223). Human eye, mouth, and hand have all been replaced with the mechanical. His mask, as Mayerson realizes, infiltrates the lives of all who see him (p. 181). Eldritch's power of manipulation creates a hallucination that the settlers accept as reality or an adequate substitute for reality. By the novel's end the outer appearances and inner awarenesses of the characters are transformed into a writhing, multiplying chaos of mechanical eyes and metal hands. The grinning metal devil is ubiquitous.

The Simulacra and *The Penultimate Truth* move from Mars back to Earth to study military dictatorship, economic exploitation, and bureaucratic manipulation. In each novel a simulacra serves as a figurehead president. The masses of little people, seeing them from a distance, mistakenly assume they are real. *The Simulacra* creates doubly inauthentic leaders: Nicole Thibodeaux, an actress trained to play the role of the matriarchal ruler, and her husband, der Alte, a simulacrum who is replaced every four years. Typical Dickian complexity of meaning abounds here. The hidden rulers, controlling from behind the scene, provide the public the appearance of a ruler, who mouths the words

of the scripts they write. The public gains the illusion of democratic process by being allowed to elect the ruler's husband every
four years, but he is in reality a mere machine. Electronic technology makes possible all these manipulations of reality whereby
the artificial and fake substitute for the authentic. In *The Penultimate Truth*, Stanton Brose, the hidden economic dictator, controls both the military and the government. President Talbot
Yancy, a simulacrum programmed to send phony video messages of hope to the mass of underground factory workers, is a
metaphor for the fantasy of honest government and earnest leaders. Script writers create presidents and manipulate masses.

In *Dr. Bloodmoney*, Dick has mastered the complex narrative
structure often obscuring the meaning in *Simulacra* and *Penultimate Truth*. The finest of his dystopian novels simulating the
postholocaust world, it ends not in despair but with the hope of
the homunculus Bill, born from the womb of a little girl. Children
bring the salvation of a regenerative vision, one freed from ma-
terialism. Dr. Bluthgeld, the mad scientist who created the bomb,
and Hoppy, the mad technologist and mutant life form spawned
by radiation, struggle for the power of world domination. Hoppy,
by the time he destroys Bluthgeld, has become as paranoid and
power-mad as the scientist. Dangerfield, a modern Everyman
encapsulated in his artificial mechanical environment, is first de-
flected from his course into endless circular orbit by Bluthgold's
bombs, then nearly killed by Hoppy's electronic invasion. In
Palmer Eldritch, an evil god with a metal face penetrated the
planetary system from outside and threatened every man. In *Dr.
Bloodmoney* a reversal occurs.

The killing, the slow destruction of Dangerfield, Bonny thought,
was deliberate, and it came—not from space, not from beyond—
but from below, from the familiar landscape. Dangerfield had not
died from the years of isolation; he had been stricken by careful
instruments issuing up from the very world which he struggled
to contact. If he could have cut himself off from us, she thought,
he would be alive now. At the very moment he listened to us,
received us, he was being killed—and did not guess.[22]

Man's alienation and despair, Dick now suggests, grow from the new settings and the new forms that his technology has spawned and the power to manipulate that they provide. Hoppy metaphors[23] the merging of the animate and the inanimate, a new life form seeded by the cross-pollination of science and technology. Dick explains,

The greatest change growing across our world these days is probably the momentum of the living towards reification, and at the same time a reciprocal entry into animation by the mechanical. We hold now no pure categories of the living versus the non-living; this is going to be our paradigm: My character, Hoppy.[24]

Dick's early robots were aliens sent by enemy forces to attack man. In his middle period the robot or simulacrum became the paradigm for the capitalist-fascist-bureaucratic structures locking the individual in a prison of false illusions created through electronic constructs. The technologist became a demonic artificer serving the devil of economic greed. In the fiction of the late sixties another spiral of evolution in his imagination moves Dick's alien from the outer space of the social realm to the inner world of the mind. The robot no longer walks wasteland streets or peers from videoscreens in electronic images; he haunts the human consciousness and stares out through a mask of flesh.[25] Dick has become aware, he tells us now, that "the greatest pain does not come down from a distant planet, but up from the depth of the human heart."[26] His attention moves to the human as a machine or android.

His Vancouver speech defines the characteristics of the android mind that separate it from the authentic human: a paucity of feeling, predictability, obedience, inability to make exceptions, and an inability to alter with circumstances to become something new.[27] In his last fiction exploring the mechanical, his earlier view of androids as artificial constructs masquerading as humans gives way to a view of androids as humans who become machines. Now robot and man have reversed roles. *Do Androids*

Dream of Electric Sheep? (1968) creates a metaphor for this process. *We Can Build You* was an earlier and unsuccessful attempt to portray the schizoid or machine man who has lost the ability to respond with genuine feelings.[28]

Read as a dramatization of inner space, *Do Androids Dream* merits recognition as one of Dick's finest novels, a view contrary to most of the current critical judgment. Stanislaw Lem in "Science Fiction: A Hopeless Case—With Exceptions" recognizes the novel as "not unimportant" but then dismisses it as disappointing because it does not offer unequivocal answers to the questions of internal logic that Dick raises.[29] But the point is Dick is picturing the inner world which is without the logical consistency that Lem demands. For Dick the clear line between hallucination and reality has itself become a hallucination. Man has a bimodal brain, or more precisely, according to Dick, two brains housed within the same skull. He recently applauded the research done in this area by Robert E. Ornstein at Stanford University but indicates he had not been aware of it when he wrote *Do Androids Dream*.[30]

Given its task of inner exploration, the novel discards the multiple-foci narrative technique of his previous novels and uses a single point of view. Superficially *Do Androids Dream* traces the adventures of policeman Rick Deckard, a bounty hunter who receives $1000 for each android he kills. The androids, now so sophisticated that they can scarcely be differentiated from humans, have been developed to serve as slave labor to the Luna colonists. Occasionally a few rebel and flee to Earth where they masquerade as humans and are hunted down and killed by men like Rick. Most of the population has gone into space to escape radiation-polluted Earth where almost no forms of life survive. Owning a living animal is a mark of status on Earth because they have become so expensive; many people must settle for cheaper electronic simulations, as does Rick. His dream is to accumulate enough money to buy a real sheep. His means to this end is killing androids.

This gestalt of action is a parable for Rick's inner journey as he discovers that he possesses both a rational and an intuitive self. Two plot lines metaphor the two selves: Rick is the intellectual, unfeeling self; he is the left hemisphere of the brain. John Isidore, the mutant with subnormal I.Q., is the intuitive self who empathizes with all forms; he is the right brain lobe. The novel sets up a series of opposites: people—things; subject—object; animate—inanimate; loving—killing; intuition—logic; human—machine. Double character sets abound; Rick Deckard and Phil Resch; Rachael Rosen and Pris Stratton, John Isidore and Wilbur Mercer. One can know only the penultimate truth; one is always a reflection away from reality and sees it as in a mirror. Thus the double characters mirror truths to each other. For Dick this encounter not of truth but only a reflection of truth is caught best in an image used by St. Paul, who speaks of seeing "as if by the reflection on the bottom of a polished metal pan."[31]

The complexity of structure and ideas in this rich novel points up the evolutionary process of the Dickian imagination in the fifteen years since the first short stories about robot warfare appeared. But the question for which Dick invents his array of answers is the same: What happens when man builds machines programmed to kill? The answer he fears is that man will become the machine that kills. This is what Rick Deckard learns about himself, that in pursuing the enemy android with a view to kill or be killed, he takes on the characteristics of the enemy and becomes an android. In one of the most powerful chapters of the novel (chapter 12) Rick encounters his double, android bounty-hunter Phil Resch, who enjoys killing. The mirror episode reflects to Rick the insight that he has become transformed into an android-killing machine.

The female androids Pris and Rachael both attract and repel Rick. Rachael is "the belle dame sans merci" who fascinates to destroy.[32] She makes love to Rick without loving because she, a mere machine, lacks emotional awareness and so is unable to empathize with others. She is, she realizes, not much different from an ant. She and her double, Pris, are mere "chitinous reflex-machines who aren't really alive."[33]

The secondary plot of the novel records the encounter of John Isidore, the subnormal chickenhead, with the androids. Contrary to Rick, who hunts androids to kill, John empathizes with them. He is a follower of Mercerism, and easily able to identify with every other living thing. Wilbur Mercer is a mysterious old man whose image on the black empathy box serves as a focus for the theological and moral system called Mercerism. Its followers unite through empathy, the energy capable of transporting the human mind through the mirror so that it unites with the opposite and sees from the reverse direction. Mercer, in a gentle endurance that transcends suffering as he endlessly toils up a barren hill, is reminiscent of Albert Camus' Sisyphus. John Isidore, grasping the handles of the black empathy box, undergoes a crossing-over, a physical merging with others accompanied by mental and spiritual identification, as happens

for everyone who at this moment clutched the handles, either here on Earth or on one of the colony planets. He experienced them, the others, incorporated the babble of their thoughts, heard in his own brain the noise of their many individual existences. They—and he—cared about one thing; this fusion of their mentalities oriented their attention on the hill, the climb, the need to ascend. Step by step it evolved, so slowly as to be nearly imperceptible. But it was there. Higher, he thought as stones rattled downward under his feet. Today we are higher than yesterday, and tomorrow—he, the compound figure of Wilbur Mercer, glanced up to view the ascent ahead. Impossible to make out the end. Too far. But it would come (pp. 21–22).

The novel mushrooms with a pyrotechnic display of self-negating inventions. Rick's lovemaking with the android Rachael Rosen—an act of identification with the other—explodes his will to kill into nauseated rejection of his work. But threatened by Rachael's double, Pris, carrying a laser gun, he kills and thus violates his newly found identity. He is instructed by Wilbur Mercer about this curse of man:

You will be required to do wrong no matter where you go. It is the basic condition of life, to be required to violate your own identity. At some time, every creature which lives must do so. It is the ultimate shadow, the defeat of creation; this is the curse at work, the curse that feeds on all life. Everywhere in the universe (p. 119).

Reversals and negations like Rick's in loving and killing are compounded throughout the novel. Mercer, the mystic, turns out to be a fake, not a religious leader but an alcoholic has-been actor. The real toad Rick discovers on his desert journey and cherishes as an omen of spiritual rebirth turns out to be an electric one. What does it all mean? Rick's final insight answers the question: "Everything is true, everything anybody has ever thought" (p. 149). He could as well have said everything is false. It all depends on the direction from which you view "reality." Language limits because the statement can encompass only one view at a time. Thus irony provides the only escape from language through language; irony contains a negation of the assertion. Given Dick's view of a puzzling, undefined, metamorphosing cosmos, irony is essential to him in creating his fictional worlds mirroring that view.

How does one survive in this universe of uncertainty where everything is both true and false? Like John Isidore, one empathizes with and responds to the needs of all forms, blinding one's eyes to the inauthentic division between living and nonliving, machine and man. Like the shadowy Wilbur Mercer, one endlessly climbs up, suffering the wounds of rocks mysteriously thrown and never reaching a destination. Mercer's hill mirrors Sisyphus's fate, his rocks the stones of martyred Stephen, his empathy the forgiving, uniting love of Christ.

Only when the divisions Dick has mirrored in the novel are healed by an inner unity growing from an acceptance of all things will artificiality be replaced by authentic existence. If you hold the nineteenth-century view of yourself as a unique concrete thing, says Dick, you can never merge with the noosphere. The left-hemisphere brain, the isolating android intellect, must merge with the right-hemisphere brain, the collective intuition we all share. Its dream images, if we will listen, partake of the creative power that can transform us from mere machines into authentic humans.

At the same time that he was writing *Do Androids Dream*, Dick created one of the greatest short stories in all literature exploring man's perception of himself as a machine, "The Electric Ant." It contains all the lightning inventiveness and the abrupt yoking of the impossible in calm ironic understatement that shocks the reader into a new way of seeing. This is Dick's literary genius: his metaphorical brilliance, a gift lying closer to the art of the poet than of the traditional novelist.

"The Electric Ant" [34] is an example of the qualities in Dick's writing that remind his critics of Franz Kafka. One thinks immediately of "The Metamorphosis," in which the first sentence matter-of-factly announces that Gregor Samsa awoke one morning from uneasy dreams to find himself transformed into a gigantic insect. Similarly in "The Electric Ant" Garson Poole awakes in his hospital bed after an accident that amputated his right hand and discovers that he is not a man but a robot. His skin covers not flesh and blood but wires, circuits, and miniature components. The objective, restrained prose describing the metamorphosis of Poole's self-image from that of a free human agent to a programmed machine lies in awful tension with the emotional intensity of the event and gives the story its terrible power. All the issues raised by the philosophy of mechanism are metaphored here. Is man only bits of matter, controlled by the laws of physics governing inanimate matter? If so, then man's cherished free will is nothing but an illusion. How can man ever know true reality if his perceptions of himself and the world around him turn out to be unreliable? My summary comments are the language of philosophical abstraction: Dick's language is the metaphor of the particular. Listen to Garson Poole after his discovery that he is a mere robot utilized by Tri-Plan Electronics Corporation.

Christ, he thought, it undermines you, knowing this. I'm a freak, he realized. An inanimate object mimicking an animate one.

But—he felt alive. Yet . . . he felt differently, now. About himself. Programmed. In me somewhere, he thought, there is a matrix fitted in place, a grid screen that cuts me off from certain thoughts, certain actions. And forces me into others. I am not free. I never was, but now I know it; that makes it different (p. 399).

Having discovered that he is a machine with a programmed "reality" tape, Poole next realizes that this insight gives him the option of altering his tape. He thinks, "If I control my reality tape, I control reality. At least so far as I am concerned. My subjective reality . . . but that's all there is. Objective reality is a synthetic construct, dealing with a hypothetical universalization of a multitude of subjective realities" (p. 401).

The critical difference for Poole is the knowledge of his robotic state, a fact that forever alters his consciousness of himself. The reader who participates in Dick's creative process is also released to a new awareness: he knows his reality tape is a subjective fiction that he has written just as certainly as is Dick's story.

When the reader ceases his labyrinthian journey through Dick's phantasmagoric worlds of evolving intelligence, human and artificial, he knows that he has not escaped the puzzling trap of consciousness. He reaches no conclusions, realizes there are none, and now perhaps he is willing to settle for a peaceful, exhilirating delight at being lost in the metaphorical maze of Dick's and his own imaginations. He shares his guide's awareness that nothing can be preserved, either by machines or by man. Dick's most recent words interrupt but do not conclude the process of his awareness.

We humans, the warm-faced and tender, with thoughtful eyes— we are perhaps the true machines. And those objective constructs, the natural objects around us and especially the electronic hardware we build, the transmitters and microwave relay stations, the satellites, they may be cloaks for authentic living reality inasmuch as they may participate more fully and in a way obscured to us in the ultimate Mind. Perhaps we see not only a deforming veil, but backwards. Perhaps the closest approximation to truth would be to say: "Everything is equally alive, equally free, equally sentient, because everything is not alive or half-alive or dead, but rather *lived through*.[35]

What future will unfold for artificial intelligence? Will it increasingly assume and perhaps eventually subsume human intelligence? What of the human brain's capacity to dream, to throw up fireworks of possibility lying outside mundane reality? Will machine intelligence achieve that gift, too? What is the answer to Dick's question, Do androids dream of electric sheep? Dick, according to his own philosophy, would want the reader to accept only the answer he discovers as he looks in the mirror of the fiction and sees his own awareness reflected back. But the reader can also be certain of his answer. Yes, as each form contains within itself the shadow image of the potential forms that seed its inevitable transformation, so androids also dream.

Conclusion

Some Critical Questions and Speculations

How am I to answer the questions asked at the beginning of this study? Has SF moved beyond entertainment to become literature? Has it accomplished the task of mythmaking as literature traditionally has done in earlier cultures? Does it reveal a vision of the universe and suggest man's role in that vision? I can answer tentatively: Yes, but . . . .

The finest of the cybernetic tales transform the traditional image of man as earthbound; transcending his earlier limitations, he becomes a questor among the stars. A trinity of images mirrors this new vision. The spaceship metaphors the escape from earth to the heavens. Inventive intelligence created the design and the artifice of the machine implements it. The robot metaphors this union of mind and machine. Fire is the third image, the fire thrusting the ship into outer space as the fire of the imagination thrusts the mind into new inner spaces.

These SF myths creating a new image of man mushroom from archetypal forms appearing in Greek culture as the Prometheus and Daedalus myths. Prometheus's gift of fire, the magic of the gods that creates and transforms, metaphors man's transforming intelligence. Mary Shelley first used the myth. In cybernetic SF her chemist uses his knowledge to create biological intelligence and becomes the engineer who builds machine intelligence. The fabulation of the myth suggesting that man's computers are the next step in the evolution of intelligence in the universe is one of the most creative acts of cybernetic SF. It is original in asking us to transform our definition of intelligence, to extend it to include what we have regarded as inanimate, to consider that alien intelligence in the universe might be in this form. The theory of chemical biogenesis has led us to recognize the real probability that forms of intelligence exist elsewhere in the universe. SF has been the avant garde literature in proposing this idea, and alien machine intelligence is a part of the concept.

Two elements of the Daedalus myth fascinate the SF imagination: man's need to escape the labyrinth of the present reality in which he finds himself trapped, and the potential of mechanical inventions to make his escape possible. Daedalus, flying to freedom, splits into a complementary vision—the wise old artificer who succeeds and the impetuous son who attempts too much and falls to destruction. The Daedalus myth is often retold in SF.

Unfortunately too few of the tales in the canon of cybernetic SF achieve a distinction meriting their designation as literature, and the best stories tend to have occurred in the first rather than the last half of the forty-eight-year period from 1930 to 1978. With too few exceptions, the fiction gives no evidence that it is aware of information theory or computer technology. It is almost atavistic in its attitude toward cybernetic automata. Alfred Chapius in *The History of Automata* suggests three separate stages in the history of automata: the age of Gods, the age of men, and the age of machines. The ancients believed in the divinity of certain moving statues; the seventeenth and eighteenth centuries wanted to make automata in human form; and in our age we want the robot to have practical value. But the SF about computers often unexpectedly gives the machine supernatural characteristics and turns it into a god, a surprising throwback to the attitude of the ancients. The portrayal of computer technology is too often inaccurate and distorted, and computer applications are not anticipated. How is this failure of the imagination in cybernetic SF to be explained? Not easily, nor accurately, of course. I am exploring a complex phenomenon and a large body of material. But a few tentative possibilities can be suggested and a few questions raised that seem worthy of further investigation.

First, that remarkable mathematician, Norbert Wiener, who had both a brilliant mind and an unusual social sensitivity, had a far-reaching influence. Works such as *Cybernetics* (1948) and *The Human Use of Human Beings* (1950) made lucid, nonmathematical, comprehensive statements about the theory of control in man and machines and the social implications of computer development early in the development of the field. Weiner was truly prophetic in his vision and he was widely read by workers in the field of computer science. Possibly there was less left for the SF writer to say because Wiener had said it first and said it so well.

There are other possibilities that seem more likely, although Wiener's influence cannot be disregarded. World War II created intellectual and cultural shocks whose vibrations still affect society. Some of them may be influencing the quality, character, and timeliness of SF. Is it possible that the shroud of secrecy covering research related to the military before, during, and after the war has made it almost impossible for the writer to stay abreast of the most recent developments in science and technology? The first substantial research and development on the computer was done for the military during the war and was top secret, as was the later development of the SAGE and NORAD systems. The secrecy of scientific research is a problem that late nineteenth- and early twentieth-century writers of SF did not face.

Consider another factor that may influence the quality of recent SF. Is it possible that contemporary science and technology have become too complicated to portray with visual imagery? The theory of information is a long distance from the theory of evolution. One requires mathematical modeling; the other uses layman's language and images for its expression. Modern theories of physical reality use mathematical language; concrete models like the billiard ball model of gases or the planetary model of atoms are no longer functional. Miniaturized electronic circuitry hardly allows the possibility for imaginative literary responses offered by the long view of time stretching back to primitive life emerging from a colloidal soup or by the far-reaching picture of the starry heavens filled with endless galaxies.

Is it possible that the complex, technical nature of the material in computer science and the incredible speed of developments in the field make it impossible for the literary imagination to keep abreast of the material? The age of science today is the age of specialization, a situation that did not exist until well into the twentieth century, and certainly not when SF originated. It is impossible to write *science* fiction without knowing science; given the knowledge explosion, that is a demanding accomplishment.

As we move to large systems views of the world, will the literary imagination find it increasingly difficult to transpose those systems to the materials of fiction—specific people in specific settings experiencing particular events? Communication networks have linked nations; the word of an event is spread through the world immediately, and so it has an impact around the world. One cannot avoid thinking in terms of large systems because the world is turning into a single system. How is that reality to be dealt with in fiction?

While all these factors have been influences in the large amount of disappointing SF, a more fundamental cause may well be the closed-system model from which the dystopian imagination seems to work and the concomitant technique of invention by extrapolation. The resultant metaphors are not new but produced merely by magnifying certain aspects of existing society. They are examined with horror in the fiction and then violently smashed. In cybernetic fiction the computer is the target. Smashing the computer is rather like staring at a pimple on one's face under a magnifying glass and finding it so distressing that one decides to blow up the pimple, forgetting that it is attached to one's face. Creativity does not seem to proceed by the magnifying device of extrapolation. In that mode a necessary connection between present and future determines the possibility even before one arrives at it.

In contrast is the small body of excellent SF working from an open-system model. It seems to perceive the human organism, the social organism, the earth, and even the universe as an indeterminate system in which unexpected change occurs. It is an

expanding, infinite system in which transcendence is always possible. The journey of the imagination in this expanding universe
is made through speculative jumps, not extrapolations.

The lover of SF is disappointed with the quality and content
of much cybernetic fiction. The genre has held so much promise.
It has seemed to offer the first really workable mediation between
the humanities and the sciences, a slender span that might model
a means of breaching the two-culture gap. But it can mediate
only if it is willing to immerse itself in both humanistic values
and scientific knowledge. And in the field of cybernetic SF that
knowledge must be basic physics and mathematics, information
theory, and computer technology.

We need to remind ourselves constantly that science and
poetry are not separate universes; the working of the scientific
imagination and the literary imagination parallel each other. Arthur Koestler in *The Act of Creation* notes that a sense of wonder
is shared by poet and scientist. The scientist wonders about a
great many things, which at first may be but superficial problems;
then he advances to more perplexing problems. After much puzzling, he creates a hypothesis. Thus the approach of the scientist
is remarkably like that of the SF writer. The scientist begins, "Let
us suppose that . . ." or "Let us imagine that . . . ." Having
made his supposition, the scientist then sets out to test it by
mathematical or experimental proof. He thus ties his speculative
thinking to reality. In *Imagination and the Growth of Science* (1967)
A. M. Taylor maintains that "to a remarkable degree the growth
of science has depended on the scientist's faculty of mental imagery, of making, as it were, models to simulate the behavior of
the observable world."[1]

SF can unite the prescientific consciousness of childhood with
the logic of scientific thought. Here the poet's sense of wonder
and delight joins the scientist's need for logic and proof. The
poet's invention of images represents the daydreaming activity
necessary to every man; the inner fire of his imagination must
shimmer, dance, and burn if his intellect is to remain alive, for
life is motion, process, change. As Gaston Bachelard reminds us

in *The Psychoanalysis of Fire,* childhood is a basic archetypal value; the sense of wonder with which a child discovers realities for the first time has a potency vital to a creative adult life. The poet, meditating and daydreaming, creates new poetic images, images carrying with them archetypal truths reawakening us to the universe of childhood.

The SF writer can keep that sense of wonder alive, for he is the poet of science. His is the fire of the imagination, consuming old images of reality, igniting new possibilities. Every man needs occasionally to sit down by that fire, gaze quietly into it, let its heat and light transform his mind. He will leave such mental fire gazing with his own imagination rekindled.

SF has the potential for giving us mental images of the future—that world not yet observable—that can serve as guides in directing our course. Most of those ideas about the future will not be productive. But new ideas are to the evolution of thought what mutations are to the biological process. Most are harmless and disappear, but a few survive, take root, and produce change. We need the kind of imagination that is able to dive into the unconscious and the unknown, to bring to the light of our awareness an array of future dreams. However, the future we are moving into will be built on scientific concepts and technological innovations. That trend seems inevitable. If the SF imagination hopes to have any influence in shaping the future, it cannot ignore the development and direction of science and technology in the present world. As the good scientist verifies his hypothesis by testing, so the good writer of SF needs to test his future models against the reality of what is known in science. If what is known negates the possibility of ever arriving at his future, his imaginary world can offer the reader nothing more than escapist entertainment. Too many of the writers of cybernetic SF have ignored this requirement of grounding their work in science. The resultant fiction is depressing, reactionary, even ridiculous to those whose knowledge of the computer is not totally naive. In no way does it uphold the claim of SF that it prepares the reader to understand and accept change. When SF no longer anticipates the future, but lags behind the present, the death of the genre may be at hand.

If SF is to remain equal to or exceed its greatest achievements, it must grow with science; it cannot react against science and still be *science* fiction. Perhaps a new category—*futuristic* fiction—is needed, less supernatural than fantastic fiction, but less rigorously grounded in science than SF. Writers working primarily from a base in the humanities and social sciences but not interested in the demanding task of educating themselves in science could work in this subgenre. *Science* fiction could continue as a mode for the writer who is willing to master the underlying scientific concepts of a field before he begins to play imaginatively with its future possibilities. Our present culture is shaped by science; the future will be even more deeply grounded in and formed by science. SF that is antiscientific in its attitude or ignores science as it models the future will be, except by the mere chance of lucky speculation, nothing more than entertainment and escapist reading. In contrast, the literary imagination that immerses itself in science before and during its imaginative leap may provide genuinely creative insights that will lead us, intelligently and humanely, into our future.

Notes

Notes to Introduction

1. Darko Suvin, "On the Poetics of the Science Fiction Genre," *College English* 34 (December 1972): 380–381.

Notes to Chapter 1

1. Marjorie Nicolson, *Science and Imagination*, pp. 3, 47–48, 81.

2. Ibid., pp. 194–195.

3. Erwin Schrödinger, *Science and Humanism*, p. 26.

4. Rollo May, *The Courage to Create*, p. 36.

5. Kenneth E. Boulding, *The Image*.

6. Ibid., pp. 5–7.

7. Norbert Wiener, "Cybernetics," *Scientific American*, November 1948. Reprinted in *Mathematics in the Modern World: Readings from Scientific American* (San Francisco: W. H. Freeman & Co., 1968), p. 378.

8. Plato, *Republic* I, 264 B; A. M. Ampere, *Essay on the Philosophy of Science*, 1838; J. C. Maxwell, *Proceedings of the Royal Society* 16 (London, 1868): 270–283.

9. Norbert Wiener, *The Human Use of Human Beings: Cybernetics and Society*, p. 24.

10. Bertram Raphael, *The Thinking Computer*, p. 5.

11. Three good sources to consult for an in-depth study of artificial intelligence are Edward Feigenbaum and Julian Feldman, eds., *Computers and Thought*; Philip C. Jackson, Jr., *Introduction to Artificial Intelligence*; Leonard Uhr, *Pattern Recognition, Learning, and Thought*.

12. For a good overview of the status of robot development today see Carl Sagan, "In Praise of Robots." See also James S. Albus and J. M. Evans, Jr., "Robot Systems," *Scientific American*, February 1976, pp. 76–86.

13. Saul Rosen, "Electronic Computers." Nigel Hawkes's *The Computer Revolution* contains a good history of computers.

14. Ludwig von Bertalanffy, *Robots, Men, and Minds*, p. 64.

15. Ervin Laszlo, *Introduction to Systems Philosophy*, p. 12.

16. For a good discussion of man as a machine, see Jacob Bronowski, *The Identity of Man*, or Dean E. Wooldridge, *Mechanical Man*.

17. Two of the most thorough studies are C. C. Gotlieb and A. Borodin, *Social Issues in Computing*, and James Martin and Adrian R. D. Norman, *The Computerized Society*.

18. Joseph Weizenbaum, *Computer Power and Human Reason*, pp. 232–234.

19. Paul Armer, "The Individual," p. 20.

20. Stanislaw Lem, "Robots in Science Fiction," p. 320.

21. Keith Gunderson, *Mentality and Machines*, p. 16.

22. Ibid., pp. 27–29.

23. See, for instance, Hurbert Dreyfus's *What Computers Can't Do*, Alan Ross Anderson's *Minds and Machines*, and Stanley L. Jaki's *Brain, Mind, and Computers*.

Notes to Chapter 2

1. Edith Hamilton, *Mythology* (Boston: Little, Brown and Co., 1943), pp. 77–94. Miss Hamilton draws on the accounts in Hesiod, Aeschylus, Aristophanes, Pausanias, and Horace.

2. Ihab Hassan, *Paracriticisms*. In "A Digression of Prometheus" (pp. 127–131) Hassan surveys the various figures and fables of Prometheus that have appeared in literature. He cites Hesiod, Aeschylus, Goethe, Percy and Mary Shelley, and the contemporary physicist Gerald Feinberg. Hassan notes that Prometheus's name means foresight, one who looks ahead. "A natural trickster, he represents the creative principle of intelligence, creative yet essentially flawed because it is ignorant of its limit, its purpose" (p. 127).

3. Derek de Solla Price, "Automata and the Origins of Mechanism and Mechanistic Philosophy," in *Science Since Babylon*, p. 50.

4. John Cohen, *Human Robots in Myth and Science*, pp. 15–17.

5. Price, *Science Since Babylon*, p. 55.

6. Ibid., p. 31.

7. Cohen, *Human Robots in Myth and Science*, p. 30.

8. Ibid., p. 33.

9. John Cohen, "Human Robots and Computer Art," *History Today*, August 1970, pp. 559–560.

10. Cohen, *Human Robots in Myth and Science*, p. 43.

11. Robert Plank, "The Golem and the Robot," pp. 13–14. Also see "Genesis

II: The Evolution of Synthetic Man," by Harry M. Geduld in *Robots, Robots, Robots,* ed. Harry M. Geduld and Ronald Gottesman, pp. 5–11.

12. J. W. Smeed, *Faust in Literature,* p. 13.

13. St. Augustine, *The Confessions,* Book V.

14. *Encyclopedia of Philosophy* (New York: Macmillan Co., 1967).

15. Cohen, *Human Robots in Myth and Science,* p. 86.

16. Paul M. Abrahm and Stuart Kenter, "Tik-Tok and the Three Laws of Robotics," *Science-Fiction Studies* 5 (March 1978): 67–80. This essay suggests that L. Frank Baum's robot Tik-Tok embodied Asimov's Three Laws over two and a half decades before *I, Robot.*

17. Letter from Asimov, January 30, 1978.

18. Conversation with Engelbarger, November 7, 1978.

19. A comprehensive listing of films about robots can be found in Geduld and Gottesman's *Robots, Robots, Robots,* pp. 241–246.

20. See Aija Ozolins, "Recent Works on Mary Shelley and *Frankenstein.*" This article provides a comprehensive review of critical works on *Frankenstein.* Among the most helpful are Christopher Small's *Mary Shelley's Frankenstein,* Martin Tropp's *Mary Shelley's Monster,* and William A. Walling's *Mary Shelley.*

21. Tropp, *Mary Shelley's Monster,* p. 53. Tropp notes that Mary Shelley might well have encountered E. T. A. Hoffmann's short stories "Automatons" (1812) and "The Sandman" (1814), two German tales dealing with clockwork dolls that simulate life.

22. Mary Shelley, *Frankenstein: or, the Modern Prometheus* (New York: Collier Books, 1961), p. 10.

23. Small, *Mary Shelley's Frankenstein,* p. 258.

24. Hassan, *Paracriticisms,* p. 131.

25. P. Morrison and E. Morrison, *Charles Babbage and his Calculating Engines,* p. 121.

26. *The Complete Tales and Poems of Edgar Allen Poe* (New York: Modern Library, 1938), p. 423.

27. In *Science-Fiction Thinking Machines,* ed. Groff Conklin (New York: Vanguard Press, 1954), p. 8.

28. Samuel Butler, *Erewhon and Erewhon Revisited* (New York: Modern Library, 1927), pp. 231, 232, 234.

29. Herbert L. Sussman, *Victorians and the Machine* (Cambridge, Mass.: Harvard U. Press, 1968), pp. 138, 140.

30. Ibid., p. 155.

31. E. M. Forster, "The Machine Stops," in *Classics of Modern Fiction* (New York: Harcourt Brace Jovanovich, 1972), p. 241.

32. Ibid., p. 246.

33. Ibid., p. 258.

34. Mark R. Hillegas, *The Future as Nightmare*, p. 69.

35. Ibid., p. 102.

36. For a comprehensive treatment of this aspect of *We*, see Carolyn H. Rhodes's "Frederick Winslow Taylor's System of Scientific Management in Zamiatin's *We*."

37. The influence of Dostoevsky is examined in Patricia Warrick's "The Sources of Zamiatin's *We* in Dostoevsky's *Notes from the Underground*," *Extrapolation* 17 (December 1975): 63-77.

38. Hillegas, *The Future as Nightmare*, p. 83.

39. Quoted in Ibid., p. 96.

Notes to Chapter 3

1. Sam Moskowitz, *Seekers of Tomorrow*, p. 42.

2. "Robbie" first appeared in *Super Science,* September 1940, under the title "Strange Playfellow." Vincent's "Rex" was published in *Astounding,* June 1934; del Rey's "Helen O'Loy" in *Astounding,* December 1938; Binder's "I, Robot" in *Amazing,* January 1939. "I, Robot" was the first of ten robot stories that Binder wrote between 1939 and 1942, all featuring the robot Adam Link. Seven of the stories were collected and published under the title *Adam Link— Robot* in 1965. Binder's is the first series of robot stories to be written from the robot's point of view. The name Eando Binder was used by Earl and Otto Binder when they collaborated on stories. Earl dropped out of the collaboration about 1940.

3. Letter from Asimov, September 23, 1976.

4. Letter from Frederik Pohl, September 14, 1978.

5. Isaac Asimov, "On Computers," *DP Solutions*, April 1975, p. 2.

6. Isaac Asimov, "Prediction as a Side Effect," *Boston Review of the Arts*, July 1972.

7. Isaac Asimov, "That Thou Art Mindful of Him," in *The Bicentennial Man* (Garden City, N.Y.: Doubleday & Co., 1976), p. 67.

8. The name is clearly derived from Marvin Minsky of MIT, a longtime friend of Asimov's, who is more enthusiastic about the possibility of duplicating human intelligence than almost any other researcher in the field of artificial intelligence.

9. Joseph F. Patrouch, Jr., *The Science Fiction of Isaac Asimov*, p. 42.

10. Philip C. Jackson, Jr., *Introduction to Artificial Intelligence*, p. 396. Also see Bertram Raphael, *The Thinking Computer*, p. 249.

11. Asimov, "Prediction as a Side Effect."

12. *The Rest of the Robots* (New York: Pyramid, 1964), p. 51.

13. Isaac Asimov, *I, Robot* (New York: Gnome, 1950), p. 169.

14. "The Life and Times of Multivac," in *The Bicentennial Man*, p. 118.

15. *The Caves of Steel* (Greenwich, Conn.: Fawcett Crest, 1953), p. 48.

16. "Feminine Intuition," in *The Bicentennial Man*, p. 9.

17. "That Thou Art Mindful of Him," in *The Bicentennial Man*, p. 83.

18. See "The Myth of the Machine," by Asimov, in *SF: Contemporary Mythology*, eds. Patricia Warrick, M. Greenberg, and J. Olander. In this essay Asimov expresses a similar view of machine intelligence.

19. "The Bicentennial Man," in *The Bicentennial Man*, p. 152.

20. William James, "The Scope of Psychology," in *The Nature of Human Consciousness*, ed. Robert E. Ornstein, pp. 7–12.

21. J. B. Watson, *Psychological Review* 20 (1913): 158–167.

22. Thomas S. Kuhn, *The Structure of Scientific Revolutions*, viii.

23. A comprehensive discussion of the physical basis of intelligent life can be found in Dean E. Wooldridge's *Mechanical Man*.

24. Ibid., p. 183.

25. Robert E. Ornstein, *The Psychology of Consciousness*, pp. 51–52.

26. Pratima Bowes, *Consciousness and Freedom*, p. 217.

27. Louis de Broglie, "The Philosophical Meaning and Practical Consequences of Cybernetics"; Erwin Schrödinger, *What Is Life?*

28. Schrödinger, *What Is Life?*, p. 102.

29. Ibid., p. 107.

30. Arthur Koestler, *The Ghost in the Machine*, p. 205.

31. Gregory Bateson, *Steps to an Ecology of Mind*, p. 444.

Notes to Chapter 4

1. Robert Scholes, *Structural Fabulation*, pp. 7, 42.

2. Quoted in Darko Suvin, "On the Poetics of the Science Fiction Genre," p. 374. Suvin expands his discussion in the first chapter, "Poetics," of his *Metamorphoses of Science Fiction*.

3. Ibid., p. 375.

4. Joanna Russ, "Towards an Aesthetic of Science Fiction," p. 112.

5. Damon Knight calls this feeling of awe a "sense of wonder" in his *In Search of Wonder*.

6. Russ, "Towards an Aesthetic," p. 113.

7. Werner Heisenberg, *Across the Frontiers*, p. 148.

8. Ibid., p. 150.

9. Ibid., p. 146.

10. Isaac Asimov comments that the demands of creating a convincing and scientifically plausible setting make science fiction the most difficult of all forms of writing. See "*ALGOL* Interview: Isaac Asimov," by Darrell Schweitzer, *ALGOL* 14 (Winter 1977): 22-26.

11. Arthur Koestler, *The Ghost in the Machine*, p. 183.

12. Ihab Hassan, "Beyond Arcadians and Technophiles: New Convergences in Culture?" pp. 17-18.

13. Heisenberg, "The Meaning of Beauty in the Exact Sciences," in *Across the Frontiers*, pp. 174-178.

14. Clausius's second law of thermodynamics asserts that the universe is running down like a clockwork because its energy is being steadily and inexorably degraded, dissipated into heat.

15. Ludwig von Bertalanffy, *General System Theory*, p. 93.

16. Ervin Laszlo, *A Strategy for the Future*, p. 117.

17. J. Bronowski, *The Common Sense of Science*, p. 26.

18. Ibid., p. 46.

19. Ibid., p. 63.

20. A. M. Taylor, *Imagination and the Growth of Science*, pp. 39-56.

21. Bertalanffy, *General System Theory*, p. 39.

22. Schrödinger, *What is Life?*, p. 76.

23. See chapters 3 and 4 of Ervin Laszlo's *Introduction to Systems Philosophy* for a clear presentation of multilevel hierarchies.

24. J. O. Bailey, *Pilgrims through Space and Time*, p. 262.

Notes to Chapter 5

1. Sam Moskowitz, ed., *The Coming of the Robots*, p. 13.

2. Other Campbell robot and computer stories are "The Metal Horde" (1930), "Twilight" (1934), "The Machine" (1935), *The Mightiest Machine* (1935).

3. Loren Eiseley, *The Firmament of Time*, p. 16.

4. Lester del Rey, "Though Dreamers Die" in *The Robot and the Man*, ed. Martin Greenberg (New York: Gnome Press, 1953), p. 183.

5. Lester del Rey, *Early del Rey* (Garden City, N.Y.: Doubleday & Co., 1975), p. 281.

6. Harry Bates, "Farewell to the Master," in *Famous Science Fiction Stories*, ed. Raymond J. Healy and J. Francis McComas (New York: Modern Library, 1946), p. 783.

7. Roger Zelazny, "For a Breath I Tarry," in *Modern Science Fiction*, ed. Norman Spinrad (New York: Anchor Press, 1974), p. 369.

8. Isaac Asimov, "The Machine and the Robot," in *Science Fiction: Contemporary Mythology*, ed. Patricia Warrick, M. Greenberg, and J. Olander, p. 253.

9. Marvin Minsky, "Computer Science and the Representation of Knowledge."

10. Christopher Anvil, "The Hunch," *Analog Science Fact & Fiction*, July 1961, p. 82.

11. A more recent work presenting a thorough study of the use of the computer in war games is Andrew Wilson's *The Bomb and the Computer*.

12. Claude E. Shannon, "A Chess-Playing Machine," p. 104.

13. Ibid, pp. 105–107.

14. *Analog* (April 1977), in a brief biographical note on science fiction writer George R. R. Martin, comments on his August 1972 article "The Computer Was a Fish" in *Analog*. In that article Martin, a class A chess player, treated factually the same achievements of computer intelligence portrayed in Lieber's story.

15. James Martin and Adrian R. D. Norman, *The Computerized Society*, p. 49.

16. Stanley Rothman and Charles Mosman, *Computers and Society*, pp. 247–248.

17. Edmund Berkeley and Lawrence Wainwright, *Computers: Their Operation and Applications* (New York: Reinhold Publishing, 1956), p. 291.

18. Martin and Norman, *Computerized Society*, p. 164.

19. Donn B. Parker, *Crime by Computer*, p. 11.

20. Joseph Weizenbaum, *Computer Power and Human Reason*, pp. 3–4.

21. Charles Beaumont's "Last Rites" (1955) is another excellent story about a priest who is a robot.

Notes to Chapter 6

1. Leonardo De Vinci had earlier proposed that through mechanical inventions nature could be controlled and made to serve man.

2. Frank E. Manuel, ed., *Utopias and Utopian Thought*, and Lewis Mumford,

The Story of Utopias, both contain good discussions of the utopian tradition and literature.

3. Jack Williamson's *H. G. Wells: Critic of Progress* is a thorough study of Wells's early dystopian fiction.

4. Actually, the glass-domed city is an image that Zamiatin seems to have borrowed from H. G. Wells's *When the Sleeper Wakes.*

5. Quoted in Arthur Koestler, *The Sleepwalkers,* p. 503.

6. Ibid., pp. 525–526.

7. Chad Walsh, *From Utopia to Nightmare,* p. 136.

8. Kurt Vonnegut, *Player Piano* (New York: Avon, 1952), p. 169.

9. David Ketterer, *New Worlds for Old,* p. 126.

10. Norbert Wiener, *Cybernetics,* p. 25.

11. Bernard Wolfe, *Limbo* (New York: Ace Books, 1952), p. 52.

12. Jack Williamson, "With Folded Hands," in *The Science Fiction Hall of Fame,* ed. Ben Bova (Garden City, N.Y.: Doubleday & Co., 1973), p. 513.

13. Olof Johannesson is the pseudonym of Hannes Alfven, a Swedish cosmologist.

14. Olof Johannesson, *The End of Man?* (New York: Award Books, 1966), p. 19.

15. Norbert Wiener, *God and Golem, Inc.,* chaps. 4, 5. John G. Kemeny, *Man and the Computer,* chaps. 5, 6.

16. J. Bronowski, *The Ascent of Man,* p. 334.

17. Isaac Asimov, "Social Science Fiction," pp. 285–290.

18. Marshall D. Sahlins, "Notes on the Original Affluent Society," pp. 85–86.

19. Arthur Koestler, *The Ghost in the Machine,* p. 48.

20. Ibid.

21. Alexandre Koyre, *From the Closed World to the Infinite Universe,* p. 6.

22. Fred Polak, *The Image of the Future,* pp. 15–16.

23. Ibid., pp. 192, 22.

24. Oscar Wilde, "The Soul of Man under Socialism," in *The Works of Oscar Wilde,* vol. 8. (New York: Lamb Publishing Co., 1909), p. 148.

Notes to Chapter 7

1. Ira M. Freeman, *Physics,* pp. 548–549.

2. See Ludwig von Bertalanffy, "The Theory of Open Systems in Physics and Biology," pp. 23–29.

3. K. G. Kenbigh, *An Inventive Universe*, p. 163.

4. Arthur C. Clarke, *The City and the Stars* (New York: Signet, 1956), preface.

5. For an interesting reading of *The City and the Stars* as a dramatization of the pastoral-urban conflict in human history, see pp. 216–221 of William Irwin Thompson's *At the Edge of History*.

6. See Jacques Monod, *Chance and Necessity*, pp. 193–196, for a good summary explanation of DNA and the genetic code.

7. Alexei Panshin, *Heinlein in Dimension*, p. 118.

8. Samuel R. Delany, *Nova* (Garden City, N.Y.: Doubleday & Co., 1968), p. 52. Subsequent references are to this edition.

9. Samuel R. Delany, *The Einstein Intersection* (New York: Ace Books, 1967), p. 128.

10. Darrell Schweitzer, "*ALGOL* Interview: Samuel R. Delany," *ALGOL*, Summer 1976, p. 18.

11. Arthur C. Clarke, *2001: A Space Odyssey* (New York: Signet, 1968), p. 149.

12. Frank Herbert, *Destination: Void* (New York: Berkley Medallion, 1966), p. 34. Herbert published a revised edition of this novel in 1978. This later edition deletes some mathematical discussion, and incorporates epigraphs at the beginning of each chapter. Several of the epigraphs are from Mary Shelley's *Frankenstein*.

13. Isaac Asimov originally proposed the computer programming of moral laws in his Three Laws of Robotics. In Boyd's novel some moral laws have actually been implemented.

14. John Boyd, *The Last Starship from Earth* (New York: Berkley Medallion, 1968), pp. 99–100.

15. See Jane Hipolito, "The Last and First Starship from Earth," in *SF: The Other Side of Realism*, ed. Thomas D. Clareson, pp. 186–192, for an excellent analysis of Boyd's parallel worlds and time travel between them.

16. Yevgeny Zamiatin, *We* (New York: Bantam Books, 1972), pp. 116–117.

17. Stanislaw Lem, "In Hot Pursuit of Happiness," in *View from Another Shore*, ed. Franz Rottensteiner (New York: Seabury Press, 1973), p. 4.

18. Franz Rottensteiner, ed., *View from Another Shore* (New York: Seabury Press, 1973), p. xiv.

19. Darko Suvin, "Afterword: The Open-Ended Parables of Stanislaw Lem and *Solaris*," in *Solaris* (New York: Berkley Medallion, 1971), p. 221.

20. Michael Kandel, "Stanislaw Lem on Men and Robots," p. 14.

21. "The Sanatorium of Dr. Vliperdius," in *Mortal Engines*, tr. Michael Kandel (New York: Seabury Press, 1977), pp. 133–134.

22. "The Sixth Sally," in *The Cyberiad*, tr. Michael Kandel (New York: Seabury Press, 1974), pp. 148-149.

23. "The Seventh Sally," in *The Cyberiad*, pp. 167-168.

24. Monod, *Chance and Necessity*, p. 154.

25. Ibid., p. 160.

26. Ibid., p. 165.

27. Schrödinger, *What Is Life?*, p. 36.

28. See Arthur Koestler, *The Act of Creation*, pp. 178-181, for an expanded discussion of the imagination's speculative leap.

29. Michael Moorcock, "Sea Wolves," in *Science against Man*, ed. Anthony Cheetham (New York: Avon, 1970), pp. 193, 203.

Notes to Chapter 8

1. Bruce Mazlish, "The Fourth Discontinuity," in *Perspectives on the Computer Revolution*, ed. Zenon W. Pylyshyn, pp. 195-197.

2. Ibid., p. 197.

3. Ibid.

4. J. C. R. Licklider, "Man-Computer Symbiosis," in *Perspectives on the Computer Revolution*, ed. Zenon W. Pylyshyn, pp. 307-308.

5. "The Preserving Machine," in *The Preserving Machine* (New York: Ace Books, 1968), p. 5.

6. Conversation with Philip K. Dick, November 14, 1978.

7. William Tindall, *The Literary Symbol*, pp. 51-61.

8. Other stories not discussed here are "The Variable Man," "The Great C," "Progeny," "War Veteran," and "Service Call."

9. "Second Variety," in *The Best of Philip K. Dick*, ed. John Brunner (New York: Ballantine Books, 1970), p. 24.

10. Paul Dickson, in *The Electronic Battlefield*, describes the conversion of warfare to contests between electronic devices. This process began in the sixties, a decade after Dick's stories; thus his imaginary creations were amazingly prophetic.

11. "Autofac," in *The Best of Philip K. Dick*, p. 280.

12. *The Best of Philip K. Dick*, p. 449.

13. *Vulcan's Hammer* (New York: Ace Books, 1960), p. 115.

14. In *Science-Fiction Studies* 2 (March 1975): 8-22.

15. *The Best of Philip K. Dick*, p. 446.

16. "If There Were No Benny Cemoli," in *The Best of Philip K. Dick.*

17. Letter from Philip K. Dick, July 1978.

18. See Angus Taylor's brief but insightful comments in his *Philip K. Dick and the Umbrella of Light.*

19. *The Three Stigmata of Palmer Eldritch* (Garden City, N.Y.: Doubleday & Co., 1964), p. 276.

20. The source for the Palmer Eldritch face is the war mask of the Attic Greeks, says Dick in "Man, Android, and Machine," in *Science Fiction at Large,* ed. Peter Nicholls (New York: Harper & Row, 1976).

21. Darko Suvin, "P. K. Dick's Opus," p. 14.

22. *Dr. Bloodmoney* (New York: Ace Books, 1965), p. 256.

23. I am aware that in using *metaphors* as a verb instead of a noun, I am either violating or augmenting the English language. But because Dick constantly creates images of processes rather than describing states, a verb form seems necessary. I prefer *metaphors* to the more mathematical verb *models.*

24. "Man, Android, and Machine," in *Science Fiction at Large,* p. 203.

25. Ibid., p. 204.

26. *The Best of Philip K. Dick,* p. 444.

27. In *Philip K. Dick: Electric Shepherd,* ed. Bruce Gillespie (Melbourne, Australia: Norstrilia Press, 1975), pp. 57, 63.

28. *We Can Build You* was written before 1964 and was not published at that time, according to Dick's statement in a letter dated July 31, 1978. Several years later Ted White serialized it in *Amazing,* and it was then published as a novel by Daw in 1969.

29. In *Philip K. Dick: Electric Shepherd,* p. 86.

30. Dick, "Man, Android, and Machine," pp. 211–212.

31. Ibid., p. 206.

32. The story of a man destroyed by his love for a femme fatale has been told repeatedly in fairy tales, myths, and poems. One of the best-known treatments is John Keats's poem, "Le Belle Dame sans Merci."

33. *Do Androids Dream of Electric Sheep?* (New York: Signet, 1968), p. 129.

34. In *The Best of Philip K. Dick.*

35. "Man, Android, and Machine," p. 220.

Conclusion

1. A. M. Taylor, *Imagination and the Growth of Science,* p. 24.

Nonfiction Bibliography

Achinstein, Peter. *Concepts of Science*. Baltimore, Md.: Johns Hopkins Press, 1968.

Aldiss, Brian W. *Billion Year Spree*. New York: Schocken Books, 1975.

Amis, Kingsley. *New Maps of Hell*. New York: Harcourt Brace, 1960.

Anderson, Alan Ross, ed. *Minds and Machines*. Englewood Cliffs, N.J.: Prentice-Hall, 1964.

Arbib, Michael A. *Brains, Machines, and Mathematics*. New York: McGraw-Hill, 1964.

———. *The Metaphorical Brain*. New York: John Wiley & Sons, 1972.

Armer, Paul. "The Individual: His Privacy, Self-Image, and Obsolescence." *Computers and People*, June 1975, pp. 16–22.

Armytage, W. H. G. *Yesterday's Tomorrows*. Toronto: U. of Toronto Press, 1968.

Ash, Brian. *Faces of the Future*. New York: Tapplinger, 1975.

Asimov, Isaac. "Social Science Fiction." In *Science Fiction: The Future*, ed. Dick Allen. New York: Harcourt Brace Jovanovich, 1971.

Atheling, William, Jr. *The Issue at Hand*. Chicago: Advent Publishers, 1964.

Bachelard, Gaston. *The Psychoanalysis of Fire*. Boston: Beacon Press, 1964.

———. *The Poetics of Space*. Boston: Beacon Press, 1969.

Bailey, J. O. *Pilgrims through Space and Time*. Westport, Conn.: Glenwood Press, 1947.

Barron, Neil. *Anatomy of Wonder*. New York: Bowker, 1976.

Bateson, Gregory. *Steps to an Ecology of Mind*. New York: Ballantine Books, 1972.

Beer, Stafford. *Designing Freedom*. New York: John Wiley & Sons, 1974.

Berger, Albert I. "The Magic That Works: John W. Campbell and the American Response to Technology." *Journal of Popular Culture* 5 (Spring 1972): 867–942.

Berkeley, Edmund. *Giant Brains, or Machines That Think*. New York: John Wiley & Sons, 1949.

Berry, Adrian. *The Next Ten Thousand Years*. Saturday Review Press/ E. P. Dutton & Co., 1974.

Bertalanffy, Ludwig von. *General System Theory*. New York: George Braziller, 1968.

————. *Robots, Men, and Minds*. New York: George Braziller, 1967.

————. "The Theory of Open Systems in Physics and Biology." *Science* III (January 13, 1950): 23–29.

Boguslaw, Robert. *The New Utopians: A Study of System Design and Social Change*. New York: Prentice-Hall, 1965.

Bloch, Robert. "Imagination and Modern Social Criticism." In *The Science Fiction Novel: Imagination and Social Criticism*, ed. Basil Davenport. Chicago: Advent Publishers, 1959.

Boulding, Kenneth E. *The Image*. Ann Arbor, Mich.: U. of Michigan Press, 1966.

Bowes, Pratima. *Consciousness and Freedom*. London: Methuen & Co., 1971.

Bowman, Daniel. *Industrial Robots: A Practical Handbook*. Monroeville, Pa.: International Material Management Society, 1976.

Bretnor, Reginald, ed. *Modern Science Fiction*. New York: Coward-McCann, 1953.

————. *Science Fiction, Today and Tomorrow*. New York: Harper & Row, 1974.

Broglie, Louis de. "The Philosophical Meaning and Practical Consequences of Cybernetics." In *New Perspectives in Physics*, tr. A. J. Pomerans. New York: Basic Books, 1962.

Bronowski, Jacob. *The Ascent of Man*. Boston: Little, Brown & Co., 1973.

————. *The Common Sense of Science*. Cambridge, Mass.: Harvard U. Press, 1966.

————. *The Identity of Man*. Garden City, N.Y.: Natural History Press, 1965.

————. *Science and Human Values*. New York: Harper & Row, 1965.

Bundy, Robert, ed. *Images of the Future*. Buffalo, N.Y.: Prometheus Books, 1976.

Cannon, W. B. *The Wisdom of the Body*. New York: W. W. Norton & Co., 1963.

Carter, Paul A. *The Creation of Tomorrow*. New York: Columbia U. Press, 1977.

Chapius, Alfred, and Droz, Edmond. *Automata*. Translated by Alec Reid. London: B. T. Batsford, 1958.

Clareson, Thomas D., ed. *SF: The Other Side of Realism*. Bowling Green, Ky.: Bowling Green U. Popular Press, 1971.

Clarke, Arthur C. *Profiles of the Future*. New York: Harper & Row, 1973.

————. *Report on Planet Three*. New York: Harper & Row, 1972.

Clarke, I. F. *Voices Prophesying War, 1763–1984*. London: Oxford U. Press, 1966.

Cohen, John. *Human Robots in Myth and Science*. Cranbury, N.J.: A. S. Barnes & Co., 1967.

Crosson, Frederick J., and Sayre, Kenneth M., ed. *The Modeling of Mind*. Notre Dame, Ind.: U. of Notre Dame Press, 1963.

Davenport, Basil, ed. *The Science Fiction Novel*. Chicago: Advent, 1959.

Dechert, Charles R. *The Social Impact of Cybernetics*. Notre Dame, Ind.: U. of Notre Dame Press, 1966.

Dertouzos, Michael L., and Moses, Joel, eds., *The Computer Age: A Twenty-Year View*. Cambridge, Mass.: MIT Press, 1979.

Dick, Philip K. "The Android and the Human." In *Philip K. Dick: Electric Shepherd*. Edited by Bruce Gillespie. Melbourne, Australia: Norstrilia Press, 1975.

————. "Man, Android, and Machine." In *Science Fiction at Large*. Edited by Peter Nicholls. New York: Harper & Row, 1976.

Dickson, Paul. *The Electronic Battlefield*. Bloomington, Ind.: Indiana U. Press, 1976.

Diebold, John. *Automation: The Advent of the Automatic Factory*. Princeton, N.J.: D. Van Nostrand Co., 1952.

Dorf, Richard C. *Computers and Man*. San Francisco: Boyd and Fraser, 1974.

Dreyfus, Hurbert. *What Computers Can't Do*. New York: Harper & Row, 1972.

Eiseley, Loren. *The Firmament of Time*. New York: Atheneum Publishers, 1974.

Elliott, Robert C. *The Shape of Utopia*. Chicago: U. of Chicago Press, 1970.

Eurich, Neil. *Science in Utopia*. Cambridge, Mass.: Harvard U. Press, 1967.

Feigenbaum, Edward, and Feldman, Julian, eds. *Computers and Thought*. New York: McGraw-Hill, 1963.

Fenichel, Robert R., and Weizenbaum, Joseph. *Computers and Computation*. San Francisco: W. H. Freeman & Co., 1971.

Franklin, H. Bruce. *Future Perfect*. New York: Oxford U. Press, 1966.

Freeman, Ira M. *Physics*. New York: McGraw-Hill, 1973.

Geduld, Harry M., and Gottesman, Ronald, eds. *Robots, Robots, Robots*. Boston: New York Graphic Society, 1978.

George, F. H. *The Brain as a Computer.* Oxford: Pergamon Press, 1973.

Gingerich, Owen. *The Nature of Scientific Discovery.* Washington, D.C.: Smithsonian Institution Press, 1974.

Goble, Neil. *Asimov Analyzed.* Baltimore, Md.: Mirage, 1972.

Gotlieb, C. C., and Borodin, A. *Social Issues in Computing.* New York: Academic Press, 1974.

Greenberger, Martin, ed. *Computers, Communication, and the Public Interest.* Baltimore, Md.: Johns Hopkins Press, 1971.

Gunderson, Keith. *Mentality and Machines.* New York: Anchor Books, 1971.

Gunn, James E. *Alternate Worlds.* Englewood Cliffs, N.J.: Prentice-Hall, 1975.

Halacy, D. S., Jr. *Computers—The Machines We Think With.* New York: Harper & Row, 1962.

Hassan, Ihab. "Beyond Arcadians and Technophiles: New Covergences in Culture?" *Massachusetts Review,* Spring 1976, pp. 7–18.

———. *Paracriticisms.* Urbana, Ill.: U. of Illinois Press, 1975.

Hatt, Harold E. *Cybernetics and the Image of Man.* New York: Abingdon Press, 1968.

Hawkes, Nigel. *The Computer Revolution.* New York: E. P. Dutton & Co., 1971.

Heinlein, Robert A. "Science Fiction: Its Nature, Faults and Virtues." In *The Science Fiction Novel: Imagination and Social Criticism,* ed. Basil Davenport. Chicago: Advent Publishers, 1959.

Heisenberg, Werner. *Physics and Philosophy.* New York: Harper & Brothers, 1958.

———. *Across the Frontiers.* New York: Harper & Row, 1975.

Hillegas, Mark R. *The Future as Nightmare.* Carbondale, Ill.: Southern Illinois U. Press, 1967.

Hook, Sidney, ed. *Dimensions of Mind.* New York: New York University Press, 1960.

Jackson, Philip C., Jr. *Introduction to Artificial Intelligence.* London: Mason & Lipscomb Publishers, 1974.

Jaki, Stanley L. *Brain, Mind, and Computers.* New York: Herder & Herder, 1969.

Jaynes, Julian. *The Origin of Consciousness in the Breakdown of the Bicameral Mind.* Boston: Houghton Mifflin, 1976.

Jeans, Sir James. *The Mysterious Universe.* New York: Macmillan Co., 1930.

Kandel, Michael. "Stanislaw Lem on Men and Robots." *Extrapolation* 14, no. 1 (December 1972): 13–24.

Kemeny, John G. *Man and the Computer.* New York: Charles Scribner's Sons, 1972.

Kenbigh, K. G. *An Inventive Universe.* New York: George Braziller, 1975.

Ketterer, David. *New Worlds for Old.* Garden City, N.Y.: Doubleday & Co., 1974.

Kline, Morris, ed. *Mathematics in the Modern World: Readings From Scientific American.* San Francisco: W. H. Freeman & Co., 1968.

Knight, Damon. *In Search of Wonder.* Chicago: Advent Publishers, 1967.

Koestler, Arthur. *The Act of Creation.* New York: Dell Publishing, 1964.

———. *The Ghost in the Machine.* New York: Macmillan Co., 1967.

———. *The Sleepwalkers.* New York: Macmillan Co., 1959.

Kornbluth, C. M. "The Failure of the Science Fiction Novel as Social Criticism." In *The Science Fiction Novel: Imagination and Social Criticism,* ed. Basil Davenport. Chicago: Advent Publishers, 1959.

Koyre, Alexander. *From the Closed World to the Infinite Universe.* New York: Harper & Row, 1957.

Kuhn, Thomas S. *The Structure of Scientific Revolutions.* Chicago: U. of Chicago Press, 1962.

Kuhns, William. *The Post-Industrial Prophets: Interpretations of Technology.* New York: Weybright & Talley, 1971.

Lami, Edward L., and DeBolt, Joe. "The Computer and Man: The Human Use of Non-Human Beings in the Works of John Brunner." In *The Happening Worlds of John Brunner,* ed. Joseph W. DeBolt. Port Washington, N.Y.: Kennikat Press, 1975.

Laszlo, Ervin. *Introduction to Systems Philosophy.* New York: Harper & Row, 1972.

———. *A Strategy for the Future.* New York: George Braziller, 1974.

———. *The Systems View of the World.* New York: George Braziller, 1972.

Lem, Stanislaw. "Robots in Science Fiction." In *SF: The Other Side of Realism,* ed. Thomas D. Clareson. Bowling Green, Ky.: Bowling Green U. Popular Press, 1971.

Luria, Salvador E. *Life: The Unfinished Experiment.* New York: Charles Scribner's Sons, 1973.

Malone, Robert. *The Robot Book.* New York: Jove Publications, 1978.

Manuel, Frank E., ed. *Utopias and Utopian Thought.* Boston: Houghton Mifflin, 1965.

Martin, James, and Norman, Adrian R. D. *The Computerized Society.* Englewood Cliffs, N.J.: Prentice-Hall, 1970.

Marx, Leo. *The Machine in the Garden*. London: Oxford U. Press, 1964.

Massey, Sir Harrie. *The New Age in Physics*. New York: Basic Books, 1966.

May, Rollo. *The Courage to Create*. New York: W. W. Norton & Co., 1975.

Minsky, Marvin L. "Computer Science and the Representation of Knowledge." In *The Computer Age: A Twenty-Year View*, ed. Michael L. Dertouzos and Joel Moses. Cambridge, Mass.: MIT Press, 1979.

Monod, Jacques. *Chance and Necessity*. New York: Alfred A. Knopf, 1971.

Morrison, P., and Morrison, E. "The Strange Life of Charles Babbage." *Scientific American* 186 (April, 1952): 66–71.

Morrison, P., and Morrison, E. *Charles Babbage and His Calculating Engines*. New York: Dover Publications, Inc., 1961.

Moskowitz, Sam. *Explorers of the Infinite*. Cleveland, Ohio: World, 1963.

———. *Seekers of Tomorrow*. New York: Ballantine Books, 1967.

Mowshowitz, Abbe. *The Conquest of Will: Information Processing in Human Affairs*. Reading, Mass.: Addison-Wesley, 1976.

Mumford, Lewis. *Technics and Civilization*. New York: Harcourt, Brace & Co., 1934.

———. *The Myth of the Machine*. New York: Harcourt, Brace & World, 1966.

———. *The Story of Utopias*. New York: Viking Press, 1962.

Nelson, Theodor. *Computer Lib*. 1974. (No publisher)

Neumann, John von. *The Computer and the Brain*. New Haven, Conn.: Yale U. Press, 1958.

Newman, James R. *Science and Sensibility*. New York: Simon & Schuster, 1961.

Nicolson, Marjorie. *Science and Imagination*. Ithaca, N.Y.: Cornell U. Press, 1956.

Nozick, Robert. *Anarchy, State, and Utopia*. New York: Basic Books, 1974.

Ornstein, Robert E., ed. *The Nature of Human Consciousness*. San Francisco: W. H. Freeman & Co., 1973.

———. *The Psychology of Consciousness*. San Francisco: W. H. Freeman & Co., 1972.

Ozolins, Aija. "Recent Works on Mary Shelley and *Frankenstein*." *Science-Fiction Studies* 3 (July 1976): 187–202.

Panshin, Alexei. *Heinlein in Dimension*. Chicago: Advent Publishers, 1969.

Parker, Donn B. *Crime by Computer*. New York: Charles Scribner's Sons, 1976.

Parkman, Ralph. *The Cybernetic Society*. New York: Pergamon Press, 1972.

Parsegian, V. L. *This Cybernetic World of Men, Machines, and Earth Systems.* Garden City, N.Y.: Doubleday & Co., 1972.

Patrouch, Joseph F., Jr. *The Science Fiction of Isaac Asimov.* Garden City, N.Y.: Doubleday & Co., 1974.

Perry, James M. *The New Politics: The Expanding Technology of Political Manipulation.* New York: Clarkson N. Potter, 1968.

Philmus, Robert. *Into the Unknown.* Berkeley and Los Angeles: U. of California Press, 1970.

Pierce, J. R. *Symbols, Signals and Noise: The Nature and Process of Communication.* New York: Harper & Brothers, 1961.

Plank, Robert. "The Golem and the Robot." *Literature and Psychology* 15 (Winter 1965): 12–28.

Plattel, Martin G. *Utopian and Critical Thinking.* Pittsburg, Pa.: Duquesne U. Press, 1972.

Polak, Fred. *The Image of the Future.* San Francisco: Jossey-Bass, 1973.

Pool, Ithiel de Sola, Abelson, Robert P., and Popkin, Samuel L. *Candidates, Issues, and Strategies: A Computer Simulation of the 1960 and 1964 Presidential Elections.* Cambridge, Mass.: MIT Press, 1964.

Price, Derek de Solla. *Science Since Babylon,* enl. ed. New Haven, Conn.: Yale U. Press, 1975.

Pylyshyn, Zenon W., ed. *Perspectives on the Computer Revolution.* Englewood Cliffs, N.J.: Prentice-Hall, 1970.

Raphael, Bertram. *The Thinking Computer.* San Francisco: W. H. Freeman & Co., 1976.

Reginald, Robert. *Contemporary Science Fiction Authors.* New York: Arno Press, 1975.

Reichenback, Hans. *Philosophic Foundations of Quantum Mechanics.* Berkeley and Los Angeles: U. of California Press, 1944.

———. *The Rise of Scientific Philosophy.* Berkeley and Los Angeles: U. of California Press, 1951.

Rhodes, Carolyn H. "Frederick Winslow Taylor's System of Scientific Management in Zamiatin's *We.*" *Journal of General Education* 38 (Spring 1976): 31–42.

Rose, Mark, ed. *Science Fiction.* Englewood Cliffs, N.J.: Prentice-Hall, 1976.

Rose, Steven. *The Conscious Brain.* New York: Random House, 1973.

Rosen, Saul. "Electronic Computers: A Historical Survey." *Computing Surveys* 1 (March 1969): 7–36.

Rosenberg, Jerry M. *The Computer Prophets.* London: Macmillan & Co., 1969.

Rosenblueth, Arturo. *Mind and Brain*. Cambridge, Mass.: MIT Press, 1970.

Rothman, Stanley, and Mosman, Charles. *Computers and Society*. Chicago: Science Research Associates, 1972.

Russ, Joanna. "Towards an Aesthetic of Science Fiction." *Science-Fiction Studies* 2 (July 1975): 112–119.

Ryle, Gilbert. *The Concept of Mind*. New York: Barnes & Noble, 1949.

Sagan, Carl. "In Praise of Robots." *Natural History*, January 1975, pp. 8–20.

Sahlins, Marshall D. "Notes on the Original Affluent Society." In *Man the Hunter*, ed. Richard B. Lee and Irven DeVore. Chicago: Aldine, 1968.

Sanders, Donald. *Computers in Society*. New York: McGraw-Hill, 1973.

Scholes, Robert. *Structural Fabulation*. Notre Dame, Ind.: U. of Notre Dame Press, 1975.

Schrödinger, Erwin. *Science and Humanism*. London: Cambridge U. Press, 1951.

————. *What Is Life?* Cambridge: Cambridge U. Press, 1946.

Shannon, Claude E. "A Chess-Playing Machine." *Scientific American*, February 1950. Reprinted in *Computers and Computation: Readings from Scientific American*. San Francisco: W. H. Freeman & Co. 1971.

————. "The Mathematical Theory of Communication." In *The Mathematical Theory of Communication*. Shannon, Claude E. and Weaver, Warren. Urbana: The U. of Illinois Press, 1949.

Simon, Herbert A. *The Sciences of the Artificial*. Cambridge, Mass.: MIT Press, 1969.

Singh, Jagjit. *Great Ideas in Information Theory, Language, and Cybernetics*. New York: Dover Publications, 1966.

Small, Christopher. *Mary Shelley's Frankenstein*. Pittsburgh, Pa.: U. of Pittsburgh Press, 1973.

Smeed, J. W. *Faust in Literature*. New York : Oxford U. Press, 1975.

Spencer, Sharon. *Space, Time, and Structure in the Modern Novel*. New York: New York U. Press, 1971.

Sussman, Herbert L. *Victorians and the Machine*. Cambridge, Mass.: Harvard U. Press, 1968.

Suvin, Darko. "On the Poetics of the Science Fiction Genre." *College English* 34 (December 1972): 372–381.

————. *Metamorphoses of Science Fiction*. New Haven: Yale U. Press, 1979.

————. "The Open-Ended Parables of Stanislaw Lem and *Solaris*." Afterword in *Solaris*. New York: Berkley Medallion, 1971.

————. "P. K. Dick's Opus: Artifice as Refuge and World View." *Science-Fiction Studies* 2 (March 1975): 8–22.

Taylor, A. M. *Imagination and the Growth of Science.* New York: Shocken Books, 1967.

Taylor, Angus. *Philip K. Dick and the Umbrella of Light.* Baltimore, Md.: T. K. Graphics, 1975.

Thompson, William Irwin. *At the Edge of History.* New York: Harper & Row, 1971.

Tindall, William. *The Literary Symbol.* Bloomington, Ind.: Indiana U. Press, 1965.

Todorov, Tzvetan. *The Fantastic.* Translated by Richard Howard. Ithaca, N.Y.: Cornell U. Press, 1972.

Toffler, Alvin, ed. *The Futurists.* New York: Random House, 1972.

Tomeski, Edward A., and Lazarus, Harold. *People-Oriented Computer Systems.* New York: Van Nostrand Reinhold Co., 1975.

Travis, Irene, ed. *Computer Impact.* Englewood Cliffs, N.J.: Prentice-Hall, 1970.

Tropp, Martin. *Mary Shelley's Monster.* New York: Houghton Mifflin, 1976.

Turing, A. M. "Computing Machinery and Intelligence." In *Perspectives on the Computer Revolution.* ed. Zenon W. Pylyshyn. Englewood Cliffs, N.J.: Prentice-Hall, 1970.

Turn, Rein. *Computers in the 1980s.* New York: Columbia U. Press, 1974.

Uhr, Leonard. *Pattern Recognition, Learning, and Thought.* Englewood Cliffs, N.J.: Prentice-Hall, 1973.

Van Tassel, Dennie L. *The Compleat Computer.* 1976. (No publisher)

Walsh, Chad. *From Utopia to Nightmare.* Westport, Conn.: Greenwood Press, 1962.

Warrick, Patricia. "The Sources of Zamiatin's *We* in Dostoevsky's *Notes from the Underground.*" *Extrapolation* 17 (December 1975): 63–77.

Warrick, Patricia, Greenberg, M., and Olander, J., eds. *Science Fiction: Contemporary Mythology.* New York: Harper & Row, 1978.

Weizenbaum, Joseph. *Computer Power and Human Reason.* San Francisco: W. H. Freeman & Co., 1976.

Wiener, Norbert. *Cybernetics or Control and Communication in the Animal and the Machine.* New York: John Wiley & Sons, 1948.

————. *God and Golem, Inc.* Cambridge, Mass.: MIT Press, 1964.

————. *The Human Use of Human Beings: Cybernetics and Society.* Boston: Houghton Mifflin, 1950.

Wigner, Eugene P. *Symmetries and Reflections.* Bloomington, Ind.: Indiana U. Press, 1967.

Williamson, Jack. *H. G. Wells: Critic of Progress.* Baltimore, Md.: Mirage Press, 1973.

Wilson, Andrew. *The Bomb and the Computer.* New York: Dell Publishing, 1968.

Wollheim, Donald A. *The Universe Makers.* New York: Harper & Row, 1971.

Wooldridge, Dean E. *Mechanical Man.* New York: McGraw-Hill, 1968.

Indexes

Contento, William. *Index to Science Fiction Anthologies and Collections.* Boston: G. K. Hall Co., 1978.

Day, Donald B. *Index to the Science Fiction Magazines, 1926-1950.* Portland, Oregon: Perri Press, 1952.

Index to the Science Fiction Magazines, 1966-1970. Cambridge, Mass: New England Science Fiction Assn., 1971.

The MIT Science Fiction Society Index to the S-F Magazines, 1951-1965. Erwin S. Strauss, comp. Cambridge, Mass., 1966.

Tuck, Donald H. *The Encyclopedia of Science Fiction and Fantasy*, Vol. 1. Chicago: Advent Publishers, 1974.

———. *The Encyclopedia of Science Fiction and Fantasy*, Vol. 2. Chicago: Advent Press, 1978.

Fiction Bibliography

Most of the science fiction stories used in this study were originally published in the pulp magazines, often in serial form for longer works. The best short stories were later reprinted in various anthologies. Longer works were often reprinted as novels, in either hard or soft cover or both. Much of this material is now out of print and not easily available, although very recently several publishers have begun to publish reprint series. Because a story may have appeared in a variety of places, the place of publication has not been given in this bibliography. The date listed is that of first publication.

Literary Antecedents

Bierce, Ambrose. "Moxon's Master." 1894.

Butler, Samuel. *Erewhon.* 1872.

Capek, Karel. *R. U. R.* 1921.

Cook, William Wallace. *Round Trip to the Year 2000.* 1903.

Forster, E. M. *The Machine Stops.* 1909.

Hamilton, Edmond. "The Metal Giants." 1926.

Merritt, A. *The Metal Monster.* 1920.

————. *The Moon Pool.* 1919.

Poe, Edgar Allen. "Maelzel's Chess Player." 1836.

Shelley, Mary. *Frankenstein: or, the Modern Prometheus.* 1818.

Williamson, Jack. "The Metal Man." 1928.

Wright, S. Fowler. "Automata." 1929.

Zamiatin, Yevgeny. *We.* 1922.

Fiction 1930–1977

Alban, Antony. *Catharsis Central.* 1969.

Aldiss, Brian W. "But Who Can Replace a Man?" 1958.

————. "The Hunter at His Ease." 1970.

Aldiss, Brian W. "The New Father Christmas." 1957.

Anderson, Poul. "The Critique of Impure Reason." 1962.

———. "Epilogue." 1962.

———. "Goat Song." 1972.

———. "Quixote and the Windmill." 1950.

———. "Sam Hall." 1953.

Anfilov, Gleb. "Erem." 1963.

Anvil, Christopher. "The Hunch." 1961.

Asimov, Isaac. "All the Troubles in the World." 1958.

———. "The Bicentennial Man." 1976.

———. "Catch That Rabbit." 1944.

———. *The Caves of Steel*. 1953.

———. "The Computer That Went on Strike." 1972.

———. "Death Sentence." 1943.

———. "Escape." 1945

———. "Evidence." 1946.

———. "The Evitable Conflict." 1950.

———. "The Feeling of Power." 1957.

———. "Feminine Intuition." 1969.

———. "First Law." 1956.

———. "Franchise." 1955.

———. "Galley Slave." 1957.

———. "The Last Question." 1956.

———. "Liar." 1941.

———. "Lenny." 1958.

———. "Let's Get Together." 1956.

———. "The Life and Times of Multivac." 1975.

———. "Little Lost Robot." 1947.

———. "The Machine That Won the War." 1961.

———. "Mirror Image." 1972.

———. *The Naked Sun*. 1956.

———. "Profession." 1957.

———. "Reason." 1941.

———. "Risk." 1955.

———. "Robbie." 1940.

———. "Robot AL-76 Goes Astray." 1942.

———. "Runaround." 1942.

———. "Satisfaction Guaranteed." 1951.

———. "Someday." 1956.

———. "Stranger in Paradise." 1974.

———. "The Tercentenary Incident." 1976.

———. "That Thou Art Mindful of Him." 1974.

———. "Victory Unintentional." 1942.

Banks, Raymond E. "Walter Perkins Is Here!" 1970.

Bates, Harry. "Farewell to the Master." 1940.

Beaumont, Charles. "Last Rites." 1955.

Bester, Alfred. *The Computer Connection.* 1974.

Biggle, Lloyd, Jr. "In His Own Image." 1968.

———. "Spare the Rod." 1958.

Binder, Eando. "Adam Link in Business." 1940.

———. "Adam Link, Champion Athlete." 1940.

———. "Adam Link Faces a Revolt." 1941.

———. "Adam Link Fights a War." 1940.

———. "Adam Link in the Past." 1941.

———. "Adam Link, Robot Detective." 1940.

———. "Adam Link Saves the World." 1942.

———. "Adam Link's Vengeance." 1940.

———. "I, Robot." 1939.

———. "The Trail of Adam Link." 1939.

Blish, James. "Solar Plexus." 1941.

Bloch, Alan. "Men Are Different." 1954.

Bone, J. F. "Triggerman." 1958.

Boucher, Anthony. "The Quest for Saint Aquin." 1951.

Boulle, Pierre. "The Man Who Hated Machines." 1969.

———. "The Perfect Robot." 1969.

Bounds, Sydney J. *The Robot Brains.* 1969.

Bova, Ben. "The Next Logical Step." 1962.

———. *THX 1138*. 1971.

———. "The Perfect Warrior." 1963.

Bova, Ben, and Ellison, Harlan. "Brillo." 1970.

Boyd, John. *The Last Starship from Earth*. 1968.

Bradbury, Ray. "There Will Come Soft Rains." 1950.

Brown, Frederic. "Answer." 1954.

Brunner, John. "The Invisible Idiot." 1970.

———. "Judas." 1967.

———. *The Jagged Orbit*. 1969.

———. *The Shockwave Rider*. 1975.

———. "Thou Good and Faithful." 1953.

———. "You'll Take the High Road." 1973.

Budrys, Algis. "First to Serve." 1954.

———. *Michelmas*. 1978.

Burdick, Eugene. *The 480*. 1964.

Burdick, Eugene, and Wheeler, Harvey. *Fail-Safe*. 1962.

Caidin, Martin. *The God Machine*. 1968.

Cameron, Lou. *Cybernia*. 1972.

Campbell, John W., Jr. "The Last Evolution." 1932.

———. "The Machine." 1935.

———. "The Metal Horde." 1930.

———. *The Mightiest Machine*. 1935.

———. "Twilight." 1934.

———. "When The Atoms Failed." 1930.

Carrigan, Richard and Nancy. *The Siren Stars*. 1970.

Chandler, A. Bertram. "The Left-Hand Way." 1967.

———. "The Soul Machine." 1969.

Chapdelaine, Perry A. "We Fused One." 1968.

Clarke, Arthur C. "A Meeting with Medusa." 1973.

———. *The City and the Stars*. 1956.

———. "Dial 'F' for Frankenstein." 1966.

———. "The Nine Billion Names of God." 1953.

———. "Superiority." 1951.

———. *2001: A Space Odyssey*. 1968.

Clement, Hal. "Answer." 1947.

Clifton, Mark, and Riley, Frank. *They'd Rather Be Right*. 1957.

Compton, D. G. *The Steel Crocodile*. 1970.

———. *Synthajoy*. 1968.

Conley, Rick. "The War of the Words." 1972.

Coupling, J. J. "Period Piece." 1948.

Crichton, Michael. *The Terminal Man*. 1972.

Crossen, Kendell Foster. *Year of Consent*. 1954.

Delany, Samuel R. *Nova*. 1968.

del Rey, Lester. "Helen O'Loy." 1938.

———. "Instinct." 1951.

———. "Into Thy Hands." 1945.

———. "Though Dreamers Die." 1944.

———. "To Avenge Man." 1964.

Dick, Philip K. "Autofac." 1955.

———. "The Defenders." 1953.

———. *Do Androids Dream of Electric Sheep?* 1968.

———. *Dr. Bloodmoney*. 1965.

———. "The Electric Ant." 1969.

———. "The Great C." 1953.

———. "Imposter." 1953.

———. *Martian Time Slip*. 1964.

———. *The Penultimate Truth*. 1964

———. "The Preserving Machine." 1953.

———. "Progeny." 1954.

———. "Second Variety." 1953.

———. "Service Call." 1955.

———. *Simulacra*. 1964.

———. *The Three Stigmata of Palmer Eldritch*. 1964.

———. "The Variable Man." 1953.

———. *Vulcan's Hammer*. 1960.

Dick, Philip K. "War Veteran." 1955.

———. *We Can Build You.* 1972.

Dickson, Gordon. "Computers Don't Argue." 1965.

———. "The Monkey Wrench." 1961.

———. *Necromancer.* 1962.

Dunsany, Lord Edward. *The Last Revolution.* 1951.

Durham, Jim. "F. O. D."

Eklund, Gordon. "Second Creation." 1974.

Elliot, Bob, and Goulding, Ray. "The Day the Computer Got Waldon Ashenfelter." 1967.

Ellison, Harlan. "I Have No Mouth and I Must Scream." 1967.

Ellison, Harlan, and Bova, Ben. "Brillo." 1970.

Fairman, Paul W. *I, The Machine.* 1968.

Friborg, Albert Compton. "Careless Love." 1953.

Gallum, Raymond Z. "Derelict." 1935.

———. "The Scarab." 1936.

Garrett, Randall. "The Hunting Lodge." 1954.

———. "A Spaceship Named McGuire." 1961.

George, Peter. *Two Hours to Doom.* 1958.

Gerrold, David. *When Harlie Was One.* 1972.

Goulart, Ron. *What's Become of Screwloose? and Other Inquiries.* 1971.

Gunn, James E. "The Message." 1972.

Hadley, Arthur. *The Joy Wagon.* 1958.

Harrison, Harry. "Arm of the Law." 1958.

———. "I See You." 1959.

———. "The Repairman." 1959.

———. "The Robot Who Wanted to Know." 1962.

———. "Simulated Trainer." 1958.

———. "Survival Planet." 1961.

———. "The Velvet Glove." 1956.

———. "War With the Robots." 1962.

Heinlein, Robert. *The Moon Is a Harsh Mistress.* 1966.

Herbert, Frank. *Destination: Void.* 1966. Revised edition, 1978.

Hock, Edward. *The Transvection Machine*. 1971.

Hodder-Williams, Christopher. *Fistful of Digits*. 1968.

Hogan, James. *The Genesis Machine*. 1978.

———. *The Two Faces of Tomorrow*. 1979.

Hoyle, Fred, and Elliot, John. *A for Andromeda*. 1962.

———. *Andromeda Breakthrough*. 1964.

Jameson, Malcolm. "Pride." 1942.

Johannesson, Olof. *The End of Man?* 1966.

Jones, D. F. *Colossus*. 1966.

———. *The Fall of Colossus*. 1974.

Jones, Raymond F. *The Cybernetic Brains*. 1950.

———. "Rat Race." 1966.

Kelleam, Joseph E. "Rust." 1939.

Koontz, Dean R. *Demon Seed*. 1973.

Kornbluth, C. M. "With These Hands." 1951.

Kuttner, Henry. "Jesting Pilot." 1966.

Kuttner, Henry, and Moore, C. L. "Two Handed Engine." 1955.

Lack, G. L. "Rogue Leonardo." 1960.

Lafferty, R. A. *Arrive at Easterwine*. 1971.

Laumer, Keith. *The Great Time Machine Hoax*. 1963.

———. "Eurema's Dam." 1972.

Leiber, Fritz. "Answering Service." 1967.

———. "A Bad Day for Sales." 1953.

———. "The Mechanical Bride." 1954.

———. *The Silver Eggheads*. 1961.

———. "64-Square Madhouse." 1962.

Leinster, Murray. "A Logic Named Joe." 1946.

———. "The Wabbler." 1952.

Lem, Stanislaw. *The Cyberiad: Fables for the Cybernetic Age*. 1974.

———. "In Hot Pursuit of Happiness." 1973.

———. *Mortal Engines*. 1977.

Leman, Grahame. "Conversational Mode." 1972.

Levin, Ira. *This Perfect Day*. 1970.

Long, Frank Belknap. *It Was the Day of the Robot*. 1963.

McCaffrey, Anne. "The Ship Who Sang." 1961.

MacDonald, John D. "Mechanical Answer." 1938.

McIntosh, J. T. "Machine Mode." 1951.

———. "Spanner in the Works." 1963.

McIntyre, Vonda N. "The Genius Freaks." 1973.

Mackin, Edward. "Key to Chaos." 1964.

———. "The Trouble With H.A.R.R.I." 1957.

Malec, Alexander. "10:01." 1966.

Martin, George R. R. "The Last Superbowl Game." 1975.

Mead, Shepherd. *The Big Ball of Wax*. 1954.

Miller, Walter M., Jr. "Dumb Waiter." 1952.

———. "I Made You." 1954.

Monteleone, Thomas F. "Chicago." 1973.

Moorcock, Michael. *The Final Programme*. 1968.

———. "Sea Wolves." 1969.

Padgett, Lewis. "Deadlock." 1939.

———. "Ex Machine." 1949.

———. "The Twonky." 1942.

Perkins, Lawrence. "Delivered with Feeling." 1965.

Philips, Peter. "Lost Memory." 1952.

Pierce, John R. "See No Evil." 1966.

Pohl, Frederik. *The Age of the Pussyfoot*. 1969.

———. "Day Million." 1966.

———. *Gateway*. 1977.

———. "The Schematic Man." 1969.

Reynolds, Mack. *Computer War*. 1967.

———. *Computer World*. 1970.

———. "Criminal in Utopia." 1968.

Riley, Frank. "The Cyber and Justice Holmes." 1955.

Roshwald, Mordecai. *Level 7*. 1959.

Rothmand, Milton A. "Getting Together." 1972.

Russell, Eric Frank. "Boomerang." 1953.

Saberhagen, Fred. *Berserker.* 1967.

——. *Berserker's Planet.* 1974.

Seabright, Idris. "Short in the Chest." 1954.

Shaara, Michael. "Soldier Boy." 1953.

——. "2066: Election Day." 1956.

Shaw, Bob. "Harold Wilson at the Cosmic Cocktail Party." 1970.

Sheckley, Robert. "Can You Feel Anything When I Do This?" 1969.

——. "Fool's Mate." 1953.

Silverberg, Robert. "Getting Across." 1973.

——. "Going Down Smooth." 1968.

——. "Good News from the Vatican." 1971.

——. "The Macauley Circuit." 1956.

Simak, Clifford. *City.* 1952.

——. "Limiting Factor." 1949.

——. "Skirmish." 1950.

——. "Lulu." 1957.

——. "Univac: 2200." 1973.

Sladek, John. *The Muller-Fokker Effect.* 1971.

——. *The Reproductive System.* 1968.

Smith, George O. "Counter Foil." 1964.

Sturgeon, Theodore. "Agnes, Accent, and Access." 1973.

Temple, William. *The Automated Goliath.* 1962.

Tenn, William. "The Jester." 1951.

Thomas, Dan. *The Seed.* 1967.

Townes, Robert Sherman. "Problem for Emmy." 1952.

Tremaine, Orlin F. "True Confession." 1939.

Vance, Gerald. *We, The Machine.* 1951.

Van Vogt, A. E. "Final Command." 1948.

——. "Fulfillment." 1950.

——. *The World of Null A.* 1945.

Vincent, Hart. "Rex." 1934.

Vinge, Vernon. "The Accomplice." 1967.

——. "Long Shot." 1972.

Vonnegut, Kurt, Jr. "EPICAC." 1950.

———. *Player Piano.* 1952.

Wellen, Edward. "No Other Gods." 1972.

Williams, Robert Moore. "Robot's Return." 1938.

Williamson, Jack. *The Humanoids.* 1963.

———. "With Folded Hands." 1947.

Wodhams, Jack. "Sprog." 1971.

Wolfe, Bernard. *Limbo.* 1952.

———. "Self Portrait." 1951.

Wolfe, Gene. "Alien Stones." 1972.

Wyndham, John. "Compassion Circuit." 1954.

———. "The Lost Machine." 1932.

Young, Michael. *The Rise of the Meritocracy.* 1958.

Zelazny, Roger. "For a Breath I Tarry." 1966.

Zebrowski, George. "Starcrossed." 1973.

Zebrowski, George, and Carrington, Grant. "Fountain of Force." 1972.

Anthologies

Ashley, Mike, ed. *Souls in Metal.* 1977.

Binder, Eando. *Adam Link—Robot.* 1965.

Conklin, Groff, ed. *Science-Fiction Thinking Machines.* 1954.

del Rey, Lester. *Robots and Changelings.* 1957.

Elwood, Roger, ed. *Invasion of the Robots.* 1965.

Goulart, Ron. *What's Become of Screwloose? and Other Inquiries.* 1973.

Greenberg, Martin, ed. *The Robot and the Man.* 1953.

Harrison, Harry. *War with the Robots.* 1968.

Knight, Damon, ed. *The Metal Smile.* 1968.

Kuttner, Henry. *Robots Have No Tails.* 1952.

Lewis, Arthur O., ed. *Of Men and Machines.* 1963.

McCaffrey, Anne. *The Ship Who Sang.* 1970.

Moskowitz, Sam, ed. *The Coming of the Robots.* 1963.

Mowshowitz, Abbe, ed. *Inside Information: Computers in Fiction.* 1977.

Russell, Eric Frank, ed. *Men, Martians, and Machines.* 1958.

Saberhagen, Fred. *Berserker*. 1967.

Silverberg, Robert, ed. *Men and Machines*. 1968.

Van Tassel, Dennie L., ed. *Computers, Computers, Computers*. 1977.

Index